NME ROCK'N'ROLL
DECADES
THE SEVENTIES

NEW MUSICAL EXPRESS ROCK'N'ROLL

DECADES

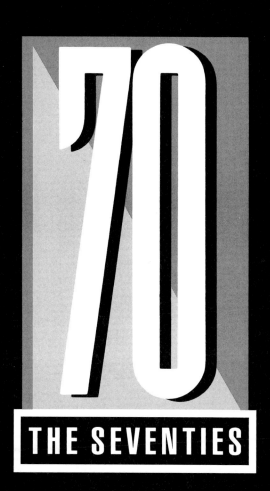

'70

THE SEVENTIES

WHSMITH

EXCLUSIVE ·BOOKS·

THE SEVENTIES

Consultant Editor: John Tobler

Contributors: Fred Dellar, Hugh Fielder, Dave McAleer,
David Sandison.

Editor: David Heslam
Assistant Editor: Mike Evans

Designed by Christopher Matthews

CONTENTS

The publishers wish to thank the New Musical Express (NME) for their kind assistance and access to archive material without which this project would not have been possible. All American chart information is © 1955-1992 BPI Communications Inc. and appears courtesy of Billboard magazine.

This edition produced exclusively for WH Smith

Published by Octopus Illustrated Publishing
Michelin House, 81 Fulham Road, London SW3 6RB
part of Reed International Books Limited.

Copyright © Reed International Books Ltd and
IPC Magazines Ltd 1992

ISBN 0 600 57534 9

Printed in Slovenia

Debbie Harry

Pink Floyd

David Bowie

THE SEVENTIES

If rock music behaved logically – and thank goodness it doesn't know how to – it would surely have understood that the end of the 1960s was no better or more enjoyable than the start of that decade, and that somewhere a mistake had been made. Fortunately, the more wasteful tendencies of the early 1970s, which resulted in the premature deaths of rock starts like Duane Allman, Janis Joplin and Jim Morrison, didn't become an epidemic, but for the first time in the rock era, British and American tastes seriously diverged. America was attracted – some may say fatally – to the hysteria, the excess and the posturing, not to mention the volume, of Heavy Metal music.

The first metal superstars were Led Zeppelin, ironically a British quartet whose musical abilities were frequently forgotten in the euphoria induced by their loud, hard-driving R&B. They arrived as The Beatles fell apart, and became the biggest act in the world during the first half of the Seventies. More recently, Heavy Metal has become the easiest and most obvious route to wealth and stardom for both British and American bands, while the US has retained an interest in head-banging music, even if few metal musicians are individually as celebrated as the groups to which they belong.

Britain's first major trend of the 1970s was something called glam-rock, whose stated aim was to restore the fun and innocence to pop music. It's first and probably best practitioners were Marc Bolan and David Bowie. Along with several other acts, they further exaggerated and virtually lampooned psychedelic fashions, at the same time trying, with some success, to ridicule the intellectual overkill of a breed of singer/songwriters who appealed to young adults, and who were threatening to alienate the teenage populations on both sides of the Atlantic with their often overbearing sensitivity. Most of the glam-rockers, like Slade and Gary Glitter, didn't really catch on in the States, because over there the era of the stadium band was beginning in the wake of metal's noisy childhood. Supergroups like Crosby, Stills, Nash & Young attracted huge crowds to stadium concerts, although some, like Blind Faith (featuring Eric Clapton and Steve Winwood), found the pressure too restrictive and split long before their sell-by date. British groups formed in the Sixties, like The Stones, The Who, Jethro Tull, Pink Floyd and, of course, Led Zeppelin, became huge international attractions, even if some of them went off the rails – taking a year and a half to complete a new album and competing to see who could spend the most money on perfecting their latest studio creation almost became an Olympic event.

After 1976, the musical paths of Britain and America became even more widely separated. Britain's disaffected youth, which had collectively been the victim of a major economic recession, showed its resentment at the seemingly endless stream of rich American rock stars singing the praises of sun-bronzed Californian goddesses. Neither did they neglect the British counterparts of these American stars, hurtfully sneering at and vilifying the British rock aristocracy as exemplified by establishment figures like Elton John, Fleetwood Mac, Queen and all the others who spent more time in America where they were bigger stars and sold many more albums and concert tickets. The unemployed kids weren't even that excited by the perfect pop songs which became a catchy trademark for Abba, the Swedish quartet whose records outsold everyone else in the world in the Seventies. Potentially the biggest international act

The Sex Pistols

Nash, Crosby, Stills and Young

Elton John

since The Beatles, Abba failed to gain entry at the final frontier of America, but nine chart-topping singles in Britain, especially after having the stigma of winning the Eurovision Song Contest delaying their advance, was a considerable achievement. The 1970s was the decade which produced an ABC of accomplished soft rockers: Abba, Bread (whose chart-topping compilation album, 'The Sound of Bread', pioneered prime time TV marketing) and the brilliant and desperately romantic (thus sneer-provoking) music of The Carpenters, a brother and sister who further epitomized the Californian dream.

Rock music has always appealed to the non-conformist element with rebellious tendencies, and in 1977 angry British urchins like The Sex Pistols, The Clash, The Stranglers, The Jam and The Boomtown Rats provided a far less polished but infinitely more exciting alternative to disco music, which was itself epitomised by the keening harmonies of another British group from the 1960s, The Bee Gees. Punk rock brought back the confrontation and outrage which had been absent from popular music since the Sixties, and gave the kids a weapon with which they could again annoy older generations. It couldn't catch on in the same way in America, where things weren't so bleak for teenagers, although British punk rock was ironically inspired by a handful of influential American cult heroes. These punk godparents mainly emerged from urban wastelands in industrial cities like New York, Cleveland and Detroit. Motown had moved out of Detroit to the more glamorous and luxurious surroundings of Los Angeles, California, and therby forfeited its street credibility, but at the start of the Seventies, America's major Motor City had produced some of the most uncompromising acts in rock history, like The Stooges, fronted by the charismatic and ridiculously named Iggy Pop, and the revolutionary MC5.

Inevitably New York ultimately became America's most innovative musical city of the 1970s, not only producing influential originators like Lou Reed, who fronted The Velvet Underground (which also included classically trained Welsh cello player John Cale), but also the neo-transvestite New York Dolls and self-styled punk poetess Patti Smith, plus the vast majority of credible leaders of the so-called New Wave (a term invented by marketing men who objected to their acts being referred to as 'punks'): Television, The Ramones, Talking Heads and Blondie. New York was simultaneously also the disco capital of the world, and rode out the 1970s as the centre of the rock universe.

Ultimately, a lot of great rock music was produced in the Seventies on both sides of the Atlantic, and the profitability of the music industry began to escalate so dramatically that the accountants and lawyers began moving in during the second half of the decade. As a result, rock music has rarely been well enough to leave its sick bed ever since.

Everything seemed to be proceeding in more or less the right direction as the end of the 1970s approached – but new movements in the following decade would only remain popular for months rather than years. The businessmen had overestimated the attention span of the record-buying public, and had foolishly – as became clear in retrospect – encouraged punters to expect and demand frequent changes of direction and to constantly discard their heroes in favour of new models. Maybe Andy Warhol had it right when he said that everyone would have just 15 minutes of fame . . .

1970

- Pentangle are writing the soundtrack score to 'Tam Lin', a movie starring Ava Gardner and Ian McShane.

- The Bonzo Dog Band has split in the wake of a London Lyceum gig.

- Carl Wayne is to play his final date as lead singer with The Move at Stockport, England on January 31.

CHARTS

US45	Raindrops Keep Falling On My Head	*B.J. Thomas*
USLP	Abbey Road	*Beatles*
UK45	Two Little Boys	*Rolf Harris*
UKLP	Abbey Road	*Beatles*

— WEEK 2 —

US45	Raindrops Keep Falling On My Head	*B.J. Thomas*
USLP	Abbey Road	*Beatles*
UK45	Two Little Boys	*Rolf Harris*
UKLP	Abbey Road	*Beatles*

— WEEK 3 —

US45	Raindrops Keep Falling On My Head	*B.J. Thomas*
USLP	Led Zeppelin II	*Led Zeppelin*
UK45	Two Little Boys	*Rolf Harris*
UKLP	Abbey Road	*Beatles*

— WEEK 4 —

US45	Raindrops Keep Falling On My Head	*B.J. Thomas*
USLP	Abbey Road	*Beatles*
UK45	Two Little Boys	*Rolf Harris*
UKLP	Abbey Road	*Beatles*

— WEEK 5 —

US45	I Want You Back	*Jackson Five*
USLP	Led Zeppelin II	*Led Zeppelin*
UK45	Reflections Of My Life	*Marmalade*
UKLP	Abbey Road	*Beatles*

SHEP BEATEN TO DEATH

James 'Shep' Sheppard, lead singer with The Heartbeats and Shep & The Limelites, was found dead in his car on the Long Island Expressway on January 24, having been beaten and robbed. Sheppard wrote and recorded 'A Thousand Miles Away', a top 10 single in the American R&B charts during 1956, and one of the best loved doo wop anthems of the decade.

In 1961 he formed The Limelites and immediately scored massively with 'Daddy's Home', a US top 5 single that was an answer record to 'A Thousand Miles Away'. Signed to the Hull label during the early sixties, Shep & The Limelites also had minor hits with 'Ready For Your Love', 'Three Steps To The Altar' and 'Our Anniversary.'

Shep And The Limelites (from the top) Charles Baskerville, Clarence Bassett and James 'Shep' Sheppard, once one of New York's finest doo-wop outfits

ELVIS AND THE NUN

NBC-Universal International Productions have just released *'Change Of Habit'*, a movie in which Elvis Presley portrays ghetto doctor John Carpenter, while toothsome Mary Tyler Moore is Sister Michelle, a plain-clothes nun who, for moments of drama, reverts to haute couture and carefully applied eye-liner.

BILLY STEWART KILLED IN CRASH

Sweet soul, stutter-scat hit-maker Billy Stewart (32) and three members of his band were tragically killed when their car crashed off a bridge and into the River Neuse, in North Carolina. Stewart will best be remembered for such Chess waxings as 'Summertime', 'Secret Love', 'I Do Love You' and 'Sitting In The Park'.

THE ALBERT VETOES LENNON-WHO SHOW

The future of all pop concerts at London's Royal Albert Hall is in doubt because the venue has refused to host a charity event planned for March. The show, involving John Lennon, The Who, The Incredible String Band and King Crimson, was to have benefitted Britain's National Council for Civil Liberties, plus Release, the organisation that aids drug offenders.

But the RAH, who turned down a Rolling Stones concert last December, will not allow the gig to take place, and now the Musicians Union have threatened to blacklist the venue, which normally presents around 40 rock concerts each year.

ELLIS QUITS LOVE AFFAIR

Steve Ellis, often called 'The Last of the Teen Idols', has quit as lead singer with Love Affair to pursue a solo career. Says Ellis: 'We never really made it big anywhere but Britain and I think that if we had started to happen in America, I wouldn't have left.'

Dr Elvis discusses swapping T-shirts with Sister Mary Tyler Moore in a scene from Universal's Change Of Habit, El's 30th movie since 1956

PETER TO PART WITH THE GREEN STUFF

Peter Green says he would like to give some of his money away. The Fleetwood Mac guitarist is quoted as saying that he would like to provide financial help to those who are starving or merely lack a good education and opportunities.

Home after a three month tour of America, Green said, as he reversed his £700 white Jaguar out of a Richmond, Surrey, car park: 'Not that I have millions and millions, but there are some big chunks coming in compared to what the average man earns. I would like to go yachting. I would like to buy an A.C.Cobra. But before I do, I would like to know that everyone is getting their bowlful of rice every day. You know, I used to be just as happy when I was a butcher earning five pounds a week.'

LED ZEP BECOME NOBS

Just one of the nobs – Robert Plant

Led Zeppelin have been forced to play Copenhagen under the pseudonym The Nobs because Eva Von Zeppelin has objected to the group using her family name. It's Zep's third setback this month. Earlier, a proposed Singapore concert was cancelled by the local authority because of objections to the length of the group's hair, while at the start of the month singer Robert Plant was involved in a road accident after attending a Spirit concert.

STARR STARS IN MOVIE

The movie *'The Magic Christian'* premiered in New York City on February 11. Directed by Joseph McGrath and featuring a screenplay by McGrath, novelist Terry Southern and Peter Sellers, with additional material by Monty Python's John Cleese and Graham Chapman, it's a wacky offering about the world's wealthiest man (Sellers) and his protegé (Starr), who wreak havoc on the world at large in an effort to prove that people do anything for money.

Apple have released an album by Liverpool group Badfinger called 'Magic Christian Music' which contains songs from the film plus other items. One of the movie songs is 'Come And Get It', written and produced by Paul McCartney.

The Tull's award winning 'Stand-Up' sleeve

THE GRAPEVINE

- Joni Mitchell has announced her retirement in the wake of her London Royal Albert Hall show.
- The Who have taped a Leeds University gig for a live album.
- The NME awards for the best sleeve designs of the past year have been awarded to 'Motown Chartbusters' (EMI), Jethro Tull's 'Stand Up' (Chrysalis), Keef Hartley's 'Half Breed' (Decca) and The Who's 'Tommy' (Track).

STAR QUOTE

FRANCOISE HARDY

'Elvis – all those tight suits look sexy on him. It's unbelievable to think he's 34. I can't think of anybody but Elvis I'd put myself in trouble for.'

BLUES TRIBUTE AT THE FILLMORE

On February 11, The Butterfield Blues Band played a benefit for legendary bluesman Magic Sam at the Fillmore West in San Francisco. Also on the bill were Mike Bloomfield, Elvin Bishop Group, Charlie Musselwhite and Nick Gravenites.

THE GRAPEVINE

■ Country Joe McDonald has been charged with obscenity and fined $500 for doing his Fish cheer ('Gimme an F . . .') at a Massachusetts gig.

■ Andrew Loog Oldham's record label Immediate has gone into liquidation.

■ Peter Yarrow, of Peter, Paul And Mary, has pleaded guilty to 'taking immoral liberties' with a 14 year-old girl.

Human windmill Cocker

TAMMI TERRELL DEAD

Tamla Motown star Tammi Terrell, best known for her series of duets with Marvin Gaye – 'Ain't No Mountain High Enough', 'Your Precious Love', 'Ain't Nothing Like The Real Thing', 'If This World Were Mine', 'You're All I Need To Get By', 'What You Gave Me' and others – died at Graduate Hospital, Philadelphia on March 16, after undergoing the last of several brain tumour operations she had in the past eighteen months.

A one-time student at the University of Pennsylvania, where she studied psychology and pre-med until she quit to take up singing, Tammi signed to Mowtown in 1965 and had a couple of solo hits before becoming a major star via the Gaye duets.

During 1967 she collapsed in Gaye's arms during a show at Virginia's Hampton-Sydney college, her partner carrying her off into the wings. Initially, her collapse was believed to be due to exhaustion, but doctors later discovered a brain tumour. Tammi, real name Tammy Montgomery, was 24.

JOE COCKER GETS FRESH HELP

Joe Cocker has split with The Grease Band, with whom he recorded such hits as 'With A Little Help From My Friends' and 'Delta Lady'. He arrived in LA on March 11 to recuperate from months of strength-sapping road work with The Grease Band, but was informed by entrepreneur Dee Anthony that he had been contracted to commence a seven week tour due to begin on March 19, and that to cancel out would seriously jeopardise his chances of ever working in the USA again.

Singer-pianist-guitarist Leon Russell has assembled a 43-strong circus of singers and musicians (including former Grease Band keyboardist Chris Stainton and singer Rita Coolidge) to embark on the cross-America jaunt which will be known as The Mad Dogs And Englishmen Tour.

BOWIE WEDS

March 20: 'Space Oddity' hit-maker David Bowie, who's currently working with theatrical group The Hype, married Cyprus-born model Angela Barnett at London's Bromley Register Office.

The wedding began an hour and a half late because the two-some had overslept. Bowie's latest single, 'Prettiest Star', featuring Marc Bolan on guitar, was released by Mercury on March 6.

Bowie and spouse

CHARTS

US45	Bridge Over Troubled Water	*Simon & Garfunkel*
USLP	Bridge Over Troubled Water	*Simon & Garfunkel*
UK45	Wanderin' Star	*Lee Marvin*
UKLP	Bridge Over Troubled Water	*Simon & Garfunkel*
	WEEK 2	
US45	Bridge Over Troubled Water	*Simon & Garfunkel*
USLP	Bridge Over Troubled Water	*Simon & Garfunkel*
UK45	Wanderin' Star	*Lee Marvin*
UKLP	Bridge Over Troubled Water	*Simon & Garfunkel*
	WEEK 3	
US45	Bridge Over Troubled Water	*Simon & Garfunkel*
USLP	Bridge Over Troubled Water	*Simon & Garfunkel*
UK45	Wanderin' Star	*Lee Marvin*
UKLP	Bridge Over Troubled Water	*Simon & Garfunkel*
	WEEK 4	
US45	Bridge Over Troubled Water	*Simon & Garfunkel*
USLP	Bridge Over Troubled Water	*Simon & Garfunkel*
UK45	Bridge Over Troubled Water	*Simon & Garfunkel*
UKLP	Bridge Over Troubled Water	*Simon & Garfunkel*

PAUL McCARTNEY GOES SOLO

Paul McCartney has released 'McCartney', his first solo album. 'I made it because I've got a Studer four track machine at home, practised on it, liked the result and decided to make an album', he's reported as saying. A week earlier, a specially prepared McCartney 'interview', designed to accompany the release of the album, was leaked to the British press, causing 'Beatles Breakup' headlines around the world.

Earlier in the month, on April 3, Ringo released his solo effort 'Sentimental Journey'. But though the Fab Four may be falling apart, Apple Records still seem to be in full flight, and have signed Billy Preston to a solo contract.

THE SCHWARZ CAPER

New band Brinsley Schwarz hired a 707 jet and took 133 British media people to see them play live at New York's Fillmore East. However, the charter plane was delayed and arrived late, causing most of the extremely 'tired and emotional' scribes to miss the group's tepid, bill-opening spot. Managed by Irishman Dave Robinson, Brinsley Schwarz's line-up includes vocalist and bassist Nick Lowe.

SABS 'NOT SATANIC' SAYS IOMMI

Black Sabbath, the group formed by Ozzy Osbourne, Geezer Butler, Tony Iommi and Bill Ward, have denied that their name has anything to do with black magic. Said lead guitarist Iommi: 'Everybody thinks we're a black magic group but we picked the name because we liked it. I agree some of the numbers on our album are about supernatural things, but that's as far as it goes. We're a bit worried about the black magic bit, though. In America, people might take it seriously.'

From left: Bill Ward, Ozzy Osbourne, Geezer Butler and Tony Iommi – the sadly maligned Black Sabbath

TULL – 'NO MORE SINGLES'

Jethro Tull have announced that they are finished with releasing singles. 'Singles didn't really work for us,' said Ian Anderson. 'We sold lots of copies of "Witches Promise" for instance, but not as many as we did with the last album. And we find that most of the singles were going to people who'd already bought the album and not, as we hoped, to Edison Lighthouse fans'.

Tull's new album, 'Benefit', is released this month.

CHARTS

US45	Bridge Over Troubled Water — Simon & Garfunkel
USLP	Bridge Over Troubled Water — Simon & Garfunkel
UK45	Bridge Over Troubled Water — Simon & Garfunkel
UKLP	Bridge Over Troubled Water — Simon & Garfunkel

WEEK 2

US45	Let It Be — Beatles
USLP	Bridge Over Troubled Water — Simon & Garfunkel
UK45	Bridge Over Troubled Water — Simon & Garfunkel
UKLP	Bridge Over Troubled Water — Simon & Garfunkel

WEEK 3

US45	Let It Be — Beatles
USLP	Bridge Over Troubled Water — Simon & Garfunkel
UK45	Bridge Over Troubled Water — Simon & Garfunkel
UKLP	Bridge Over Troubled Water — Simon & Garfunkel

WEEK 4

US45	ABC — Jackson Five
USLP	Bridge Over Troubled Water — Simon & Garfunkel
UK45	Spirit In The Sky — Norman Greenbaum
UKLP	Bridge Over Troubled Water — Simon & Garfunkel

THE GRAPEVINE

■ Lord Sutch has released his latest album titled 'Lord Sutch And Heavy Friends', featuring contributions from Jimmy Page, Noel Redding, Jeff Beck, John Bonham and Nicky Hopkins.

■ Tom Jones commenced his biggest-ever American tour on April 2.

■ George Goldner, co-founder of the Roulette and Red Bird labels, has died age 52: also gone is bluesman Otis Spann, who has died of cancer, age 40.

Lord Sutch reprises 'You Need Hands'!

NEW BAND ALBUM TO BE MADE AT WOODSTOCK

The Band's second Capitol album, says Robbie Robertson, was cut 'in luxurious fashion' at the former home of Sammy Davis Jr, and they plan to record the next at a studio in Woodstock – doing the whole thing in one all-night session!

The idea came from listening to tapes made of shows in the States. 'They'd make great boot-leg material,' says Robertson. 'We've tried different ways of recording our albums and for this one we're going to learn all the songs as best we can and then we'll go down to a little place, here in Woodstock town, and do it all in a night.

'Our first album, "Music From Big Pink", was written first and then we went in to record it. The new one we wrote as we went along, and it's got a more sponta-neous feel. In a way it was a miracle that it worked, because we had gone out with a hair-brained idea and actually pulled it off.'

The Band (l to r) Garth Hudson, Richard Manuel, Levon Helm, Robbie Robertson, Rich Danko

CHARTS

US45   ABC
Jackson Five

USLP   Bridge Over Troubled Water
Simon & Garfunkel

UK45   Spirit In The Sky
Norman Greenbaum

UKLP   Bridge Over Troubled Water
Simon & Garfunkel

— WEEK 2 —

US45   American Woman
Guess Who

USLP   Bridge Over Troubled Water
Simon & Garfunkel

UK45   Back Home
England World Cup Squad

UKLP   Bridge Over Troubled Water
Simon & Garfunkel

— WEEK 3 —

US45   American Woman
Guess Who

USLP   Deja Vu
Crosby, Stills, Nash & Young

UK45   Back Home
England World Cup Squad

UKLP   Bridge Over Troubled Water
Simon & Garfunkel

— WEEK 4 —

US45   American Woman
Guess Who

USLP   McCartney
Paul McCartney

UK45   Back Home
England World Cup Squad

UKLP   Bridge Over Troubled Water
Simon & Garfunkel

— WEEK 5 —

US45   American Woman
Guess Who

USLP   McCartney
Paul McCartney

UK45   Question
Moody Blues

UKLP   Bridge Over Troubled Water
Simon & Garfunkel

THE GRAPEVINE

■ The Doors' Jim Morrison revealed that he's made a film called *'Hitchhiker'* that runs for 50 minutes.

■ Tom Jones has pocketed £150,000, reckoned to be the biggest solo fee to date, for a Louisville concert held on the eve of the Kentucky Derby.

■ The Beatles' 'Let It Be' has set a new record for advance US sales with a $3.7 million upfront order.

THE POLL WINNERS CONCERT

This year's NME poll-winner's concert proved a pop bonanza, the line-up including Blue Mink, Bob & Marcia, Brother-hood Of Man, Lou Christie, Dana, Edison Lighthouse, Steve Ellis, The Johnny Howard Band, Juicy Lucy, Marmalade, Hank Marvin & The Shadows, Picket-tywitch, The Pipkins, Cliff Richard, Clodagh Rodgers, Van-ity Fare, White Plains, Love Affair, Rare Bird and Brinsley Schwarz. It was hosted by Tony Blackburn and Jimmy Savile.

GREEN FOR GO

Peter Green has quit Fleetwood Mac, playing his final gig with the band at London's Chalk Farm Roundhouse. The band is look-ing for a suitable replacement.

Meanwhile, a British tour (due to commence on June 1) has been cancelled. A Mac single featuring Peter Green, 'The Green Mahal-ishi (With The Two Prong Crown)', was released on Reprise earlier this month.

BEATLES RELEASE 'CHEAPSKATE' ALBUM

The Beatles have released a new album 'Let It Be', which bears three production credits. George Martin (assisted by Glyn Johns) produced the original tracks which – after being pronounced 'worthless' by the Fabs – were sal-vaged by Phil Spector.

Comments NME's Alan Smith: 'If The Beatles soundtrack album "Let It Be" is to be their last, then it will stand as a cheap-skate epitaph, a cardboard tomb-stone, a sad and tatty end to a musical fusion which wiped clean and drew again the face of pop music.'

A movie, also called *'Let It Be'*, documenting the making of the album, is to be premiered in New York on May 13.

ELP – THE GROUP MOST LIKELY?

New group Emerson, Lake & Palmer are currently rehearsing for their first tour. Born out of a slice of The Nice, King Crimson and Atomic Rooster respectively, the band came to be out of Emerson and Lake's informal conversations in America last year, where King Crimson and The Nice were on tour.

Bassist Greg Lake has affirmed that contractual hassles have absorbed a great deal of their time, particularly so with drummer Carl Palmer, who only got his release from Atomic Rooster at the beginning of June. Carl thought it highly amusing that his final gig on May 31 had been thought big deal enough to merit the billing 'Atomic Rooster – Last performance with Carl Palmer'.

Among the material they're rehearsing is 'Rondo', plus a delightful composition titled 'Take A Pebble'. 'It's not ready yet though,' said organist Keith Emerson, 'give us two more months to knock it together.'

RAY DAVIES FLIES 6,000 MILES FOR A WORD

Ray Davies of The Kinks made a 6,000 mile round trip from New York to London and back – just to change one word of the Kink's new single 'Lola'.

The original lyric contained a reference to Coca-Cola, which Britain's BBC Radio One – the country's most powerful station – would regard as advertising and slap a broadcasting ban on the disc.

Ray, who came back to change the reference to 'Cherry Cola', thus ensuring airplay, is currently touring the States with The Kinks, where they're fully booked until June 23, when they play Seattle. After this they move on to play dates in Canada before completing their tour at Honolulu Earth Station (June 29-July 1) and LA's Whiskey A Go-Go (July 3-5).

Ray Davies wondering whether the BBC are into soda pop

CHARTS

US45	Everything Is Beautfiul	*Ray Stevens*
USLP	McCartney	*Paul McCartney*
UK45	Yellow River	*Christie*
UKLP	Let It Be	*Beatles*

— WEEK 2 —

US45	The Long & Winding Road	*Beatles*
USLP	Let It Be	*Beatles*
UK45	In The Summertime	*Mungo Jerry*
UKLP	Let It Be	*Beatles*

— WEEK 3 —

US45	The Long & Winding Road	*Beatles*
USLP	Let It Be	*Beatles*
UK45	In The Summertime	*Mungo Jerry*
UKLP	Let it Be	*Beatles*

— WEEK 4 —

US45	The Love You Save	*Jackson Five*
USLP	Let It Be	*Beatles*
UK45	In The Summertime	*Mungo Jerry*
UKLP	Bridge Over Troubled Water	*Simon & Garfunkel*

SYD RE-APPEARS

The enigmatic Syd Barrett selected Extravaganza '70, at London's Olympia Stadium, to make his first public appearance since leaving Pink Floyd two years ago. Assisted by fellow Floydian Dave Gilmour on bass, and Humble Pie drummer Jerry Shirley, Syd played 'Terrapin', 'Gigolo Aunt', 'Effervescing Elephant' and 'Octopus' before beating a hasty retreat.

Syd Barrett – the police can now remove their missing person notices

---

A twist in fate for Chubby

THE GRAPEVINE

- Chubby Checker has been arrested at Niagara Falls after police found various forms of drugs in his car.

- Janis Joplin unveiled her Full Tilt Boogie Band in Louisville on June 12, but the gig was sparsely attended.

- Grand Funk Railroad have spent $100,000 on a New York Times Square billboard to advertise their latest release, 'Closer To Home'.

'JUST CALL ME MRS McVIE'

Christine Perfect, whose self-titled debut album was released in Britain by Blue Horizon on June 13 has announced that she is to leave the music business. Also, in future, she will be content to be known as plain Mrs John McVie.

The main reason for this, she admitted, was that her solo career was not following its predicted route. 'I was not even making enough money to pay my band,' she confided.

1970

HOW CAT FOUGHT OFF THOUGHTS OF DEATH

Cat Stevens has revealed that he became a split personality a while back. He was ill in hospital with TB and claims: 'Every morning I would see a coffin go by my window and I thought I'd had it. Then in the middle of some deep meditation, I found myself in a rainstorm. But only my outside was getting wet. You know, the real me was still dry inside and I thought: 'I'm not really ill, I just think I am.'

Stevens, whose comeback single, 'Lady D'Arbanville', has just gone Top 20 in Britain, said that his new album, 'Mona Bone Jakon', has a cover painting titled 'The Dustbin Cried The Day The Dustman Died'. 'I did that one to draw attention to dustbins - they're very underprivileged.' Cat is currently writing the music for 'Deep End', a movie directed by Jerzy Skolmowski and starring Jane Asher, Paul McCartney's ex.

Sebastian in 'festivals are no daydream' shock!

DIY PAYS OFF FOR HOTLEGS

The growing trend among groups to write their own material and produce their own records is paying off handsomely for Hotlegs, who've entered the UK charts with their 'Neanderthal Man' single. But Hotlegs have taken the process a step further by recording at Stockport's Strawberry Studios, which are part owned by their lead guitarist Eric Stewart, who used to be with The Mindbenders.

Eric's fellow members of Hotlegs are Kevin Godley (drums, percussion, vibes and vocals) and Lol Creme (acoustic guitars, records, piano, bass and vocals). Both Kevin and Lol are basically graphic artists and are currently working on models to go with the Pan Books novel of the film 'Oliver Cromwell'. The next pro-ject Kevin and Lol will be undertaking is the creation of more models, this time to go with the film 'The Railway Children'.

Hotlegs – Neanderthal men

ATLANTA FESTIVAL – 'A DISASTER ZONE'

The Governor of Georgia, Lester Maddox, is attempting to have rock festivals banned in his state following drug-related problems at the recent Atlanta Festival, which spanned July 3-5.

A crowd of 200,000 attended the show, which featured Jimi Hendrix, John Sebastian, Mountain, Procol Harum, Poco, Jethro Tull, Johnny Winter, B.B. King and others, but the drug-control system quickly deteriorated, causing local medics to attempt to have the area declared an official health disaster zone.

CHARTS

US45	The Love You Save *Jackson Five*
USLP	Let It Be *Beatles*
UK45	In The Summertime *Mungo Jerry*
UKLP	Bridge Over Troubled Water *Simon & Garfunkel*
WEEK 2	
US45	Mama Told Me Not To Come *Three Dog Night*
USLP	Woodstock *Soundtrack*
UK45	All Right Now *Free*
UKLP	Bridge Over Troubled Water *Simon & Garfunkel*
WEEK 3	
US45	Mama Told Me Not To Come *Three Dog Night*
USLP	Woodstock *Soundtrack*
UK45	All Right Now *Free*
UKLP	Let It Be *Beatles*
WEEK 4	
US45	(They Long To Be) Close To You *Carpenters*
USLP	Woodstock *Soundtrack*
UK45	All Right Now *Free*
UKLP	Bridge Over Troubled Water *Simon & Garfunkel*

THE GRAPEVINE

■ The Everly Brothers now have their own series of one-hour TV shows in the States. The series goes out over the ABC network and runs until September 16.

■ The Rolling Stones have split from manager Allen Klein and his company, ABKCO.

■ The FBI is mounting an investigation into counterfeit record rings following a flood of bootleg releases in the States.

FLOYD IN THE PARK

Pink Floyd are to headline a free concert in London's Hyde Park on July 18. Also booked for the gig are Roy Harper, Edgar Broughton, Kevin Ayers, Robert Wyatt, Lol Coxhill and Formerly Fat Harry.

NO MORE IOW FESTIVALS SAY FOULKS

Even before the third Isle of Wight festival was over, the Foulk brothers of Fiery Creations, the shindig's promoters, announced that there would be no more in the series because their losses totalled some £90,000 ($180,000). As a musical experience, however, the festival, which took place over the August Bank Holiday weekend, was an enormous success, the line-up including Melanie, Procol Harum, Chicago, Taste, Family, Cactus, Emerson Lake & Palmer, The Doors, Joni Mitchell, Ten Years After, The Who, Sly & The Family Stone, Donovan, Leonard Cohen,

Moody Blues, Jimi Hendrix, Joan Baez, Voices Of East Harlem, Miles Davis, Tiny Tim, Richie Havens, Free, Arrival, and Jethro Tull.

Joni Mitchell's set was marred when one spectator jumped on stage and began yelling to people on a nearby hill – but she recovered to complete an act that proved worthy of four encores.

There was also a pause in the proceedings on the Sunday night, when one DJ ambled to the mike and casually informed the crowd: 'There's something I have to tell you – the stage is on fire.' This flare-up, caused by a stray firework, proved momenta-

Peace! Or something ruder

rily spectacular, but was got under control eventually without much hassle.

That, though, was the least of the Foulks' problems. They'd laid out nearly £500,000 ($1 million) up front – about half going on talent costs alone – and it seems highly improbable that they will be able to recoup much on movie rights, unlike the Woodstock Festival promoters. Nevertheless, British Rail claims to be happy, reckoning that, during the period of the festival, 600,000 people used their ferries to reach the island.

Dave Clark ready-steady-going with Kathy McGowan (second right)

DAVE CLARK CALLS IT A DAY

After selling 35 million records since they turned professional in March 1964, The Dave Clark Five have disbanded. Though Clark says that the group will never again appear in public, he has stockpiled over 60 tracks to be released periodically.

Additionally, another Dave has been involved in a split this week. Stax soulmen Sam and Dave are going their separate ways after a 10-year partnership, which included such modern classics as 'Hold On, I'm Coming', 'You Don't Know Like I Know' and 'Soulman'.

CHRISTINE JOINS THE MAC

Christine McVie has confirmed rumours that she is to join Fleetwood Mac. The band's manager Clifford Davis revealed that she had been invited to join after sitting in with them at their Hampstead hideout and immediately accepted the offer.

1970

RIGHT SONG SAVES THE CARPENTERS

ELVIS ON TOUR

Elvis Presley has begun his first US tour in almost 14 years – and finished it! The tour began in Phoenix, Arizona on September 9 and visited St Louis (10), Detroit (11), Miami (12), Tampa (13) and Mobile (14). In Phoenix a bomb scare delayed the start of the show.

INVICTUS – THE NEW MOTOWN?

The Invictus label has Britain's two top singles – Freda Payne's 'Band Of Gold' holding the pole position while Chairman Of The Board's 'Give Me Just A Little More Time" is at No. 2.

This represents a remarkable achievement for Holland-Dozier-Holland, the songwriting and production team that left Motown to form a rival record company. Now, after just a brief life span, Invictus is already proving a worthy challenger to Berry Gordy's previously all-conquering label.

The Carpenters are snowed under with requests for in-person concerts and TV appearances and their records are selling by the boatload – all thanks to 'Close To You', a song written six years ago by Burt Bacharach and Hal David for Dionne Warwick.

But only a couple of months ago, the brother/sister act were wondering if they'd still be working together by the end of the year. Now, in the wake of success with 'Close To You', a US No. 1 which is also riding high in the UK charts, the couple look certain to achieve further kudos with 'We've Only Just Begun', their latest US release. All of which causes Richard Carpenter to declare: 'Everything is going according to plan.'

Richard does all the arranging and orchestrations on the Car-

Singing drummer Karen Carpenter with keyboard-playing relative

penters' albums, on which sister Karen takes lead vocals. In addition, Richard wrote 10 songs on their A&M debut album and four on the second. Herb Alpert signed the group after hearing them sing 'Ticket To Ride' on the radio.

HENDRIX 'NO JUNKIE' SAYS PATHOLOGIST

A coroner's inquest into the death of Jimi Hendrix, who died at a London, Notting Hill, flat on September 18, has established that the guitarist died of 'suffocation from inhalation of vomit'. Pathologist Professor Donald Teare added that there was no evidence that Hendrix had been a drug addict and had no needle marks anywhere on his body. Jimi was 27.

CANNED HEAT MEMBER FOUND DEAD

Al 'Blind Owl' Wilson, singer and guitarist with Canned Heat, has been found dead in fellow band member Bob Hite's garden in Topanga Canyon, California. Aged 27, he was discovered with an empty bottle of barbiturates at his side.

Wilson's death casts doubt on the continued survival of Canned Heat, who have scored major international hits with 'On The Road Again', 'Going Up The Country' and 'Let's Work Together', although the band have been preparing to record with blues veteran John Lee Hooker.

Al Wilson and hip harp

■ Bing Crosby has been awarded a second platinum disc by US Decca for record sales in excess of 300 million.

■ Fleetwood Mac have released their first post-Peter Green album, 'Kiln House' (Reprise).

■ Miami authorities have acquitted 'Flasher' Jim Morrison on a charge of lewd behaviour, but have adjudged him guilty of indecent exposure and profanity.

CHARTS

US45	War *Edwin Starr*
USLP	Cosmo's Factory *Creedence Clearwater Revival*
UK45	Tears Of A Clown *Smokey Robinson & Miracles*
UKLP	A Question Of Balance *Moody Blues*

WEEK 2

US45	War *Edwin Starr*
USLP	Cosmo's Factory *Creedence Clearwater Revival*
UK45	Tears Of A Clown *Smokey Robinson & Miracles*
UKLP	A Question Of Balance *Moody Blues.*

WEEK 3

US45	Ain't No Mountain High Enough *Diana Ross*
USLP	Cosmo's Factory *Creedence Clearwater Revival*
UK45	Tears Of A Clown *Smokey Robinson & Miracles*
UKLP	A Question Of Balance *Moody Blues*

WEEK 4

US45	Ain't No Mountain High Enough *Diana Ross*
USLP	Cosmo's Factory *Creedence Clearwater Revival*
UK45	Band Of Gold *Freda Payne*
UKLP	Bridge Over Troubled Water *Simon & Garfunkel*

JANIS O.D.s

Janis Joplin was found dead of a drug overdose in a room at Hollywood's Landmark Hotel on October 4. She was discovered laying face down with fresh puncture marks in her arm. The singer had frequently suffered from drink and drugs problems in the past, yet things seemed to be taking an upturn in her career.

She claimed to be extremely happy with her new Full Tilt Band and had just completed work on 'Pearl', a forthcoming CBS album. Additionally, she'd recently become engaged to Seth Morgan, the son of a prestigious New York family and a student at Berkeley.

Earlier in the year, referring to Jimi Hendrix's death, she said: 'I can't go out this year because he was a bigger star.'

CHARTS

US45	Ain't No Mountain High Enough	*Diana Ross*
USLP	Cosmo's Factory	*Creedence Clearwater Revival*
UK45	Band Of Gold	*Freda Payne*
UKLP	Bridge Over Troubled Water	*Simon & Garfunkel*

— WEEK 2 —

US45	Cracklin' Rosie	*Neil Diamond*
USLP	Cosmo's Factory	*Creedence Clearwater Revival*
UK45	Band Of Gold	*Freda Payne*
UKLP	Bridge Over Troubled Water	*Simon & Garfunkel*

— WEEK 3 —

US45	I'll Be There	*Jackson Five*
USLP	Cosmo's Factory	*Creedence Clearwater Revival*
UK45	Band Of Gold	*Freda Payne*
UKLP	Paranoid	*Black Sabbath*

— WEEK 4 —

US45	I'll Be There	*Jackson Five*
USLP	Abraxas	*Santana*
UK45	Band Of Gold	*Freda Payne*
UKLP	Paranoid	*Black Sabbath*

— WEEK 5 —

US45	I'll Be There	*Jackson Five*
USLP	Led Zeppelin III	*Led Zeppelin*
UK45	Black Night	*Deep Purple*
UKLP	Led Zeppelin III	*Led Zeppelin*

STAR NAMES FOR TV

Ray Stevens, Lesley Gore, Jerry Reed and Esther Ofarim are flying to Britain for guest spots on BBC 1's new series hosted by Australian Rolf Harris, beginning on Saturday, October 24. Other guests set to appear include Dusty Springfield, The Hollies, Lulu, Italy's Caterina Valente and Tom Paxton.

Black Sabbath, Julie Felix and Labi Siffre guest in Granada's TV 'Lift-Off' on October 21, while Mott The Hoople and Bridget St John are showcased in BBC 2's 'Disco 2' on October 10.

Nashville picker Jerry Reed

TAYLOR-MADE STAR OF FILM AND TV

James Taylor, in Britain to play a Sunday concert at the London Palladium, has been filming an 'In Concert' programme for BBC Television. Talking about shooting the movie *'Two Lane Blacktop'*, in which he plays the driver of a cross-country dragster, Taylor said: 'That took us all over the Midwest: Macon, Georgia, Little Rock, Arkansas, Boswell, Oklahoma, and everywhere like that. That movie took about two months and involved working 13 hours a day, at least.'

Taylor opened his TV concert with 'With A Little Help From My Friends', and continued with 'Fire And Rain', before indulging in a very funny take-off of Ray Charles's 'Things Go Better With Coca-Cola', which may be edited out of the show before screening. 'Sweet Baby James', 'Carolina On My Mind' and 'Sunny Skies' were also included, along with 'Steamroller', a song written when James was with New York group Flying Machine, in 1966.

MOVE BECOMES 10-PIECE

Roy Wood's ambitious plans to augment The Move into a 10-piece ensemble named The Electric Light Orchestra have, at last, been realised. The project, which was first reported last year, has finally reached fruition this month with the news that the much enlarged outfit is currently rehearsing.

The line-up includes a string quartet, a french horn and two miscellaneous instruments – plus Jeff Lynn on piano and lead guitar, Roy Wood on bass, acoustic guitar and oboe, and Bev Bevan on drums. It is, however, stressed that The Move will still continue to operate as a small group.

BEE GEES TOGETHER AGAIN

"Maurice only has courgettes" – Barry Gibb in the upcoming Cucumber Castle

The first record by the newly-reunited Bee Gees, 'Two Years On', gains a release at the end of the month. The group have been arguing for ages but, as Robin Gibb explains: 'We actually came together on Friday, August 21. We had been together the night before – but with our lawyers, arguing about the same things that we had been fighting over for months. Next day, we met at Robert Stigwood's office to carry on the argument and suddenly it was all over. We just threw it out the window and decided to go straight into the studio again.'

Maurice Gibb has now returned from Ireland, where he went to attend the premiere of Richard Harris's latest film, 'Bloomfield', for which he wrote part of the score.

Other Bee Gee news involves a forthcoming TV spectacular called 'Cucumber Castle'. Shortly to be screened by the BBC, the show was shot before Robin rejoined the group and includes appearances by Lulu, former Goon Spike Milligan and horror king Vincent Price.

BEACH BOY GENIUS FIGHTS DEAFNESS

Brian Wilson – his return to live work was brief

Brian Wilson is fighting against total deafness. This development has apparently been caused by The Beach Boys, the group he nurtured, playing too loudly! Brian has experienced ear trouble for some years and this was given as the reason he gave up playing regularly with the group to assume a more background role.

However, earlier this month, he decided to sit in with the Beach Boys when they were playing LA's Whiskey A Go-Go – the first time he's played with the group in public for some five years. But, after having to be helped off stage, Brian is now undergoing treatment in LA. It's said that even if he does retain his hearing, Brian will be unlikely ever to risk playing with the group again on a full-time basis.

CLAPTON IN NASHVILLE

Eric Clapton is in Nashville recording the TV debut of his new band, The Dominoes, for the Johnny Cash Show. Earlier, he'd been in Miami producing an album for blues giants Junior Wells and Buddy Guy. Asked if he'd played on the sessions, he replied: 'Are you kidding? With cats like that, there's really no reason to play. I just produced it for them.'

Talking about his role as lead vocalist with The Dominoes, Eric said: 'I was hoping Duane Allman would come up and do the Cash show with me. We're doing a couple of songs Duane did with me on the album, and with him playing lead I would have more chance to get into my singing.'

Allman, for his part, claimed: 'Eric Clapton's the only English guitarist I respect. He's a gas to work with and just a totally nice dude.'

STAR QUOTE

JOE JACKSON
(The Jackson 5's father)

'All the boys have to clean their own rooms, wash dishes, mop and wax the floors. We want them to be good boys and respect their mother and father.'

CHARTS

US45	I'll Be There – Jackson Five
USLP	Led Zeppelin III – Led Zeppelin
UK45	Woodstock – Matthews' Southern Comfort
UKLP	Motown Chartbusters, Vol. 4 – Various

WEEK 2
US45	I'll Be There – Jackson Five
USLP	Led Zeppelin III – Led Zeppelin
UK45	Woodstock – Matthews' Southern Comfort
UKLP	Led Zeppelin III – Led Zeppelin

WEEK 3
US45	I Think I Love You – Partridge Family
USLP	Led Zeppelin III – Led Zeppelin
UK45	Woodstock – Matthews' Southern Comfort
UKLP	Led Zeppelin III – Led Zeppelin

WEEK 4
US45	I Think I Love You – Partridge Family
USLP	Abraxas – Santana
UK45	Voodoo Chile – Jimi Hendrix
UKLP	Led Zeppelin III – Led Zeppelin

PURPLE AND THE FRAULEIN

Ian Gillan gets ready to duck

Deep Purple are the latest band to suffer from the deplorable antics of German 'fans' who want all concerts to be free. At the slightest suggestion of an entrance fee, upwards of 1,000 troublemakers gather at the hall and then provoke everybody in sight into damaging property. 'They had battering rams in Heidelberg and they were trying to get at the band,' claimed Purple's Ian Paice. 'We saw a girl driving round in a car with a loudspeaker on top, organising the riots. She was at Heidelberg and in Hanover too. At Hanover, we were about four floors up and they were throwing lumps of rock up at the windows.'

BEATLES – THE FINAL CHAPTER?

Paul McCartney has filed a writ in the London High Court against 'The Beatles Co', seeking the legal dissolution of the Beatles' partnership. Just prior to Christmas, speculation favoured a Beatles reunion, despite the fact that during 1970 the four members of the group all emerged as highly successful solo artists.

CHARTS

US45	I Think I Love You	Partridge Family
USLP	Abraxas	Santana
UK45	I Hear You Knocking	Dave Edmunds
UKLP	Led Zeppelin III	Led Zeppelin

WEEK 2

US45	Tears Of A Clown	Smokey Robinson & The Miracles
USLP	Abraxas	Santana
UK45	I Hear You Knocking	Dave Edmunds
UKLP	Led Zeppelin III	Led Zeppelin

WEEK 3

US45	Tears Of A Clown	Smokey Robinson & The Miracles
USLP	Abraxas	Santana
UK45	I Hear You Knocking	Dave Edmunds
UKLP	Motown Chartbusters, Vol.4	Various

WEEK 4

US45	My Sweet Lord	George Harrison
USLP	Abraxas	Santana
UK45	When I'm Dead And Gone	McGuinness Flint
UKLP	Led Zeppelin III	Led Zeppelin

THE GRAPEVINE

■ Both John Lennon and Yoko Ono have released albums titled 'The Plastic Ono Band'.

■ The Rolling Stones' documentary *'Gimme Shelter'* had its US premiere on December 6, the first anniversary of Altamont.

■ Beach Boy Dennis Wilson and Rumbo's single 'Sound Of Free' has been given a release in the UK only on Stateside.

MORRISON RECORDS POEMS

The Doors' Jim Morrison spent several hours of his 27th birthday, December 8, recording poetry at Elektra's LA studio. The Doors have since played two sell-out shows in Dallas (December 10) where they previewed their forthcoming album and received two encores after each set. They also played New Orleans (December 11), but this was reportedly a disaster, Morrison picking up the mike in frustration, smashing it repeatedly into the stage until the wood shattered, after which he threw the stand into the crowd and then slumped down, sitting motionless before a stunned audience.

ROCKFIELD NO BARN SAYS EDMUNDS

Though Dave Edmunds has a massive UK hit in 'I Hear You Knockin', he says that his band, Rockpile, is not yet ready to tour and he intends to complete an album first. Said Edmunds: 'The papers are saying there's a lot of money behind me – but that is complete rubbish. I'm not part of the manufactured pop world, I paid for my own sessions and worked hard to produce the sound I want.

'I would also like to correct a statement put out by my publicist. I do not own Rockfield Studio, where I work – it's owned by two very good friends of mine, Charles and Kingsley Ward. And it is NOT a barn!'

Dave Edmunds who's covered Smiley Lewis' 1955 R&B biggie

BYE BYE BEATLES – THE FAB FOUR FALL APART

The precise date when The Beatles, the most successful and popular group of the rock era, split up is difficult to pinpoint. The process was gradual and probably began in August 1967 when their manager Brian Epstein died, ostensibly of an accidental overdose of sleeping pills.

Epstein had tried, usually with some success, to provide a barrier between the group and the rest of the world. With his absence, the individual Beatles found that they lacked an objective critic who could talk them out of their worst excesses. While the group had provided employment for several old friends from Liverpool like Mal Evans and Neil Aspinall, none of these mates felt sufficiently confident to question the unlikely schemes dreamed up by John, Paul, George and Ringo, who were pleased to have stepped off the touring treadmill, but were also rather bored.

Another significant occurrence came with the romance between John Lennon and Japanese avant-garde artist Yoko Ono, which would result before long in Lennon's divorce from his first wife, Cynthia. This affair coincidentally took place around the same time that Paul McCartney's long-running relationship with actress Jane Asher started to disintegrate, and Paul met Linda Eastman, a photographer from New York, who later became his wife.

The presence of two new close companions forced the Beatles' main songwriting partnership to spend more time away from each other and the rest of the group than had been their habit since coming to fame.

Added to these new attachments was the increased pressure on all The Beatles to keep producing hit records. One of the reasons for the group's deciding to stop touring after 1965 was that it would leave them greater opportunities for writing and recording.

But when Epstein died, the group found itself without a decision-maker. Lennon was too besotted with Yoko Ono to want to spend time thinking about the group's career, yet he was also resentful towards McCartney for undertaking duties which many felt he should have assumed himself. In the wake of Epstein's death, many powerful managers were offering their services to The Beatles, and while Lennon was most interested in a New York accountant named Allen Klein, who had previously worked with The Rolling Stones, his songwriting partner (not surprisingly) favoured the New York law practice of Eastman & Eastman, run by his future father-in-law and brother-in-law.

Ultimately, George and Ringo sided with John Lennon, supposedly after Klein had provoked Lee Eastman into a verbal attack which the group witnessed. Lennon, in particular, was impressed by what he felt he had in common with Klein who thus represented 75 per cent of The Beatles during the early 1970s, while the Eastmans looked after Paul's business. It was hardly an ideal situation, especially as the group was now firmly divided into two camps, each of which seemed to be pulling in different directions much of the time.

Things were not helped by the shelving of what was planned as a filmed documentary about the making of a new Beatle album, to be titled 'Get Back', which eventually emerged as 'Let It Be' after it had finally become evident that The Beatles did not intend to work together again. John Lennon was far more interested in his other group, The Plastic Ono Band, which had enjoyed several hits while Paul, George and Ringo had all become involved in their

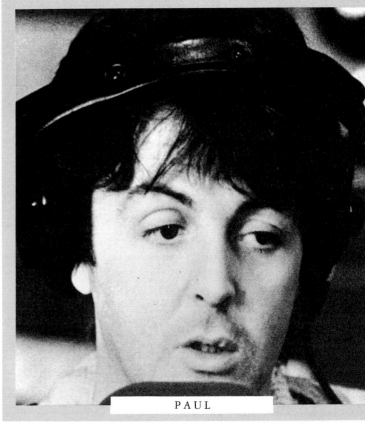

PAUL

JOHN

The peak? 'Sergeant Pepper'

own recording projects. When Paul announced that he was leaving the group and a week later released his first solo album, The Beatles officially came to an end. By the start of 1974, when McCartney released 'Band On The Run', each of the erstwhile Beatles had proved that there was life and commercial success to be found as an artist in his own right.

Nevertheless, it was only after John Lennon had been murdered in December 1980, that the world finally stopped clamouring for the biggest group in the world to reform for just one more album.

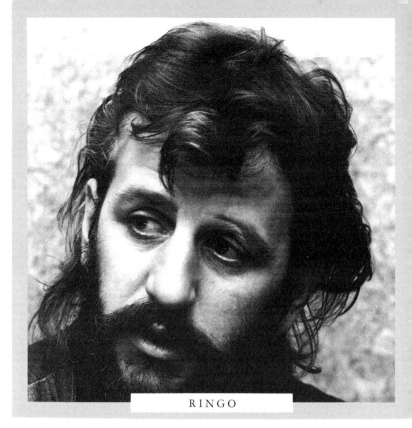

RINGO

GEORGE

End of the road 'Let It Be'

Yoko, Julian and John

Denny Laine, Linda and Paul

THE GRAPEVINE

■ Folk-rockers Fotheringay (which features ex-Fairport Convention singer Sandy Denny and her bassist hubby Trevor Lucas) are the first band of the year to announce a split - their London Queen Elizabeth Hall gig on January 30 will now be a farewell performance.

■ Diana Ross marries PR man Robert Silberstein in Las Vegas on January 21. Silberstein is also known as Robert Ellis.

ZAPPA ZAPS PRESSMEN

Frank Zappa. He'll be checking into a motel shortly

Frank Zappa, who has never disguised his low opinion of music press journalists walked out of a London press conference called to unveil plans for the filming of The Mothers Of Invention's sex, drugs and rock'n'roll fantasy, *200 Motels*, due to begin at Pinewood Studios in February.

A row began when writers complained that much of what was being announced had already appeared in a Sunday newspaper interview Zappa had done. At first he apologized, claiming that he had been duped into doing the interview – but that brought the response: 'Why didn't you check it out with United Artists, your record label?'

The discussion became increasingly heated and acrimonious, with two UK national paper writers pressing Zappa to say whether or not he trusted his PR people.

Eventually tiring of the barrage of awkward questions, Zappa began a dialogue which began: 'There's one sequence in the movie where a girl journalist comes onstage and sits in a chair and begins asking me a series of really banal questions . . .'. After which, he downed his drink and stalked out of the room.

For the record, *200 Motels* is to star Theodore Bikel, and will include acting roles for Ringo Starr, Keith Moon (who plays a nun!), former Turtles singers Mark Volman and Howard Kaylan (now members of The Mothers and re-named Flo & Eddie by Zappa), and Mothers' drummer Aynsley Dunbar. British music critic and film maker Tony Palmer is to direct, and the soundtrack will feature The Mothers Of Invention and The Royal Philharmonic Orchestra, conducted by Elgar Howarth.

DEMOB FOR BAKER'S AIRFORCE

Ginger Baker, showman supreme

Ginger Baker's Airforce, whose second album 'Airforce 2' was recently released, is to disband at the end of the group's current series of British club and concert dates.

The group's lifetime will have spanned just 17 months when the final date is played on February 20. Airforce was originally formed by the former Cream drummer for just one Royal Albert Hall concert, but has since featured such members as Steve Winwood and Chris Wood (ex Traffic), former Family bassist Ric Grech, one-time Moody Blues singer Denny Laine, jazz drummer Phil Seaman and The Plastic Ono Band's Alan White.

STAR QUOTE

GILBERT O'SULLIVAN

'When I'm dressed normally, the girls hang around and talk and maybe ask for autographs. When I get dressed up, the girls run away.'

DYLAN ON TV

Bob Dylan made a rare TV appearance on *Earl Scruggs: His Family And Friends*, a NET-TV Special aired in the US on January 100, the twosome playing 'East Virginia Rag' and 'Nashville Skyline Rag'. Scruggs, a legendary bluegrass banjoist, is best-known as half of Flatt and Scruggs, who had a 1962 hit with 'The Ballad Of Jed Clampett', theme to *The Beverly Hillbillies* TV show.

HARRISON HARASSED

George – the way he was

George Harrison's publishing company and Apple are being sued over his world-wide hit 'My Sweet Lord'.

According to papers filed by American writer/manager Ronald Mack, the ex-Beatle's song infringes the copyright of The Chiffons' 1963 million-seller 'He's So Fine', which Mack wrote while managing the Brooklyn quartet.

Details published in connection with Paul McCartney's action to dissolve The Beatles' partnership indicate that 'My Sweet Lord' will earn Harrison more than a million pounds this year, which makes the Mack lawsuit potentially huge in settlement terms, should Harrison fail to establish his innocence.

WEATHERMEN IS/ARE KING

British pop prankster Jonathan King has admitted what everyone has suspected for weeks – he is The Weathermen, whose single 'It's The Same Old Song' is currently riding high in the UK charts, and he supplied all three lead vocal voices on the disc, as well as writing and producing it.

King, a graduate of Cambridge University and until recently personal assistant to Sir Edward Lewis, chairman of British Decca Records (The Stones' label), is now looking for three singer-musicians who can go out as The Weathermen for concert appearances.

Initially, however, they'll back King whenever The Weathermen are booked to appear on TV or radio. Explains Jonathan: 'I'm willing to go on TV or radio, but I won't go back on the road again. I turned that in a long time ago.'

Music fans with long memories will recall King first achieving prominence when his 'Everyone's Gone To The Moon' was a huge British and European hit in 1965, while he was still a student. He was also the man behind Hedgehoppers Anonymous' 'It's Good News Week', and host of the ATV series 'Good Evening' in 1966.

NO RETIREMENT SAYS SANDIE

'The Lump' – as Sandie Shaw affectionately called it – has gone, and Sandie is now the proud mother of daughter Grace. But there is no way that motherhood is going to force Sandie into premature retirement, or to settling down to just being plain Mrs Banks (she's married to fashion designer Jeff).

Until a few weeks before Grace's birth, Sandie was hard at work promoting her new single 'Rose Garden', and she will return to recording as soon as she's able, and once she's found the right nanny for Grace.

"These days I can afford shoes. But it's still the park bench at night." Pop mum of the month Sandie Shaw

THE GRAPEVINE

■ Eric Burdon's UK tour with War was cancelled when it was discovered the singer had flown back to LA, seemingly suffering from 'sheer exhaustion'.

■ Balls, the new supergroup which included Denny Laine and Steve Gibbons in its line-up, has split.

■ Cabaret singer Annie Haslam has joined Renaissance, replacing American vocalist Binky.

Peter, Paul And Mary – they first got together in Greenwich Village during the early '60s, after Mary had appeared in a flop Broadway musical

'I WANTED TO BE A VET' SAYS OLIVIA

Ex-Toomorrow singer Olivia Newton-John, whose version of Bob Dylan's 'If Not For You' has gone Top 10 in Britain, says: 'I haven't always thought about going into show business professionally. I originally wanted to be a vet. I got as far as my 'O' level exams, then left school and started singing.

'I formed a duo with a friend from Australia – we were called Pat and Olivia – but we kept forgetting each other was on stage and the mike leads got tangled up!'

She describes life with supergroup Toomorrow as 'frustrating', adding: 'Our film died a death and it was all a bit of a shambles. But it was good experience.'

Olivia has just completed some guest spots on the Cliff Richard BBC TV series in London.

SINATRA QUITS

Frank Sinatra has announced that he's quitting what he describes as 'the show biz scene'. The 55 year-old entertainer plans to spend most of his time writing and possibly teaching.

It is not yet clear whether he will make any more records, but the tone of his announcement indicates that he will not. Sinatra is due to play farewell charity concerts in the States in May and June.

FLY AWAY PETER, PAUL AND MARY TOO!

Peter, Paul and Mary have broken up with Peter Yarrow, Paul Stookey and Mary Travers all agreeing to go their separate ways. First to announce plans for the future is Mary Travers, whose solo album 'Mary' has just been released in America.

She'll do an American concert tour during April and May with a specially formed quartet before spending time guesting on various TV shows in New York and LA.

Yarrow and Stookey's plans have not yet been revealed.

SECOND WOODSTOCK ALBUM – DETAILS

Editing of a second double-album 'Woodstock' compilation has now been completed. The resulting set is to be released in the States shortly, with a British release expected to follow within the next two months.

The albums are dedicated to the late Jimi Hendrix, who's featured throughout one entire side. Also showcased in this latest collection are Crosby, Stills, Nash and Young, Melanie, Joan Baez, Jefferson Airplane, The Butterfield Blues Band, Canned Heat and Mountain.

And there is still enough material left over from the legendary 1969 festival recordings for a third double-album to be issued in the future.

DIANA TO PORTRAY LADY DAY

Diana Ross has confirmed that she is to appear in her first movie role. She will portray Billie Holiday in 'Lady Sings The Blues', a film based around the life of the famous jazz singer who died in 1969.

Tamla Motown are to finance the movie to the tune of five and a half million dollars with Berry Gordy producing. Motown recently announced that it was widening the scope of its activities and would allocate 15 million dollars this year to film, stage and TV productions. Its first venture was a Diana Ross TV special.

Diana Ross (left) and the late, great Billie Holiday (right). Billie, known as Lady Day, was a one-time prostitute who eventually became acclaimed the greatest of all jazz vocalists

MAMAS AND PAPAS REFORM

The Mamas And Papas are back together four years after they announced their disbandment – and they're already fashioning a new album.

It is not known whether the quartet intend to make any live appearances in the immediate future but if the reunion is permanent, concert dates will certainly follow.

SWEET: PURE POP AND PROUD

The Sweet are the most recent new group to break into the UK Top 30, with their single 'Funny Funny'. Its appeal is strictly to the teen market – a fact the group don't try to hide. Indeed, they are positively proud of it.

'We enjoy playing pop music', guitarist Andy Scott explains. 'We do other numbers onstage which are less obviously commercial than "Funny Funny", but whatever we do is centred around vocal harmonies.'

Record producers Nicky Chinn and Mike Chapman have already written The Sweet's follow-up single, which is called 'Co-Co', Scott revealed, adding: 'We've also got an album coming out soon, for which Nicky and Mike have written four songs.'

All four members of the group, (which was formed in 1968 by drummer Mick Tucker and lead singer Brian Connolly,

along with Andy Scott and bassist Steve Priest), seem to accept that people will compare them to bubblegum supergroup The Archies.

'The Archies had a number one, didn't they?', quipped Brian Connolly.

THE GRAPEVINE

■ After a stay of eight years on UK Decca, Billie Davis has now left the label.

■ Irish singer Clodagh Rodgers, who failed to appear at the opening night of the Tommy Steele show 'Meet Me In London' at London's Adelphi Theatre, says she has been sacked.

■ Jeremy Spencer's replacement with Fleetwood Mac will be 25 year-old Bob Welch from San Francisco.

STONES LAUNCH OWN LABEL

The Rolling Stones have signed with the Kinney Group and their recordings will, henceforth, be released on a newly created label called Rolling Stones Records. The group's first album under the new deal will be released in the UK on April 23 and is titled 'Sticky Fingers'.

The album was produced by Jimmy Miller and is to be issued in a special cover designed by Andy Warhol. The first single on Rolling Stones Records will be a maxi-single containing three A-sides – 'Brown Sugar'/'Bitch'/ 'Let It Rock' – and represents tremendous value for money.

CHARTS

US45	Just My Imagination	Temptations
USLP	Pearl	Janis Joplin
UK45	Hot Love	T.Rex
UKLP	Bridge Over Troubled Water	Simon & Garfunkel

WEEK 2

US45	Just My Imagination	Temptations
USLP	Pearl	Janis Joplin
UK45	Hot Love	T.Rex
UKLP	Home Lovin' Man	Andy Williams

WEEK 3

US45	Joy To The World	Three Dog Night
USLP	Pearl	Janis Joplin
UK45	Hot Love	T.Rex
UKLP	Bridge Over Troubled Water	Simon & Garfunkel

WEEK 4

US45	Joy To The World	Three Dog Night
USLP	Pearl	Janis Joplin
UK45	Hot Love	T.Rex
UKLP	Home Lovin' Man	Andy Williams

MANFREDS OUT – KINKS IN DOWNUNDER

The Manfred Mann group have flown back from Australia, cutting short their projected month-long tour by three weeks. This follows an incident in a Melbourne motel where their tour manager Bob Foster was attacked.

A spokesman commented: 'Bob had threats made on his life and was given 24 hours to get out of Australia. Manfred feared for his own safety too and decided to return to Britain as soon as possible.'

No explanation was offered for the threats. But, as The Manfreds headed back, The Kinks announced that they are to pay their first visit down under for four years, commencing a 12 day tour on May 29.

FREE BECOME THREE!

With their current single 'My Brother Jake' standing high in the UK charts, Free have disbanded! The decision to break up was taken during the group's recent Australian tour and now the various members are planning new bands.

Announcing the split, a spokesman said: 'The boys felt they had achieved as much together as they possibly could within their existing framework. They have now decided to pursue individual careers.' The group had been together for three years.

It is expected that guitarist Paul Kossoff and drummer Simon Kirke will stay together and assemble a new group. Singer Paul Rodgers and bassist Andy Fraser will form their own separate bands.

A farewell live album, recorded at Sheffield and Croydon's Fairfield Hall, is planned for release in June, but there will be no follow-up single to 'My Brother Jake'.

STAR QUOTE

MARC BOLAN

on the eve of his sell-out UK tour

'I am so pleased that people are there, I feel I might just go on stage and burst into tears.'

STRANGELY STRANGE NO MORE

Dr Strangely Strange are to split after playing a concert with Al Stewart at London's Drury Lane Theatre on May 16. Ivan Pawls has decided that he will only play occasional gigs, Tim Booth has not yet formulated future plans, and Neil Hopwood may give up being a professional musician.

Terry and Gay Woods, who joined the outfit at the beginning of the year, will form a new group in which the emphasis will be on traditional Irish music.

Eric Clapton – who donated his own votes to B.B. King, Freddie King and Duane Allman

CLAPTON PIPS HENDRIX AS GREATEST EVER

An NME poll in which Tom Fogerty, Alexis Korner, Dave Davies, Ritchie Blackmore, Ronnie Wood, Eric Clapton, Gary Moore, Dave Edmunds and many more guitarists took part, has resulted in a narrow win for Eric Clapton (16 points) over Jimi Hendrix (15) with B.B. King third (12) and Frank Zappa fourth (11).

Buddy Guy and Robbie Robertson both received nine points, while Peter Green received eight.

Mick and missus

THE GRAPEVINE

- Mick and Bianca Jagger got married in France on May 12; guests included Paul McCartney, Ringo Starr, Steve Stills and Eric Clapton.
- Dickie Valentine was killed on May 6, in a car crash. One-time page-boy at the London Palladium, he won the NME poll as Britain's top singer from 1953 to 1957.
- Dionne Warwick has left Scepter Records after a hit-filled 10 years.

HERD REFORM

The Herd have re-formed. The group – one of Britain's top record acts a year or so back – already has a comeback single released, an album in preparation and a series of gigs planned.

At the moment, the line-up is fluid, but it is understood that The Herd's erstwhile drummer Andrew Steele will be joining the group when it starts undertaking one-nighters.

Though the single, 'You've Got Me Hangin' From Your Loving Tree', only features two original Herd members – Gary Taylor (bass and vocals) and Louis Rich (vocals) – plus session musicians, it is expected that the group will eventually settle down to the same line-up it had at the time of disbandment.

The exception will be guita-

rist/vocalist Peter Frampton, who is now an integral part of Humble Pie. There are also some contractual problems concerning keyboard player Andy Bown, but these are expected to be resolved shortly.

Gary Taylor: One of the two confirmed members of the new Herd. Their last hit, 'I Don't Want Our Loving To Die'', came way back in 1968

THE GRAPEVINE

■ Most prized current bootleg: Eric Burdon & War with Jimi Hendrix, recorded in London the night before Jimi's death.

BEACH BOY IN HOSPITAL

Dennis Wilson, the only surfing Beach Boy, a better drummer than a glazier

Beach Boys' drummer Dennis Wilson has lost the use of his right hand for several months as a result of an accident at his Cali-

■ The Celebration Of Life Festival, in Louisiana, has proved a shambles. The event opened on June 21, three and a half days late, and was closed down three days later when the promoters failed to supply food and medical facilities and with only nine of the 27 advertised acts having showed.

CHARTS

US45	Brown Sugar *Rolling Stones*
USLP	Sticky Fingers *Rolling Stones*
UK45	Knock Three Times *Dawn*
UKLP	Sticky Fingers *Rolling Stones*

— WEEK 2 —

US45	Want Ads *Honey Cone*
USLP	Sticky Fingers *Rolling Stones*
UK45	My Brother Jake *Free*
UKLP	Sticky Fingers *Rolling Stones*

— WEEK 3 —

US45	It's Too Late *Carole King*
USLP	Tapestry *Carole King*
UK45	I Did What I Did For Maria *Tony Christie*
UKLP	Sticky Fingers *Rolling Stones*

— WEEK 4 —

US45	It's Too Late *Carole King*
USLP	Tapestry *Carole King*
UK45	Chirpy Chirpy Cheep Cheep *Middle Of The Road*
UKLP	Sticky Fingers *Rolling Stones*

fornia home. He was fixing a pane of glass into a window frame when the glass shattered and severed nerves in his hand and wrist.

The Beach Boys are due to begin a 10-day tour shortly and, if Wilson is fit enough to take part, he will appear in a singing role only. a deputy drummer is meanwhile being sought.

Wilson also hopes to be fit enough to attend the New York premiere of *Two Lane Blacktop*, the movie in which he co-stars with James Taylor.

CLYDE McPHATTER DIES

Clyde McPhatter, the son of a North Carolina baptist minister, who became one of the world's finest soulmen, has died, aged 40.

Once lead singer with Billy Ward's Dominoes, he went on to form The Drifters in 1953, appearing on such hits as 'Money Honey' and 'Such A Night'. Drafted into the Air Force in 1954, upon his discharge he became a solo performer and recorded such US hits as 'A Lover's Question' and 'Lover Please', along with 'Treasure Of Love', McPhatter's only UK hit as a solo artist.

1971

ANDY WILLIAMS TV SERIES SCRAPPED

Andy Williams' weekly TV series is being taken off the air. the 1970/71 series, which is currently being screened in the UK by BBC-1, is to be his last.

Andy gave up making weekly shows three years ago in order to concentrate on occasional specials but, within 12 months, was forced back into the weekly format by public demand. But now his show is being dropped because of falling ratings in America.

THE GRAPEVINE

- In the wake of Edgar Broughton's plan to play free concerts in UK seaside towns, the city of Blackpool has slapped a ban on all such free shows for the next 25 years!

- U.K. Pop group Dando Shaft have been booked to appear in the play *You Must Be Joking*, at Coventry's Belgrade Theatre in September.

- Billy Preston has been signed to A&M and is recording an album.

THE END FOR JIM MORRISON

Jim Morrison, who ducked out from leading The Doors in order to concentrate on creative writing, died in Paris on July 3, aged 27.

On the night of July 2, Morrison regurgitated a small amount of blood, but claimed he felt fine and announced his intention of taking a bath. Early next morning, his wife Pamela found him dead in the water-filled bath, apparently from natural causes. Morrison had recently consulted a local doctor concerning a respiratory problem.

The singer-poet is to be buried in the same Paris cemetery as French chanteuse Edith Piaf and playwright Oscar Wilde, as well as a number of illustrious French authors, painters and artists.

LED ZEP: A REAL GAS

Led Zeppelin were involved in a massive riot when, playing to a crowd of over 15,000 in Milan's Vigorelli Stadium, the group's act was disrupted by charging police and soldiers wielding batons and lobbing tear-gas canisters.

Even before the show started, the stadium was ringed by hundreds of police and soldiers, while outside there were trucks full of reinforcements waiting for any sign of crowd trouble. They went into action with scarcely any provocation, and this led to a full-scale riot during which some of the group's equipment was damaged.

Said a group member: 'It'll be refreshing to come home for a bit of sanity.'

THE JAMES GANG RIDE OUT

The James Gang – Dale Peters, Joe Walsh and Jimmy Fox – who are in Britain for a tour, held a press reception at which Walsh, the band's lead guitarist, recalled: 'I did a jam with Eric Clapton and Peter Green at the Boston Tea Party a while back and I didn't know about it until 10 minutes before we did it!

'There was so much respect between those two that they were playing very quiet and I stayed out of the way, but contributed a bit. Usually when you show up for a jam, everybody's ego gets into it and that defeats the whole purpose of jamming.'

The band play the London Lyceum on July 25.

STAR QUOTE

A L   K O O P E R

'I'm so pleased to be in Britain, I could just sit and pour tea over my head.'

Anglophile Al Kooper

BIG DEAL AT WEELEY

(Far left) Lindisfarne, Newcastle Brown downers and suppliers of Weeley singalongs

(Left) One-time bopping elf Marc Bolan, now a festival favourite

A rampage by gangs of Hells Angels bikers failed to stop The Weeley Festival – held at the south of England resort of Clacton on August 28-9 – from being one of Britain's most successful-ever rock events.

Although the Angels destroyed a concession stand, reaped a deal of other damage, and savagely beat up a girl who got in their way, they were routed by a squad of festival-goers who formed themselves into a vigilante group, mounted a counter-attack and destroyed most of the Angels' prized, hand-built choppers.

But the music went on. Headliners The Faces turned in a storming set, as did T. Rex and Lindisfarne, all of whom received tumultuous receptions from the massive crowd.

Other acts appearing included Rory Gallagher, folkie Julie Felix, King Crimson, Stone The Crows, Caravan, Colosseum, Barclay James Harvest, Mott The Hoople, The Edgar Broughton Band, Juicy Lucy, Mungo Jerry and Curved Air – a bill which caused one reviewer to describe it as 'DeMille gone mad!'

The Hells Angels were not available for comment.

CHARTS

US45	How Can You Mend A Broken Heart — *Bee Gees*
USLP	Tapestry — *Carole King*
UK45	Get It On — *T.Rex*
UKLP	Bridge Over Troubled Water — *Simon & Garfunkel*

WEEK 2

US45	How Can You Mend A Broken Heart — *Bee Gees*
USLP	Tapestry — *Carole King*
UK45	Get It On — *T.Rex*
UKLP	Every Good Boy Deserves Favour — *Moody Blues*

WEEK 3

US45	How Can You Mend A Broken Heart — *Bee Gees*
USLP	Tapestry — *Carole King*
UK45	Never Ending Song Of Love — *New Seekers*
UKLP	Every Good Boy Deserves Favour — *Moody Blues*

WEEK 4

US45	How Can You Mend A Broken Heart — *Bee Gees*
USLP	Tapestry — *Carole King*
UK45	I'm Still Waiting — *Diana Ross*
UKLP	Every Good Boy Deserves Favour — *Moody Blues*

WILL THE REAL P.J. PROBY SIGN HERE?

P.J. Proby's new look nearly landed him in trouble when he opened a new nightspot in Preston, Lancashire. Some members of the audience at the club, The Piper, refused to believe he was P.J. because the singer has lost 49lbs in weight and has grown a beard for a movie he's shooting with Peter Fonda.

Suspicion spread, and the owners of the club threatened to pull out of the £1,500 deal. The police were brought in to collect specimens of Proby's signature to verify his identity.

Eventually, in order to satisfy patrons, the club owners had to offer £1,000 to anyone who could prove that the artist was not the real P.J. Proby.

P.B. Proby – we think!

THE GRAPEVINE

- Tony Kaye has left Yes, his replacement being The Strawbs' Rick Wakeman.

- Mick Jagger has made an unprintable comment regarding UK Decca's decision to release the 'Gimme Shelter' album, which has nothing to do with the movie but contains six old cuts plus extracts from the Albert Hall concert of 1966.

- Elton John made his US debut at the LA Troubadour on August 22.

Bad Jokebook raider Tony Blackburn

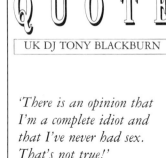
ARETHA AND STEVIE AT CURTIS FUNERAL

August 17: Stevie Wonder, Aretha Franklin, Cissy Houston, Brook Benton, Delaney and Bonnie, Duane Allman, Herbie Mann and Arthur Prysock were among those who attended the funeral of soul saxman King Curtis in New York City.

Curtis, who was born Curtis Ousley, was stabbed to death on August 13, following an argument outside his New York apartment. He was 37.

FRAMPTON CUTS UP THE PIE

Founder member Peter Frampton has quit Humble Pie in order to concentrate on a solo career. The announcement was made by Pie manager Dee Anthony, who is visiting London to finalize plans for the group's forthcoming European tour, which opens in Frankfurt on November 1.

The final album featuring Frampton with Humble Pie will be issued by A&M in October. Titled 'Performance', it's a double set which was recorded live at New York's Fillmore East earlier this year.

Peter Frampton – no longer humble

Asked for a comment, Peter Frampton replied: 'At last I'm doing something I've always wanted to do. It's time I found out if people are prepared to listen to what I can do myself.'

JAMES TAYLOR INJURY CAUSES PANIC

Panic broke out in the New York office of manager Nathan Weiss after a phone call announced that James Taylor had injured his right hand after tinkering with some machinery at his farm on Martha's Vineyard, Mass.

Initially it was suggested that James might even lose the hand, but a doctor later confirmed that it was only a severe flesh wound and that all tendons and bones had been left intact.

Even so, New Yorkers will have to wait a while before seeing Taylor in concert again. His three sell-out Carnegie Hall dates for this month have now been rescheduled for November.

The ultra-noisy Sly Stone

15,000 LIMIT FOR BANGLA DESH GIG

Only half the potential capacity of 30,000 will be allowed into the mammoth Who-Faces-Mott The Hoople-Lindisfarne Bangladesh concert at London's Oval stadium on September 18. City authority regulations have been clamped on fans, even though thousands more are allowed into the ground for cricket matches.

Atomic Rooster have now been added to the bill and will be flying in from America, where they've been touring. Also playing at the event will be The Grease Band, Quintessence, America and Eugene Wallace.

CARL WILSON SENTENCED TO SING

Carl Wilson of The Beach Boys will not have to fight in Vietnam after all. He's been opposing military service for nearly four years and, at one time, looked as if he might face a term of imprisonment because of his views.

But, at a final court hearing, he's been put on probation for three years and fined $4,000, one proviso being that, during the next two years, he must sing regularly at prisons, hospitals and orphanages.

Carl Wilson sings on but no Saigon

LENNON WANTS CLAPTON FOR BAND

A fully clothed John and Yoko

John Lennon is hoping to persuade Eric Clapton to join the band he is proposing to take on a world tour next year. Lennon has already announced that the bassist will be Klaus Voorman, while pianist Nicky Hopkins will also be in the outfit, which will be completed by Yoko Ono and drummer Jim Keltner.

Lennon also stated, in New York, that he's asked Phil Spector to produce an act for the group which he proposes to call The John & Yoko Mobile Plastic Ono Band Fun Show.

CHARTS

US45	Maggie May *Rod Stewart*
USLP	Every Picture Tells A Story *Rod Stewart*
UK45	Maggie May *Rod Stewart*
UKLP	Every Picture Tells A Story *Rod Stewart*

WEEK 2

US45	Maggie May *Rod Stewart*
USLP	Every Picture Tells A Story *Rod Stewart*
UK45	Maggie May *Rod Stewart*
UKLP	Every Picture Tells A Story *Rod Stewart*

WEEK 3

US45	Maggie May *Rod Stewart*
USLP	Every Picture Tells A Story *Rod Stewart*
UK45	Maggie May *Rod Stewart*
UKLP	Every Picture Tells A Story *Rod Stewart*

WEEK 4

US45	Maggie May *Rod Stewart*
USLP	Every Picture Tells A Story *Rod Stewart*
UK45	Maggie May *Rod Stewart*
UKLP	Every Picture Tells A Story *Rod Stewart*

WEEK 5

US45	Maggie May *Rod Stewart*
USLP	Imagine *John Lennon*
UK45	Maggie May *Rod Stewart*
UKLP	Every Picture Tells A Story *Rod Stewart*

STAR QUOTE

KEITH MOON

'Give me a mandolin and I'll play you rock'n'roll.'

AL LEAPS – AFTER THREE MONTHS

A record that has been in the stores for three months has suddenly leapt from nowhere into the NME UK singles charts. Titled 'Tired Of Being Alone', it's by American singer Al Green who, last year, was voted fifth most promising R&B singer by US publication *Cashbox*.

Originally from Forrest City, Arkansas, Green began singing spirituals with his four brothers while still at school and, by the age of 16, was part of The Creations. Later Al Green & The Soulmates' 'Back Up Train' notched up sales of 70,000, helping to put his name on the map.

STAR NAMES OVER THE RAINBOW

The Rainbow – London's newest live rock centre – is lining up an impressive list of star names for its first season of concerts. The 3,500-seater, formerly The Finsbury Park Astoria and famed in rock history as the venue for The Beatles' Christmas shows in the sixties, plans to open on November 4 with a three-day engagement by The Who.

Alice Cooper is now confirmed to follow The Who on November 7, while other acts booked for the theatre include Grand Funk, The Grateful Dead, Mountain, The Doors, The Faces, Fairport Convention, Family, Leon Russell, Climax Chicago and Barclay James Harvest.

The cost of converting the cinema to modern rock standards was £150,000 ($300,000), of which nearly £15,000 ($30,000) was spent on a new computerized lighting rig.

Alice in Rainbowland

ROD CHART SENSATION

Faces vocalist Rod Stewart has pulled off an amazing feat by having his 'Every Picture Tells A Story' album at No. 1 on both sides of the Atlantic, while his 'Maggie May' single has also gone top of the singles charts both here and in America.

'The single is a freak, a million to one chance,' said Rod. 'But the album has permanence and a lasting value. I still can't see how the single is such a bit hit. It has no melody. Plenty of character and nice chords, but no melody.'

Rod luvs Maggie true

THE GRAPEVINE

■ Gene Vincent died of a bleeding ulcer on October 12. He has lived in severe pain ever since a motorcycle accident back in 1955.

■ The death is also reported of Duane Allman, who was killed in a motorcycle crash near his Macon, Georgia home on October 29.

■ Allan Clarke has announced that he'll be leaving The Hollies before the end of the year.

1971

SLADE – NO 'NEW BEATLES' LAUNCH

Slade claim to have turned down the opportunity of being launched in America as the next Beatles. The offer would have involved a multi-million dollar campaign, including a TV series shot in the group's native Wolverhampton, plus a full-length film set in locations round the world and a heavily promoted debut tour of the States.

'But,' commented singer Noddy Holder, 'Acceptance would have meant the cancellation of many commitments here – and the last thing we want to do is to mess around the people who have put us where we are.'

Wolverhampton wanderer Noddy Holder

SUPERSTAR OUSTS PEPPER

MCA is claiming a British sales record for its 'Jesus Christ Superstar' album. The previous LP record was established by The Beatles' 'Sgt. Pepper's Lonely Hearts Club Band' which has now sold seven million copies throughout the world. Combined international sales of 'Superstar' have already passed three and a half million, and – since it is a double-album – this represents a total in excess of seven million units.

Composers Tim Rice and Andrew Lloyd Webber are to be presented with a gold disc for sales of the album in Australia. Then they're booked for Israel next year, where location work begins on a film version of the musical, to be directed by Norman Jewison. A stage version of the rock opera – already running on Broadway – is expected to open in Britain during late spring 1972.

CHARTS

US45	Gypsys, Tramps & Thieves *Cher*
USLP	Shaft *Isaac Hayes*
UK45	Maggie May *Rod Stewart*
UKLP	Every Picture Tells A Story *Rod Stewart*
— WEEK 2 —	
US45	Gypsys, Tramps & Thieves *Cher*
USLP	Santana *Santana*
UK45	Coz I Luv You *Slade*
UKLP	Every Picture Tells A Story *Rod Stewart*
— WEEK 3 —	
US45	Theme From Shaft *Isaac Hayes*
USLP	Santana *Santana*
UK45	Coz I Luv You *Slade*
UKLP	Every Picture Tells A Story *Rod Stewart*
— WEEK 4 —	
US45	Theme From Shaft *Isaac Hayes*
USLP	Santana *Santana*
UK45	Coz I Luv You *Slade*
UKLP	Imagine *John Lennon*

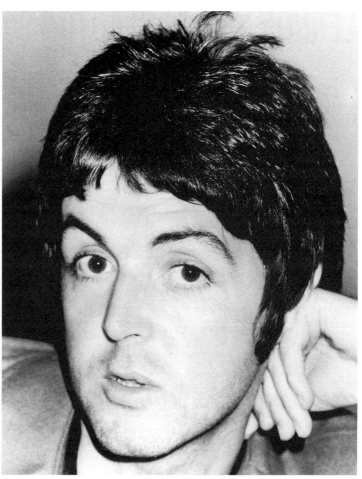

NO LOLLIPOP WANTED, SAYS PAUL

Paul McCartney has said that he's not getting out of Apple, The Beatles' own label. 'I've not got to go down, as Allen Klein said recently,' he added. But he's far from happy with the way the label has been handled.

'Apple isn't a democracy,' he complained. 'It's way out of line with what I thought was going to happen. None of The Beatles have, to this day, seen any of that money. As far as the money off The Beatles' records is concerned, The Beatles still haven't got it.

'I'd like to see the four Beatles split whatever's left of what The Beatles made. George calls it throwing a tantrum whenever I say things like that. But I only want what I earned. I'm not asking for a lollipop.'

Once B.S. & T. now gone A.W.O.L.

THE GRAPEVINE

■ Colosseum, the outfit featuring drummer Jon Hiseman and singer Chris Farlowe, has split.

■ David Clayton Thomas, lead vocalist with B.S. & T. since the departure of Al Kooper, has gone solo.

■ Wings' first album, 'Wild Life', released on November 15.

■ Donovan's current US tour, his first in two years, has proved a failure, one concert drawing only half as many people as expected.

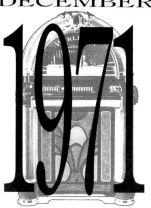
TEN YEARS AFTER SET UK TOUR

Ten Years After, who have just returned from the United States with their first gold disc – awarded for one million sales of the 'A Space In Time' album, – are to start the new year with a tour of selected British universities.

The tour opens at Reading on January 8, then visits campuses in Birmingham, Sheffield, Lancaster, Cardiff, Liverpool, Leeds, Brighton, Nottingham, Salford and Leicester.

'This tour is something we've wanted to do for a long time,' explained guitarist Alvin Lee. 'It was the university audiences, along with London clubs like The Marquee, who picked up on us in the first place.'

Supporting Ten Years After at selected gigs will be Jude, the group formed by ex-Procol Harum guitarist Robin Trower and ex-Jethro Tull drummer Clive Bunker.

GILBERT 'TOO SHY TO TOUR'

An offer of an extensive British tour for songwriter Gilbert O'Sullivan has been turned down because he is 'too shy' to appear in public.

According to manager Gordon Mills, he has also declined two major film roles for his *protégé*. So, instead of expanding his activities, Gilbert (real name Raymond) will spend the early part of 1972 in his Surrey cottage, writing material for his second album, plus new singles.

FACES ALBUM BANNED

The Faces' album, 'A Nod's As Good As A Wink To A Blind Horse', has been banned in America. Over 400,000 copies have been pressed and dispatched, but distributors are refusing to handle it, alleging that the poster included in the sleeve is obscene.

Arrangements are now being made to re-release the album without the offending poster, which is a different one to that released in Britain.

THE GRAPEVINE

■ Traffic are now down to a trio, Rich Grech and Jim Gordon having left.

■ Marc Bolan is the first artist confirmed for a triple-album set issued as a benefit for last June's UK Glastonbury Festival.

■ Because the Royal Albert Hall has banned him, Isaac Hayes' forthcoming London appearances on January 27 and 28 have been rescheduled for the Rainbow.

ZAPPA AND FURY HOSPITALIZED

"Frankly, I've been zapped!"

Mothers Of Invention leader Frank Zappa is currently in a London clinic, nursing a broken leg and his pride after being pushed into the orchestra pit by an audience member during his December 10 show at the Rainbow Theatre. Zappa also suffered concussion in the fall, which the performer claims could have been avoided if the pit had been covered over.

Initially taken to a public hospital nearby, Zappa refused to be treated there, describing it as 'absolutely filthy'. He was then taken to the private clinic, where he is expected to remain for two more months. Litigation is in the air.

Another rock star now hospitalized is British veteran Billy Fury, who was admitted to the National Heart Hospital on December 13. He is to undergo an operation for the replacement of two heart valves.

Hayes – shafted by the Albert

CHARTS

US45	Family Affair	Sly & The Family Stone
USLP	Santana	Santana
UK45	Coz I Luv You	Slade
UKLP	Imagine	John Lennon
WEEK 2		
US45	Family Affair	Sly & The Family Stone
USLP	Santana	Santana
UK45	Ernie (Fastest Milkman In The West)	Benny Hill
UKLP	Imagine	John Lennon
WEEK 3		
US45	Family Affair	Sly & The Family Stone
USLP	There's A Riot Goin' On	Sly & The Family Stone
UK45	Ernie (Fastest Milkman In The West)	Benny Hill
UKLP	Four Symbols	Led Zeppelin
WEEK 4		
US45	Brand New Key	Melanie
USLP	There's A Riot Goin' On	Sly & The Family Stone
UK45	Ernie (Fastest Milkman In The West)	Benny Hill
UKLP	Four Symbols	Led Zeppelin

THE GRAPEVINE

- Blues belter Big Maybelle died in Cleveland on January 23 at the age of 47.

- Allan Clarke, former lead singer with The Hollies, has signed with RCA as a solo act.

- Ian Matthews, who separated from Southern Comfort a year ago, has teamed with Andy Roberts, Dave Richards and Bob Ronga to form Plainsong.

IT WAS SINFIELD OR ME, SAYS FRIPP

Crimson's Robert Fripp. The band is now down to a four piece

Pete Sinfield, the founder member of King Crimson who announced his departure from the band this month, has told music journalists: 'Bob Fripp seemed to be unhappy when I complained that I was unable to do my job properly on our recent Stateside trip. The Tuesday before Christmas, he rang me up and said he couldn't continue working with me.'

Talking about the American trip, Sinfield remembered: 'When we got there, Ian (Wallace), Boz and Mel (Collins) went straight into a shop that sold Levi's and cowboy boots and bought themselves lots of American clothes so that they then looked like their audience. I refused to do this and, instead, always wore the green corduroy poet's suit.'

Asked for his comments, Robert Fripp replied: 'It was Sinfield or me, one of us had to quit. He's a very talented guy but there's a lot about Peter that I intensely dislike.'

LENNON'S NEW GROUP

John and Yoko have chosen Elephant's Memory, a New York rock outfit, to be their new band. They have taken this step because the various members of The Plastic Ono Band are now scattered around the world.

So, on the recommendation of Yippie guru Jerry Rubin, Lennon watched Elephant's Memory at a Max's Kansas City gig, then immediately invited them to work with him and Yoko.

Elephant's Memory, who have recorded for Buddah, recently received a gold disc for their contribution to the soundtrack of the movie *Midnight Cowboy*.

REXMANIA !

T. Rex, on their current UK tour, are turning the musical clock back to the early Sixties. Their Boston Gliderdrome gig saw scenes of hysteria and confusion unparalleled since the days of Beatlemania.

More than 30 people fainted, and one girl had to be taken to hospital after falling from the balcony in the excitement. Extra police were drafted in to cope with a crowd of more than 5,000 who came from all parts of the country.

DRUMMER'S INJURY DELAYS BECK TOUR

A projected British tour by The Jeff Beck Group has now been postponed. Reason is that drummer Cozy Powell recently sustained a broken hand as a result of a fall while recording in Memphis and the injury has proved more serious than was at first thought.

Powell has been forbidden by a London specialist to work for another five weeks. Consideration was given to using a stand-in drummer for the tour but it has now been decided to postpone the proposed February itinerary until March.

BEEB BAN MACCA

Macca – a legend in Nottingham's lunchtime

The BBC have banned 'Give Ireland Back To The Irish', the new Paul McCartney single, as being 'politically controversial'.

A spokesman for the Corporation explaining the ban said: 'At a time when we are striving our utmost to remain impartial, this record can only be described as inflammatory.'

Radio Luxembourg have also banned the single, but EMI Records say that they're going ahead with distribution to stores.

Meanwhile, Paul chose to break his five-year absence from live gigs with a surprise lunchtime concert, given by Wings at Nottingham University on 9 February, before an audience of around 700 disbelieving students.

BLACK OAK GO ROCK AND ROLLER-SKATE

Wheeler-dealers Black Oak Arkansas

Black Oak Arkansas have held one of the most unusual press receptions Hollywood has seen for some time.

The party was held at the Hollywood Roller Bowl and everybody spent the evening on roller skates, listening to the band play – 'everybody' included members of LA's professional skating team, The Thunderbirds, through to Phil Spector and a topless female.

The final casualty report read just one broken arm, but countless bruises.

THE GRAPEVINE

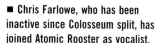

■ Chris Farlowe, who has been inactive since Colosseum split, has joined Atomic Rooster as vocalist.

■ Jazz trumpet star Lee Morgan was shot to death in a New York club. He was 33.

■ Following concentrated recording sessions with Humble Pie, Stevie Marriott has collapsed, suffering from nervous exhaustion.

Stevie Marriott, diminutive Pie man feeling the strain

POCO IN UK

Poco have arrived in Britain to play a short tour that includes shows at London's Rainbow Theatre on 4 and 5 February.

They've just flown in from Copenhagen, where reporter Nick Logan said: 'Their main strength is as a band but, vocally, Richie Furay, the one remaining ex-member of Buffalo Springfield now that Jim Messina has gone, provides no-nonsense upfronts, finding support from George Grantham, while Paul Cotton has a voice that has a compelling, quivering quality, something reminiscent of Neil Young.'

It's Poco's first time out of the States.

TULL SET POEM TO MUSIC

Jethro Tull's new album 'Thick As A Brick' is scheduled for release on 18 February. The LP is based on a poem by eight-year-old Gerald Bostock of St Cleve, Lancashire. The poem won a national prize before it was withdrawn, following psychiatric reports on Bostock.

Tull have set the poem to music and the work covers both sides of the album. There are no individually titled tracks, just one continuous piece of music lasting 45 minutes.

The group recently returned from a five-week European tour and are now set to play two consecutive nights at London's Royal Albert Hall on 21 and 22 March as part of their biggest-ever British concert tour.

BOLAN WOWS WEMBLEY

'It was a religio-sensual experience. He pulled the strings. He had the power. He used it.' So says reviewer Tony Tyler about Marc Bolan's two concerts at London's Wembley Pool on March 18.

The first T. Rex concerts to be held in Britain for six months, they attracted 20,000 fans plus Ringo Starr, who headed a film crew intent on filming the event as an Apple documentary on the Bolan phenomenon.

For Bolan, the shows proved an undoubted triumph and have been heralded as 'the concerts that changed the face of British rock'. For Ringo, it was a return to the place of former triumphs - he stood on the same stage seven years ago at an NME Pollwinners concert.

Meanwhile, in the States, T. Rex's 'Bang A Gong (Get It On)' has become a massive hit, reaching the Top 10. The single's change of name was necessary because Chase had a hit with another song called 'Get It On' during 1971, and it was decided to alter the title of the T. Rex single to avoid confusion.

John and Yoko in the queue to obtain a new US visa. It's believed that all the others in the room are actually members of the CIA!

CHARTS

US45	Without You / Nilsson
USLP	American Pie / Don McLean
UK45	American Pie / Don McLean
UKLP	Paul Simon / Paul Simon

——— W E E K 2 ———

US45	Without You / Nilsson
USLP	Harvest / Neil Young
UK45	Without You / Nilsson
UKLP	Paul Simon / Paul Simon

——— W E E K 3 ———

US45	Heart Of Gold / Neil Young
USLP	Harvest / Neil Young
UK45	Without You / Nilsson
UKLP	Paul Simon / Paul Simon

——— W E E K 4 ———

US45	A Horse With No Name / America
USLP	America / America
UK45	Without You / Nilsson
UKLP	Paul Simon / Paul Simon

THE GRAPEVINE

■ Gentle Giant are to be co-featured with the Hendrix movie *Jimi At Berkeley* in a forthcoming UK tour.

■ Bill Haley has been billed as appearing in the forthcoming UK-touring Rock & Roll Revival Show, but he writes to NME: 'I know nothing about this and have signed for no such tour.' Chuck Berry, another supposedly on the tour, also expressed surprise.

Gentle Giant have appeared as The Howling Wolves, The Road Runners and Simon Dupree and the Big Sound, and The Moles. Line-up (left to right) Kerry Minnear (keyboards, woodwinds, guitars), John Weathers (drums), Gary Green (guitar, percussion, woodwind), Ray Shulman (bass, violin, trumpet), Derek Shulman (sax, recorder, bass, vocals)

JOHN LENNON TO BECOME AN AMERICAN?

John and Yoko Lennon have bid for US citizenship in order to avoid deportation.

Earlier in the month, Lennon's visa extension was cancelled by the New York Office of Immigration, who'd granted the extension just five days earlier. The official explanation is given as John's 1968 pot bust in London, but the Lennons suspect the true reason might have something to do with their performance at Alice Tully Hall in January, given without obtaining American work permits.

There, they performed from their seats, Yoko conducting the band with the aid of an apple.

BEACH BOYS ADD TWO

The Beach Boys have become a septet with the addition of two new members. They have been joined by black musicians Blondie Chaplin (guitar) and Ricky Fatarr (drums), both of whom were previously with South African group Flame, an outfit which supported The Beach Boys on their last British dates.

MOTT HEAD ROCK CIRCUS

Ian Hunter leads the Mott in a prayer for the upcoming tour

Mott The Hoople are to head one of the most ambitious and unusual packages ever conceived for a rock group.

It will be billed as The Mott The Hoople Rock 'n' Roll Circus, and will also feature new Island group Hackensack, plus a knife-throwing act called Las Vivas, juggler Frank Paulo and – as special guest star – comedian Max Wall.

The tour plays 16 major UK venues this month, including an appearance at London's Lyceum on April 19.

A spokesman for Island Records said: 'It will be a good, solid rock show, with an element of variety to give it spice. It will be a fast, all-happening show, with the knife-throwing and juggling going on while the groups are actually performing.'

Careful with that axe, Eugene!

CHARTS

US45	A Horse With No Name	*America*
USLP	America	*America*
UK45	Without You	*Nilsson*
UKLP	Paul Simon	*Paul Simon*

—— WEEK 2 ——

US45	A Horse With No Name	*America*
USLP	America	*America*
UK45	Without You	*Nilsson*
UKLP	Fog On The Tyne	*Lindisfarne*

—— WEEK 3 ——

US45	The First Time Ever I Saw Your Face	*Roberta Flack*
USLP	America	*America*
UK45	Without You	*Milsson*
UKLP	Harvest	*Neil Young*

—— WEEK 4 ——

US45	The First Time Ever I Saw Your Face	*Roberta Flack*
USLP	America	*America*
UK45	Amazing Grace	*Royal Scots Dragoon Guards Band*
UKLP	Harvest	*Neil Young*

—— WEEK 5 ——

US45	The First Time Ever I Saw Your Face	*Roberta Flack*
USLP	First Take	*Roberta Flack*
UK45	Amazing Grace	*Royal Scots Dragoon Guards Band*
UKLP	Harvest	*Neil Young*

APRIL 1972

NME'S FREEBIE MAXI

NME are to give away a free 12-minute maxi-single with the April 29 issue. The single includes an advance preview of tracks from The Rolling Stones' new album 'Exile On Main Street', plus the title track to the new Curved Air album, 'Phantasmagoria', and 'Blind Alley', a solid rocker from all-girl group Fanny's 'Fanny Hill'.

Also included is a Mick Jagger solo blues that will never be issued elsewhere and which is undoubtedly destined to become a collector's item.

RINGO FILMS FLEET STREET

Ringo Starr is now concentrating almost entirely on his work as a film producer and cameraman. In addition to his film on Marc Bolan and T. Rex, Ringo is simultaneously working on a documentary called *Models And Fleet Street*.

Said a spokesman: 'It's about the lives of the girls who appear in various poses on pages two and three of popular UK dailies, and how they fit into London's Fleet Street scene.'

Ringo is also set to appear in a film called *Count Down* which has a Dracula-style plot.

New Island signings Vinegar Joe

THE GRAPEVINE

■ Vinegar Joe have released their debut Island album this month; the band's line-up now stands as Robert Palmer (rhythm guitar and vocals), Elkie Brooks (vocals), Pete Gage (guitar), John Hawken (piano), Mick Shaw (bass) and John Woods (drums).

■ Four people died during Puerto Rico's Mar y Sol Festival, which ran 1-3 April and included performances by The Allman Brothers, ELP, Black Sabbath, and The J. Geils Band.

FAIRPORTS BUNCH UP FOR ROCK

Various Fairport Convention members past and present, plus friends, are to release an island album as The Bunch.

The album, which will be in UK shops on 21 April, is titled 'Rock On' and features 'Nadine', 'The Loco-Motion', 'Willie and The Hand Jive' and other rock classics, performed by such singers and musicians as Richard Thompson, Linda Peters, Trevor Lucas, Sandy Denny, Dave Mattacks, Tyger Hutchings and The Dundee Horns.

Given away free with the album will be a flexi-disc of 'Let There Be Drums' featuring drummer Gerry Conway.

Drummer Dave Mattacks recently quit the Fairports to join The Albion Country Band.

Ex-Fairport Richard Thompson, rocking with the folkies

STAR QUOTE

MARC BOLAN

'I've written a film about a messiah who visits earth. He expects to find a race of Gods and what he finds is just a mess.'

MAY 1972

CINDY – A SUPREME NO MORE

After months of conflicting reports, it has been confirmed that Cindy Birdsong has left The Supremes.

She has been replaced in the Tamla group by Lynda Laurence, who has already been recording with the group and is featured on their new single, 'Automatically Sunshine', which gains a UK release on 16 June.

Cindy, who married two years ago, is retiring from show-business and says she wants to 'just settle down as a housewife, and raise a family.' She joined The Supremes in 1967, when she replaced Florence Ballard.

CHARTS

US45 The First Time Ever I Saw Your Face
Roberta Flack

USLP First Take
Roberta Flack

UK45 Amazing Grace
Royal Scots Dragoon Guards Band

UKLP Machine Head
Deep Purple

────── W E E K 2 ──────

US45 The First Time Ever I Saw Your Face
Roberta Flack

USLP First Take
Roberta Flack

UK45 Amazing Grace
Royal Scots Dragoon Guards Band

UKLP Machine Head
Deep Purple

────── W E E K 3 ──────

US45 The First Time Ever I Saw Your Face
Roberta Flack

USLP First Take
Roberta Flack

UK45 Metal Guru
T.Rex

UKLP Fog On The Tyne
Lindisfarne

────── W E E K 4 ──────

US45 Oh Girl
Chi-Lites

USLP First Take
Roberta Flack

UK45 Metal Guru
T.Rex

UKLP Bolan Boogie
T.Rex

GIANTS OF TOMORROW

NME is to sponsor a Giants of Tomorrow marquee at the massive Great Western Express Lincoln Festival on May 26-9.

Twenty up-and-coming acts will appear in the tent, the current list including: Budgie, Mark Ashton, Rab Noakes, Walrus, Skin Alley, Tea & Sympathy, Capability Brown, Bitch, Byzantium, Akido, Sleaze Band, John Martyn, Patto, Good Habit, Smith Perkins & Smith, Demick & Armstrong, Warhorse, Gnidrolog, Spreadeagle and Morgan.

Noddy, the singer you can swear by

LES HARVEY ELECTROCUTED

Stone the Crows in happier days with Les Harvey on Maggie Bell's left

Les Harvey, guitarist and co-founder of Stone The Crows, was electrocuted and killed when he came onstage to announce the first number of the group's May 3 gig at Swansea University's Coming-Out Ball, and touched a faultily connected mike-stand.

Thrown in the air by the shock, Harvey landed with his guitar in contact with the mike-stand, and other members of the group received shocks as they tried to pull him clear.

Somebody eventually managed to kick the guitar clear, but it was too late and mouth-to-mouth respiration failed to resuscitate the young Scot.

Maggie Bell, Stone The Crows vocalist, who helped Harvey found the group two years ago, was taken to a local hospital and placed under heavy sedation.

THE GRAPEVINE

■ Noddy Holder, of Slade, has been charged in Glasgow with using obscene language during the group's set at Green's Playhouse; when cautioned and asked if he had anything to say, Noddy reportedly replied, 'It's a load of old ******'

■ John Lennon, interviewed on the Dick Cavett show, has claimed that his phone is being tapped by US Security authorities.

BLUESMAN DAVIS DIES

Blues, ragtime and gospel performer the Rev. 'Blind' Gary Davis died on May 5, age 76.

An influence on Ry Cooder and Taj Mahal, he began as a street singer, then became a gospel preacher working camp meetings and country churches. He found national fame via a Newport Festival performance in 1964.

South Carolina's 'Blind' Gary Davis

FILLMORE FILM PREMIERED

Fillmore, a documentary about the final days at Bill Graham's Fillmore East, San Francisco, was premiered in New York on May 16. Performers include Santana, Grateful Dead, Quicksilver Messenger Service, Hot Tuna, It's A Beautiful Day, Boz Scaggs, Elvin Bishop Group, and Jefferson Airplane.

Creedence Clearwater Revival don't appear in the film because they failed to approve release of their segment.

BOLAN TO QUIT TOURING?

With T. Rex fan fever reaching unprecedented heights, Marc Bolan has announced that he may be forced to give up gigging in Britain after one more farewell tour of the country.

Speaking after hysterical scenes during T. Rex's Manchester concert, Bolan said: 'It's becoming almost impossible. One more tour, I should think, and that'll be the last.'

During the sell-out show, one fan suffered a broken jaw and dozens of seats were smashed to pieces as members of the audience dashed to reach the front stage. Offstage, Bolan has now been forced to become something of a recluse, stating: 'I haven't been out of my house for two weeks. It's just like living in a goldfish bowl.'

Fans now await the arrival of the new T. Rex album, 'The Slider', in mid-July.

Bolan – if he becomes too exhausted will he seek help from the National Elf Service?

CHARTS

US45	I'll Take You There *Staple Singers*
USLP	Thick As A Brick *Jethro Tull*
UK45	Metal Guru *T.Rex*
UKLP	Bolan Boogie *T.Rex*

——— WEEK 2 ———

US45	The Candy Man *Sammy Davis Jr.*
USLP	Thick As A Brick *Jethro Tull*
UK45	Metal Guru *T.Rex*
UKLP	Bolan Boogie *T.Rex*

——— WEEK 3 ———

US45	The Candy Man *Sammy Davis Jr.*
USLP	Exile On Main Street *Rolling Stones*
UK45	Vincent *Don McLean*
UKLP	Exile On Main Street *Rolling Stones*

——— WEEK 4 ———

US45	The Candy Man *Sammy Davis Jr.*
USLP	Exile On Main Street *Rolling Stones*
UK45	Vincent *Don McLean*
UKLP	Exile On Main Street *Rolling Stones*

SOLO BELL

Maggie Bell goes into the studio next month to cut her own solo album. She will be supported by members of Stone The Crows plus various well-known guests.

Meanwhile, Stone The Crows have named Les Harvey's replacement. He is 20-year-old Scottish guitarist Jim McCulloch who, until recently, let his own band. The first gig by the new Stone The Crows line-up will be at Birmingham University on June 23.

American pieman Don McLean

THE GRAPEVINE

- Dion & The Belmonts reunited for a Madison Square Garden show on June 2; the event was recorded for a possible forthcoming album.

- CBS's John Hammond, who discovered Billie Holiday, Count Basie and Bob Dylan, has signed highly rated New Jersey singer Bruce Springsteen to the label.

- The Tallahatchie Bridge, made famous by Bobbie Gentry in her 'Ode To Billy Joe', has collapsed.

Maggie Bell: "I've always wanted to work on my own album. Not just rock but maybe also using strings"

DOWNPOUR AT THE PALACE

Though 16,000 fans were drenched at London's Crystal Palace Bowl Garden Party on Saturday, June 3, the event was still a musical success. The show, hosted by Keith Moon and opened by Sha Na Na, stayed afloat until Richie Havens' set, when the rain commenced and then never ceased.

A 90-minute change-over between Havens and The Beach Boys failed to help matters and Melanie was adjudged boring, while David Blue pulled out.

But Joe Cocker and The Chris Stainton All-Stars were acclaimed as marvellous – Cocker providing a fine set including 'St James Infirmary', 'The Letter' and 'Feelin' Alright'.

ELVIS PLAYS NEW YORK – AT LAST!

Elvis Presley played his first-ever concerts in New York at Madison Square Gardens on June 9-11, and drew more than 80,000 people, none of whom received complimentary tickets – not even the mayor!

John Lennon and Bob Dylan found themselves sitting to the rear of the arena, while George Harrison could only obtain a seat in the balcony.

A billboard welcoming the King to New York was hung in Times Square and the Hilton hosted a Presley press conference that lasted just 20 minutes.

RCA recorded the evening show on June 10 for immediate album release.

HAWKWIND MOVE UP

Hawkwind, who have taken a major step towards popular acceptance through the entry of 'Silver Machine' into the UK singles charts, are to put on a six-hour party at the London Rainbow next month.

Long dismissed as a lower division U.K. band, despite a reputation as crowd pleasers, Hawkwind are also being lined-up for their first major UK tour.

CHARTS

US45	Song Sung Blue	Neil Diamond
USLP	Exile On Main Street	Rolling Stones
UK45	Vincent	Don McLean
UKLP	American Pie	Don McLean
WEEK 2		
US45	Lean On Me	Bill Withers
USLP	Exile On Main Street	Rolling Stones
UK45	Take Me Bak Ome	Slade
UKLP	American Pie	Don McLean
WEEK 3		
US45	Lean On Me	Bill Withers
USLP	Honky Chateau	Elton John
UK45	Puppy Love	Donny Osmond
UKLP	20 Dynamic Hits	Various
WEEK 4		
US45	Lean On Me	Bill Withers
USLP	Honky Chateau	Elton John
UK45	Puppy Love	Donny Osmond
UKLP	American Pie	Don McLean
WEEK 5		
US45	Alone Again (Naturally)	Gilbert O'Sullivan
USLP	Honky Chateau	Elton John
UK45	Puppy Love	Donny Osmond
UKLP	Greatest Hits	Simon And Garfunkel

EVERYBODY QUITS

Roy Wood – moving on

Roy Wood has quit the Electric Light Orchestra, and leadership of the group will be taken over by Jeff Lynne, while Hookfoot bassist and founder member Dave Glover has left the group to be replaced by Fred Gandi, formerly of Bluesology. Additionally, John Wetton is to leave Family because of what are described as 'clashes in musical policy'.

The news also comes that Andy Fraser has walked out on Free and will not be accompanying the band on their Japanese tour, which is due to begin late this month.

Fraser has been replaced in the band by Japanese bassist Tetsu, and Free, at the same time, have been augmented by the inclusion of Texan keyboardsman John Bundrick.

Announcing the changes, a spokesman added: 'Free return to Britain on 1 August, when a decision will be taken as to whether the new members remain with the band'.

Fraser – free at last?

HAIR CLOSES ON BROADWAY

The UK cast of Hair

Hair, the tribal-rock musical, closed on Broadway on 1 July after 1,729 performances. The show first opened at the off-Broadway Public Theatre in October 1967, then moved on to play the Cheetah nightclub before transferring to the Biltmore Theater.

During its run, Diane Keaton and Melba Moore were among its leads, while the tally of hit songs included 'Aquarius', 'Let The Sun Shine In', 'Ain't Got No' and 'Good Morning Sunshine'.

The British edition of the show, at London's Shaftesbury Theatre, which opened in September 1968, continues to pull audiences.

THE GRAPEVINE

■ Mott The Hoople's 'All The Young Dudes', written and produced by David Bowie, has been released by UK CBS.

■ Paul McCartney and Wings have embarked on a 26-date European tour aboard a double-decker London bus.

■ Rolling Stones' Jagger and Richards arrested in Warwick, Rhode Island, on charges of obstructing the police after a fracas with a news photographer.

THE VANDELLAS DISBAND

Martha Reeves, who has fronted The Vandellas for more than ten years, has disbanded the group and will, henceforth, pursue a solo career.

This follows the departure from the group of Sandra Tilley, who has married and is retiring from the business. Said Martha: 'Over the years, I have had five different girls in the Vandellas, and the thought of finding yet another one, made me decide to go it alone.'

Martha is to make her first solo appearance this month, on Smokey Robinson's farewell tour with The Miracles. The other remaining Vandella, Martha's sister, Lois Reeves, is to join a new group, Quiet Elegance.

Vandellas, going it alone

ROCK 'N' ROLL WEMBLEY

A rock 'n' roll revival extravaganza takes place at London's Wembley Empire Stadium on 5 August, the line-up including Chuck Berry, Little Richard, Jerry Lee Lewis, Bill Haley, Emile Ford, Heinz and Dr Feelgood, Billy Fury, Gary Glitter, Wizzard and Bo Diddley, who was recently in Kansas City, jamming with Elephant's Memory.

The Drifters, Platters and Coasters, who were originally billed, will not now take part because the promoters have been threatened with legal action over the authenticity of these groups.

'But', claimed promoters Ron and Ray Foulk, 'our main problem is that we are obliged to protect the Wembley turf by laying down coconut matting, and we're having difficulty in obtaining sufficient quantities.'

ALICE IN RECORD-LAND

Alice Cooper's hit 'School's Out' – now No. 1 in Britain, with the album in the Top 5 – has become the biggest-selling record in the history of Warner Brothers.

Said a record company spokesman in the States: 'The reaction here is fantastic. Alice has been breaking records all over the country, and the latest was at Dillon Stadium, Connecticut, at

Promoting the UK success of 'Schools Out', Alice poses with models dressed as traditional English schoolgirls

which he smashed the Stones' gross for the same venue.'

Alice shortly ends a major tour of the USA and then begins work on a new album, using the band's own 16-track mobile, parked in the grounds of a 40-room Connecticut mansion.

BOWIE'S BIG SELL-OUT

David Bowie's London Rainbow gigs on 19 and 20 August – part of a tour promoting his latest album 'The Rise And Fall Of Ziggy Stardust And The Spiders From Mars' – have completely sold out.

Bowie now plays Bristol Locarno (27) and Bournemouth Starkers (31) before moving on to a string of dates in September, one concert being scheduled for the opening date of the 3,000 seater Manchester Hard Rock, Britain's first purpose-built rock arena.

Bowie – sell-out for Ziggy

STAR QUOTE

IAN MACLAGAN
Faces keyboardist

'The Faces are a rock 'n' roll band but Rod's a bit of a folkie at heart.'

THE GRAPEVINE

■ McCartney Wings trek has been marred by drug arrests of Paul, Linda and drummer Denny Seiwell.

■ Tear gas and police truncheons floored Grace Slick and Paul Kantner at 'Airplane gig in Akron, Ohio.

■ U.K. newcomer Gilbert O'Sullivan has a first gold disc for 'Alone Again (Naturally)'.

WATTSTAX FILMED

Luther Ingram in 'Wattstax'

The Stax Organization have followed in the footsteps of Tamla Motown by making a full-length feature film. In association with producer David Wolper, Stax filmed the all-star 'Wattstax '72' charity concert, which was staged last month at Los Angeles' Memorial Coliseum.

The six-hour show featured gospel, spiritual and soul roots, the very essence of black music and the Stax-Memphis way of things and featured such acts as The Dramatics, Little Milton, Johnny Taylor, Albert King, Frederick Knight, Isaac Hayes, Eddie Floyd, Rufus & Carla Thomas, Kim Weston, The Bar-Kays and others.

A two hour film should be on cinema screens by the end of the year.

LENNON'S THE GREATEST

John Lennon has been voted The World's Greatest Vocalist, ahead of Free's Paul Rodgers, in this year's NME Musicians' poll.

The nominations were diverse – everything from Forties crooner Vera Lynn to blues guitarist Albert King! – but the final results were: 1 John Lennon, 2 Paul Rodgers, 3 Bob Dylan, 4 Maggie Bell/Mick Jagger (equal), 6 Ray Charles/Joni Mitchell (equal), 8 Stevie Wonder, 9 Joe Cocker, 10 Rod Stewart, 11 Steven Stills, 12 Billie Holiday/Aretha Franklin (equal), 14 Elton John, 15 David Bowie/Randy Newman/Paul McCartney/Van Morrison (equal).

Elton John listed Mick Jagger, Aretha Franklin and Dusty Springfield as his choices, while Rod Stewart opted for Maggie Bell, Paul Rodgers and Labi Siffre, and Marc Bolan went for Elton John, John Lennon and Al Green.

Among the many others who voted were Bryan Ferry, Ian Hunter, Rick Nelson, Ozzy Osbourne, Lou Reed, Rick Danko, Brian Wilson, Lulu, Iggy Pop and Robert Plant.

CHARTS

US45	Brandy (You're A Fine Girl)	*Looking Glass*
USLP	Chicago V	*Chicago*
UK45	You Wear It Well	*Rod Stewart*
UKLP	Never A Dull Moment	*Rod Stewart*

── WEEK 2 ──

US45	Alone Again (Naturally)	*Gilbert O'Sullivan*
USLP	Chicago V	*Chicago*
UK45	You Wear It Well	*Rod Stewart*
UKLP	Never A Dull Moment	*Rod Stewart*

── WEEK 3 ──

US45	Black & White	*Three Dog Night*
USLP	Chicago V	*Chicago*
UK45	Mama Weer All Crazee Now	*Slade*
UKLP	Never A Dull Moment	*Rod Stewart*

── WEEK 4 ──

US45	Baby Don't Get Hooked On Me	*Mac Davis*
USLP	Chicago V	*Chicago*
UK45	Mama Weer All Crazee Now	*Slade*
UKLP	Greatest Hits	*Simon And Garfunkel*

── WEEK 5 ──

US45	Baby Don't Get Hooked On Me	*Mac Davis*
USLP	Chicago V	*Chicago*
UK45	Children Of The Revolution	*T.Rex*
UKLP	Never A Dull Moment	*Rod Stewart*

VINEGAR JOE BECOME SEVEN-PIECE

Vinegar Joe are now a seven-piece unit following two personnel changes and the addition of Jim Mullen from Brian Auger's Oblivion Express.

Steve York rejoins the band from Climax, replacing Nic South. And Mike Deacon, formerly with Juicy Lucy and The Greatest Show On Earth, takes over from John Hawken on piano.

The new line-up has been recording at London's Olympic Studios with a view to a new album release in October.

REGGAE MOVIE OPENS

Jamaica's first major movie, *The Harder They Come*, makes its debut at London's Notting Hill Gaumont on September 1, where it plays for three weeks.

Directed by Perry Henzell, the film stars Jimmy Cliff as a reggae singer who gets involved in music business rip-offs and a fight against authority. Among those heard on the film's soundtrack are Desmond Dekker, The Maytals, The Melodians, The Slickers, and Cliff himself.

A soundtrack album is available through Island Records, who financed the movie.

NICK TURNER
of Hawkwind

'We wanted to play the Windsor Sex Olympics but only half the band turned up.'

Movie star Jimmy

The one-time Steven Georgiou

THE GRAPEVINE

■ Pete Townshend's 'Who Came First' album is scheduled for UK release by Track Records on September 29.

■ The Bee Gees, who were to have made a horror movie called *Castle X* in Yugoslavia, have now shelved the project.

■ Cat Stevens opens his latest US tour on 29 September at LA's Shrine Auditorium. Supporting act is Ramblin' Jack Elliott.

Ramblin' Jack – 'And I'm really Elliott Charles Adnopoz!'

MOODY MANIA IN THE STATES

The Moody Blues have suddenly and unexpectedly been swept to a new peak of acclaim in the States on the strength of their re-promoted 1967 album, 'Days Of Future Passed', and the single, 'Nights In White Satin'.

Both are now in the Top 10 of the respective US charts and are challenging for No. 1 positions.

Meanwhile, the band's opening American tour date, at Hampton Rhodes coliseum, was a double sell-out, as was their double concert at New York's Madison Square Garden. The fastest sale was at Boston Gardens, where 19,000 tickets went in just 90 minutes.

STAR QUOTE

DAVID CASSIDY

'I'm exploited by people who put me on the back of cereal boxes. I asked my housekeeper to go and buy a certain kind of cereal and when she came home, there was huge picture of me on the back. I can't even eat breakfast without seeing my face.'

Cassidy croons

CHARTS

US45	Baby Don't Get Hooked On Me *Mac Davis*
USLP	Chicago V *Chicago*
UK45	How Can I Be Sure *David Cassidy*
UKLP	Never A Dull Moment *Rod Stewart*

— WEEK 2 —

US45	Ben *Michael Jackson*
USLP	Chicago V *Chicago*
UK45	Mouldy Old Dough *Lieutenant Pigeon*
UKLP	Never A Dull Moment *Rod Stewart*

— WEEK 3 —

US45	My Ding-A-Ling *Chuck Berry*
USLP	Superfly *Soundtrack/Curtis Mayfield*
UK45	Mouldy Old Dough *Lieutenant Pigeon*
UKLP	Greatest Hits *Simon And Garfunkel*

— WEEK 4 —

US45	My Ding-A-Ling *Chuck Berry*
USLP	Superfly *Soundtrack/Curtis Mayfield*
UK45	Mouldy Old Dough *Lieutenant Pigeon*
UKLP	Greatest Hits *Simon And Garfunkel*

McCARTNEY AND WINGS FOR BOND MOVIE

Paul McCartney is writing some – and possibly all – of the music for the next James Bond movie, *Live And Let Die*, which has just gone into production in America, with Roger Moore taking over the 007 role from Sean Connery.

The exact extent of McCartney's contribution to the film hasn't yet been determined, but he has already penned the title theme and recorded it for the movie soundtrack with his group, Wings.

CREEDENCE SPLIT

Creedence Clearwater Revival have finally called it a day after a career that's encompassed seven Top 10 US hits.

The band has been falling apart for some time now and guitarist Tom Fogerty left in January 1971, just after the release of CCR's fifth album 'Pendulum'. Since his departure, the group have struggled on as a trio.

MICHAEL JACKSON'S RATTY HIT

British songwriter Don Black, who penned the words to Lulu's 'To Sir With Love' – a US No. 1 in 1967 – also provided the lyric to 'Ben', the Michael Jackson single which went to the top of the American charts on October 14.

Black, who wrote the song with composer Walter Scharf for the movie about an ailing boy who befriends a pack of rats, was the man who suggested that Michael Jackson provided the vocal.

'He's quite an animal lover,' claims Black. 'Very sensitive. He enjoys anything that crawls or flies.'

THE GRAPEVINE

- Jon Mark, leader of Mark-Almond, has been involved in an accident in Hawaii and lost most of his left-hand ring finger.

- Phil Seaman, a great jazz drummer, and the man who taught Ginger Baker, has died.

- David Essex is leaving the London production of *Godspell* to star in the film *That'll Be The Day*, with Ringo Starr, Billy Fury and Keith Moon.

Creedence – And once there was four. Tom Fogerty (left) quit the group in 1971. Now his brother John (second right) and the others are moving on

COCKER VICTIMIZED IN OZ

Joe Cocker and The Chris Stainton Band headed back to LA after leaving Australia on October 21, where they had played two Melbourne concerts. But three concerts had to be missed following drugs charges on which Cocker was convicted and which became 'a political issue with the Australian elections close at hand.'

Cocker has now been invited to appeal against the court's decision convicting him of drug offences and will be able to apply for re-entry into Australia on December 2 – after that country's general election.

Cocker – done down-under

1972

POMPEII FLOYD

A remarkable film of Pink Floyd performing in the ruins of Pompeii, in southern Italy, is to have its official British premiere on November 25.

The movie, a joint French/German/Belgian production, directed by Adrian Maben and titled *Pink Floyd At Pompeii*, was shot in the old Roman open-air amphitheatre, both by day and night.

The music performed includes 'Echoes', 'Careful With That Axe, Eugene', 'A Saucerful Of Secrets', 'One Of These Days I'm Gonna Cut You Into Little Pieces', 'Set The Controls For

Pink Floyd perform pomp rock of their own kind with an extravaganza from the ruins of Pompeii

The Heart Of The Sun', 'Mademoiselle Nobs' and 'Dark Side Of The Moon'.

Previewed at this year's Edin-burgh Film Festival, where it was greeted with considerable acclaim, it is now hopefully destined for general release.

CHARTS

US45	I Can See Clearly Now *Johnny Nash*
USLP	Superfly *Soundtrack/Curtis Mayfield*
UK45	Mouldy Old Dough *Lieutenant Pigeon*
UKLP	Greatest Hits *Simon And Garfunkel*
— WEEK 2 —	
US45	I Can See Clearly Now *Johnny Nash*
USLP	Superfly *Soundtrack/Curtis Mayfield*
UK45	Clair *Gilbert O'Sullivan*
UKLP	Greatest Hits *Simon And Garfunkel*
— WEEK 3 —	
US45	I Can See Clearly Now *Johnny Nash*
USLP	Catch Bull At Four *Cat Stevens*
UK45	Clair *Gilbert O'Sullivan*
UKLP	Greatest Hits *Simon And Garfunkel*
— WEEK 4 —	
US45	I Can See Clearly Now *Johnny Nash*
USLP	Catch Bull At Four *Cat Stevens*
UK45	My Ding-A-Ling *Chuck Berry*
UKLP	Back To Front *Gilbert O'Sullivan*

THE GRAPEVINE

■ Andy Fraser and Chris Spedding have formed a new band, Sharks.

■ Berry Oakley, bassist and vocalist with the Allman Brothers, killed in bike accident.

■ Slade's Dave Hill has had his left leg put in plaster after his six-inch high heels caused him to fall during a Liverpool Stadium gig, sustaining a broken ankle.

Jim'n'Carly get wed

ALL-STAR TOMMY FOR RAINBOW

Following the refusal of London's Royal Albert Hall to allow an all-star production of *Tommy* to be staged there, co-producer Lou Reizner has announced that he will now be presenting the show at the Rainbow Theatre on December 9.

An impressive list of guest stars has been lined-up for this event, headed by Ringo Starr, Rod Stewart, Richard Harris and Richie Havens. Also taking part are Maggie Bell, Sandy Denny, Steve Winwood and Graham Bell, plus all four members of The Who.

The work is being performed by the London Symphony Orchestra, and the star names are appearing as the LSO's guests. The orchestra initially booked the Albert Hall, only to have the booking rejected when the list of guests was seen!

CHUCK IN ROYALTY ROW

A major royalty row has blown up between Chess Records and Coventry's Lanchester Polytechnic College, where Chuck Berry recorded his 'My Ding-A-Ling'.

The track was recorded live at the college's Arts Festival last winter, and the festival committee is now claiming that a percentage of the royalties is due to them from sales of the single, which has sold nearly two million copies throughout the world.

The Festival incurred a £12,000 ($24,000) loss but this would be wiped out by the royalties to which the Polytechnic feels it is entitled. Chess, however, deny ever having made any royalty agreement with Lanchester.

Berry: royalty wrangle

CARLY BECOMES MRS TAYLOR

Carly Simon became Mrs James Taylor on November 2, the wedding ceremony being held in Carly's Manhattan apartment.

Taylor announced the splice later in the day at a Radio City Music Hall concert where he claimed: 'I don't know whether to be more nervous about the concert, or the marriage!'

DIANA FILM HONOUR

Diana Ross in her role as Billie Holliday, which despite acclaim, did not meet with universal approval

CHARTS

US45	Papa Was A Rolling Stone	*Temptations*
USLP	Catch Bull At Four	*Cat Stevens*
UK45	My Ding-A-Ling	*Chuck Berry*
UKLP	Greatest Hits	*Simon And Garfunkel*

WEEK 2

US45	I Am Woman	*Helen Reddy*
USLP	Seventh Sojourn	*Moody Blues*
UK45	My Ding-A-Ling	*Chuck Berry*
UKLP	Back To Front	*Gilbert O'Sullivan*

WEEK 3

US45	Me & Mrs. Jones	*Billy Paul*
USLP	Seventh Sojourn	*Moody Blues*
UK45	Gudbuy 'Jane	*Slade*
UKLP	Back To Front	*Gilbert O'Sullivan*

WEEK 4

US45	Me & Mrs. Jones	*Billy Paul*
USLP	Seventh Sojourn	*Moody Blues*
UK45	Long-Haired Lover From Liverpool	*Little Jimmy Osmond*
UKLP	Back To Front	*Gilbert O'Sullivan*

WEEK 5

US45	Me & Mrs. Jones	*Billy Paul*
USLP	Seventh Sojourn	*Moody Blues*
UK45	Long-Haired Lover From Liverpool	*Little Jimmy Osmond*
UKLP	Slayed	*Slade*

Diana Ross, tipped for an Academy Award, collected the Actress Of The Year award in the highly respected NAACP Annual Image Awards presentation at the Hollywood Palladium.

The Awards proved a landslide for the Tamla-Motown organisation, with five of their acts winning categories.

These were: Jackson 5 (Male Vocal Group Of The Year), Stevie Wonder (Producer Of The Year for his 'Music Of My Mind' album); The Supremes (Female Vocal Group Of The Year), The Temptations (Album Of The Year with 'All Directions') and Nicholas Ashford and Valerie Simpson (Writers Of The Year).

THE GRAPEVINE

■ James Brown arrested after a Knoxville, Tennessee show and charged with disorderly conduct.

■ It's been announced that the live double-album by The Rolling Stones and Stevie Wonder, recorded when they toured together in America, is now unlikely to be released due to contractual difficulties.

■ Roberta Flack, guitarist Cornell Dupree and bassist Jerry Jemon have been slightly injured in a Manhattan car accident.

Roberta – auto incident

NO BAN ON BERRY, BUT MACC AXED

Self-styled protector of British public morals, Mrs Mary Whitehouse, has lashed out at Chuck Berry's No. 1 hit 'My Ding A Ling'. She is demanding a UK TV and radio ban on the record because, she says, the BBC is using it 'as a vehicle for mass child molestation'.

The BBC say that they will carry on playing the record though, inconsistently, they have slapped a ban on 'Hi Hi Hi', the new single from Paul McCartney's Wings. They insist that the sexual implications of this song are too blatant and so the record has become the second Wings single to be banned this year – the other being 'Give Ireland Back To The Irish'.

Press reports had suggested that 'Hi Hi Hi' was banned because of drug assocations, but a BBC press officer explained that the ban had nothing to do with drugs, but was primarily concerned with the part of the lyric that refers to lying on a bed and getting out 'a body gun'.

Apparently 'My Ding A Ling' escapes any ban because 'it is in the tradition of the music hall.'

MARC MOVIE GETS CRITICS NO-NO

The Marc Bolan film *Born To Boogie*, which premiered at London's Brewer Street Oscar One on December 14, has been described by one *NME* writer as 'bad, atrocious, cheap, pretentious, narcissistic and noisy.'

As a rock'n'roll film it's one of those total-personality efforts – as opposed to the *Mad Dogs And Englishmen* syndrome of boring documentaries.

Bolan claims that this is a film with surrealistic overtones. Which means that it contains some embarrassing episodes which would be Fellini-esque, except that it would be an insult to use the name of that director in the context of this film.

Perhaps the only really good scene in the film is when T. Rex perform 'Tutti Frutti' with Ringo Starr on drums and Elton John playing piano. But mainly it's Marc, Marc and more Marc.

AUSTRALIA OKAYS THE STONES

The Rolling Stones, who open their Far East tour with concerts in Honolulu this month, will be admitted to Australia after all.

The band's visit was in jeopardy because of an outstanding warrant the French police had issued against Keith Richards on a

Stones to roll down under

drugs charge.

However, the Australian Government have announced that they have no objection to the tour, though Japan has banned The Stones.

It had originally been planned for the band to be in Japan for five days, but they'll now bypass that country and resume touring in Hong Kong on February 5.

Prior to leaving for their Far East dates, the Stones managed to arrange a last-minute charity concert at Los Angeles Forum on January 18, to aid victims of the recent Nicaraguan earthquake disaster. The resulting concert raised a reported $200,000.

CHARTS

US45	You're So Vain *Carly Simon*
USLP	Seventh Sojourn *Moody Blues*
UK45	Long-Haired Lover From Liverpool *Little Jimmy Osmond*
UKLP	Slayed *Slade*

— WEEK 2 —

US45	You're So Vain *Carly Simon*
USLP	No Secrets *Carly Simon*
UK45	Long-Haired Lover From Liverpool *Little Jimmy Osmond*
UKLP	Slayed *Slade*

— WEEK 3 —

US45	You're So Vain *Carly Simon*
USLP	No Secrets *Carly Simon*
UK45	The Jean Genie *David Bowie*
UKLP	Slayed *Slade*

— WEEK 4 —

US45	Superstition *Stevie Wonder*
USLP	No Secrets *Carly Simon*
UK45	Blockbuster *Sweet*
UKLP	Slayed *Slade*

ELTON IN ARGUMENT

Elton John has slammed his own management and recording company, claiming that DJM did not want his new single, 'Daniel', to be released.

The song is a track from his upcoming album 'Don't Shoot Me, I'm Only The Piano Player', as was his last hit single 'Crocodile Rock'.

Commented Elton: 'Dick James said he didn't want another single released to detract from the sales of the next album. So I've more or less forced him to put it out – he has disowned it. I'm having to pay for all the advertising, but he says he'll pay for the ads if the single makes the UK Top 10. Isn't that nice?'

Elton – single disowned

JERRY LEE RECORDS IN BRITAIN

An impressive line-up of top-flight British musicians has been assembled to support Jerry Lee Lewis on the album he is recording in London. So far confirmed are Peter Frampton, Rory Gallagher, Albert Lee, Tony Ashton, Gary Wright, Alvin Lee, Chas Hodges and Kenny Jones.

Lewis arrived in London on January 5 for his first-ever UK sessions, which are being produced by Steve Rowland. The fare will consist of mainly old rock classics.

The Killer goes UK

THE GRAPEVINE

- Neil Young stopped a New York concert and announced 'Peace has come' after learning of the ceasefire in Vietnam.

- The live double-album of Elvis Presley's concert in Hawaii on January 14 is to be rush released all over the world. Advance orders of over one million copies have already been received.

- The Sutherland Brothers and Quiver have joined forces.

PAUL AND LINDA'S ZOO GANG

Paul & Linda McCartney have been signed to write the music for an ambitious new British TV series, *Zoo Gang*, which goes into production in March.

The six one-hour shows, which star John Mills, Brian Keith, Lili Palmer and Barry Morse, are based upon the Paul Gallico book of the same name. This will be the McCartneys' first venture into TV theme music.

MIDLER FLIES IN

Bette Midler, whose 'Do You Want To Dance' recently entered the US Top 20, arrived in London to talk about herself and her debut album.

'I'm not worried about my relationship with decadence, simply because I transcend it,' she told reporters. 'I'm at once a part of it and not a part of it. For instance, there are some performers who are right in there, in the centre of it.

'I'm thinking more of Lou Reed in this sphere of decadence. The same would hold true of David Bowie. I've never seen him performing live, but I've heard his albums.'

Miss Midler, who has just appeared on the cover of *Rolling Stone* magazine, made her name performing to audiences at The Continental Baths, a New York club frequented by homosexuals.

RICK AND HANK

Rick Wakeman is releasing 'Six Wives Of Henry VIII', a concept album on which the keyboard wizard employed three drummers, three guitarists, four bass players and a six-girl choir.

Wakeman wrote the music for the album after reading *The Private Life Of Henry VIII* on a plane to Chicago. He actually began recording the project back in November 1971 and has since slotted sessions in between US tours with Yes, spending some eight months in the studio.

Asked if he would play concerts to promote the work, Wakeman said: 'I think that would be wrong. I want people to buy the album for the right reasons, not because it's forced upon them.'

Rick previewed the album on BBC TV's *Old Grey Whistle Test* show during January.

Ex-strawb Wakeman

STRAWBS SINGLE 'HARMFUL'

The Strawbs' current UK hit 'Part Of The Union' has been termed generally harmful by Conservative member of Parliament Harold Soref. But Britain's trades union leaders have come out in strong support of the record and have even launched a poster campaign throughout the country urging young people to join a union.

As a result, political controversy seems to be brewing, Soref complaining to the BBC about the record being played on the air.

He claims that it misrepresents the unions and its tone could lead to industrial troubles. However, a Conservative Party headquarters spokesman offered a bland 'no comment'.

The Strawbs — (from left) John Ford, Richard Hudson, Dave Lambert, Blue Weaver and Dave Cousins

CHARTS

US45	Crocodile Rock *Elton John*
USLP	No Secrets *Carly Simon*
UK45	Blockbuster *Sweet*
UKLP	Slayed *Slade*

——— WEEK 2 ———

US45	Crocodile Rock *Elton John*
USLP	No Secrets *Carly Simon*
UK45	Blockbuster *Sweet*
UKLP	Don't Shoot Me, I'm Only The Piano Player *Elton John*

——— WEEK 3 ———

US45	Crocodile Rock *Elton John*
USLP	The World Is A Ghetto *War*
UK45	Blockbuster *Sweet*
UKLP	Don't Shoot Me, I'm Only The Piano Player *Elton John*

——— WEEK 4 ———

US45	Killing Me Softly With His Song *Roberta Flack*
USLP	The World Is A Ghetto *War*
UK45	Part Of The Union *Strawbs*
UKLP	Don't Shoot Me, I'm Only The Piano Player *Elton John*

THE GRAPEVINE

■ Max Yasgur, whose farm housed the 1969 Woodstock Festival, died on 8 February at the age of 53.

■ Emerson, Lake & Palmer are to form their own label, Manticore.

■ German band Saturnalia have released what is claimed to be the world's first 3D picture disc.

■ David Bowie collapsed from exhaustion at the end of a Valentine's Day show in New York.

CHARTS

US45	Killing Me Softly With His Song *Roberta Flack*
USLP	Don't Shoot Me, I'm Only The Piano Player *Elton John*
UK45	Part Of The Union *Strawbs*
UKLP	Don't Shoot Me, I'm Only The Piano Player *Elton John*

— WEEK 2 —

US45	Killing Me Softly With His Song *Roberta Flack*
USLP	Don't Shoot Me, I'm Only The Piano Player *Elton John*
UK45	Cum On Feel The Noize *Slade*
UKLP	Don't Shoot Me, I'm Only The Piano PLayer *Elton John*

— WEEK 3 —

US45	Killing Me Softly With His Song *Roberta Flack*
USLP	Dueling Banjos *Eric Weissberg & Steve Mandel*
UK45	Cum On Feel The Noize *Slade*
UKLP	Don't Shoot Me, I'm Only The Piano Player *Elton John*

— WEEK 4 —

US45	Love Train *O'Jays*
USLP	Dueling Banjos *Eric Weissberg & Steve Mandel*
UK45	Cum On Feel The Noize *Slade*
UKLP	Don't Shoot Me, I'm Only The Piano Player *Elton John*

— WEEK 5 —

US45	Love Train *O'Jays*
USLP	Dueling Banjos *Eric Weissberg & Steve Mandel*
UK45	The Twelfth Of Never *Donny Osmond*
UKLP	Billion Dollar Babies *Alice Cooper*

OSMONDS IN LONDON

The Osmonds, in London for a press conference and a *Top of the Pops* TV appearance, say that Donny's voice is changing. Asked if the public had yet heard Donny's new voice, Alan Osmond replied, 'I guess "Puppy Love" is pretty near it.'

Asked why the two eldest Osmonds aren't bopping, Alan explained: 'They're both married now and they have some kids. I should explain that our two older brothers are hard of hearing. That kind of kept them from being in show business.'

Other points included the fact that the Osmonds don't even drink Coca Cola and that, though they played at a Nixon rally, they feel politics should not be brought into music.

Meanwhile, Osmondmania continues. The brothers are currently fashioning an album which Alan Osmond claims will be 'our Sgt Pepper'.

STAR QUOTE

JON LORD
of Deep Purple

'We're as valid as anything by Beethoven'.

Taking rock presentation to new extremes, so-called 'supergroup' Emerson, Lake & Palmer

DR HOOK 'COVER' VERSION

Dr Hook & The Medicine Show were featured on the cover of the March 29 edition of *Rolling Stone* magazine, thus gaining a massive plug for their current CBS single, 'The Cover Of The Rolling Stone', which recently entered the US Top 10.

The song was penned by Shel Silverstein, the *Playboy* writer and cartoonist, who also wrote Johnny Cash's 'A Boy Named Sue', Loretta Lynn's 'One's On The Way' and Dr Hook's earlier hit 'Sylvia's Mother'.

AIRPLANE ALBUM WINGS ITS WAY

Jefferson Airplane's new album '30 Seconds Over Winterland', due out in the States this month, is a half-live, half-studio affair that includes a Grunt dictionary.

Grace Slick and Paul Kantner are still slaving away at their own album, Jorma Kaukonen is working on an acoustic solo LP, and Grace is also writing songs for an upcoming solo album.

In Singapore the vice squad recently confiscated a shipment of the band's 'Long John Silver' album because it contains a photograph of marijuana.

E.L.P WORLD TREK

Emerson, Lake & Palmer have mobilized a musical caravan for their 1973 world tour, which opens in Germany at the end of this month. Operating under the banner of 'Get Me A Ladder', the production is described as the most ambitious spectacular ever for a rock group.

The presentation will involve the transportation of 50 tour personnel and 20 tons of equipment valued at $750,000. Two 40-foot articulated trucks will carry the specially designed prosecenium, a Roman-style arch and a stage which will be erected at every performance.

Supporting act on the tour will be Stray Dog, who recently signed to ELP's Manticore label.

LINDISFARNERS GO AS THEY GO GOLD

Ray Jackson of Lindisfarne

It's officially confirmed that Newcastle folk-rock bank Lindisfarne are splitting into two. Only Alan Hull and Ray Jackson of the current line-up will feature in the completely re-shaped Lindisfarne and they will be bringing in four new musicians Tommy Duffy, Charlie Harcourt, Paul Nichols and Kenny Craddock.

The three departing members of the band – Rod Clements, Simon Cowe and Ray Laidlaw – are forming a breakaway band. This will be a quartet when they are joined by a singer-songwriter whose name is not being revealed yet due to contractual difficulties, but is rumoured to be Billy Mitchell.

The full personnel for both bands will be officially

announced on May 2, when members of the old outfit will be presented with gold discs for their hit album 'Fog On The Tyne'.

NEIL YOUNG'S WEIRD JOURNEY

Journey Through The Past, a documentary about Neil Young, was screened at the US Film Festival, in Dallas, on April 8.

A surrealistic affair that's said to owe something in approach to Italian director Federico Fellini, Young claims it is: 'A film about me – a collection of thoughts. Every scene means something to me – although with some of them, I can't say what.'

Bread – likely to be sliced?

PENTANGLE FOR FINAL SPLIT

After several months of indecision, Pentangle have decided to split – but not before they have cut another album together.

At the beginning of the year they denied reports that they were breaking up but, now that their various individual projects are gathering momentum, they have finally decided to disband. However, a new-look Pentangle could still emerge.

'Certainly Jacqui McShee and John Renbourn will continue to record together,' claimed co-manager Arthur Lubin. But Bert Jansch, Danny Thompson and Terry Cox are intent on splitting, and Jansch is heading out on a solo tour this month.

RODEN JOINS DOORS

Jess Roden, the former Bronco and Alan Bown set vocalist and guitarist, has announced that he's officially joined The Doors to replace the late Jim Morrison. Says Roden: 'It's perfectly true, although I'm not at liberty to say any more at the moment.'

His statement ends weeks of on-and-off speculation about the British singer becoming part of the US group. It's also understood that keyboard player Ray Manzarek has now left The Doors, who are currently in London for recording sessions.

Roden is already laying down tracks with them.

John Densmore, Robbie Krieger and Ray Manzarek of The Doors

CHARTS

US45	The Night The Lights Went Out In Georgia *Vicki Lawrence*
USLP	Lady Sings The Blues *Diana Ross*
UK45	The Twelfth Of Never *Donny Osmond*
UKLP	Dark Side Of The Moon *Pink Floyd*

— WEEK 2 —

US45	The Night The Lights Went Out In Georgia *Vicki Lawrence*
USLP	Lady Sings The Blues *Diana Ross*
UK45	Get Down *Gilbert O'Sullivan*
UKLP	Don't Shoot Me, I'm Only The Piano Player *Elton John*

— WEEK 3 —

US45	Tie A Yellow Ribbon *Dawn*
USLP	Billion Dollar Babies *Alice Cooper*
UK45	Tie A Yellow Ribbon *Dawn*
UKLP	Houses Of The Holy *Led Zeppelin*

— WEEK 4 —

US45	Tie A Yellow Ribbon *Dawn*
USLP	Dark Side Of The Moon *Pink Floyd*
UK45	Tie A Yellow Ribbon *Dawn*
UKLP	Ooh La La *Faces*

Former Bronco-buster Jess Roden

49

SOLO MAGGIE

Maggie Bell has quit Stone The Crows and, as a result, the band's projected British tour – due to start on May 25 – has been cancelled.

Maggie's departure from the band is reportedly down to 'increasing involvement with her solo album'. The album, which is called 'Queen Of The Night', is currently being recorded at New York's Electric Ladyland Studio.

In charge is former Cream producer and Mountain main-man Felix Pappalardi, who has also been playing bass on the sessions. Reports suggest that the project should be finished towards the end of this month, and a late June release is being planned for both sides of the Atlantic.

ELTON SCRAPS ALBUM TRACKS

Elton John has scrapped most of the tracks he recorded in Jamaica before his recent British tour and has flown to France to work on his new album almost from scratch.

It is understood that Elton was dissatisfied with some of the sounds achieved in the Jamaican studios, and is quoted as saying: 'The piano wasn't good enough.'

Lyricist Bernie Taupin has accompanied him to France to work on the LP, which has the tentative title 'Silent Movies And Talking Pictures'.

Before they left, John and Taupin were presented with three gold records by DJM Records. Two were for 'Honky Chateau' and 'Don't Shoot Me, I'm Only The Piano Player', which have both sold over 100,000 copies in Britain. The third was for one million dollars' worth of US sales for 'Don't Shoot Me'.

THE GRAPEVINE

■ The new band formed by ex-Lindisfarne members Rod Clements, Ray Laidlaw and Simon Cowe has been named Jack The Lad; as rumoured, the fourth member is Billy Mitchell, a friend of Lindisfarne's for many years.

■ CBS President Clive Davis has been fired for allegedly mis-using company funds.

■ Paul Simon has embarked on his first solo tour, playing his initial date at Boston's Music Hall on May 6.

(above) Simon says it solo

(below) Maggie Bellts out!

LANE QUITS FACES

Ronnie Lane has announced his decision to quit The Faces. Lane, who has just returned from the band's seventh American tour, commented: 'It's time to move on – I feel the need for a change.'

The group are currently auditioning for a new bass player and expect to announce Lane's replacement very shortly. In an official statement, drummer Kenny Jones said: 'Ronnie obviously wants to do something on his own and there is no reason why we should stand in his way.'

Meanwhile, Mercury Records are lining up a solo Rod Stewart album for July. Titled 'Play It Again Sam', it's a compilation from his previous four albums.

Ronnie Lane in change of Face

HENDRIX FILM OPENS

The film *Jimi Hendrix* is to open at London's Warner Theatre on June 14, a date that coincides with the release of the Warner Bros' double-album soundtrack recording.

The movie, which runs for nearly two hours, includes sequences of Hendrix in action at the Monterey and Isle Of Wight festivals, London's Marquee Club, the Filmore East and at Berkeley, California. There are also extensive filmed interviews with Hendrix, as well as conversations with many of his friends

The late, great Jimi keeps rockin' on film

including Mick Jagger, Pete Townshend, Eric Clapton and Lou Reed.

The movie's producer is Joe Boyd, former head of Witchseason and the man responsible for recordings by The Incredible String Band, Fairport Convention and Sandy Denny before he sold the management/production company to Island Records and went to work for Warner Brothers.

PETER, PAUL AND MARY REUNITE FOR ONE-OFF

John Denver and Bill Withers headlined the second annual One To One Benefit at New York's Madison Square Garden in aid of retarded children at the Willowbrook Home.

Also on the bill were Eric Weissberg & Deliverance and Judy Collins, while Kris Kristofferson, Rita Coolidge, Richie Havens and Sly Stone all made unbilled appearances, along with Peter, Paul & Mary, who reunited for the evening.

"Lean On Me" says Bill

NO UNION FOR THE STRAWBS

The Strawbs have split in two. Founder member Dave Cousins and guitarist Dave Lambert retain the Strawbs name, while John Ford, Richard Hudson and Blue Weaver are forming a breakaway group with another, as yet unnamed, guitarist.

The announcement came from America, where the band have just completed a major tour. Ford and Hudson were The Strawbs members responsible for penning the band's recent 'Part Of The Union' hit.

WYATT BADLY INJURED

Robert Wyatt, drummer with Matching Mole and formerly of Soft Machine, is in Stoke Mandeville hospital near London with a broken spine, after falling from a third floor window.

Wyatt had been attending a party in London when – sometime after midnight on June 1 – he decided to leave by climbing down a drainpipe, but fell during the descent.

Doctors now fear that Wyatt will never walk or play again.

Asked if he had been taking drugs before the fall, Wyatt said that he was merely drunk, claiming: 'It was good old alcohol. You know – the legal one.'

Matching Mole's last album, 'Little Red Record', came out in October, last year, and Wyatt was said to be forming a revised version of the band at the time of his accident.

CHARTS

US45	My Love — *Paul McCartney & Wings*
USLP	Red Rose Speedway — *Paul McCartney & Wings*
UK45	See My Baby Jive — *Wizzard*
UKLP	Aladdin Sane — *David Bowie*

— WEEK 2 —

US45	My Love — *Paul McCartney & Wings*
USLP	Red Rose Speedway — *Paul McCartney & Wings*
UK45	Can The Can — *Suzi Quatro*
UKLP	The Beatles, 1962-1966 — *Beatles*

— WEEK 3 —

US45	My Love — *Paul McCartney & Wings*
USLP	Red Rose Speedway — *Paul McCartney & Wings*
UK45	Can The Can — *Suzi Quatro*
UKLP	Aladdin Sane — *David Bowie*

— WEEK 4 —

US45	My Love — *Paul McCartney & Wings*
USLP	Living In The Material World — *George Harrison*
UK45	Can The Can — *Suzi Quatro*
UKLP	Pure Gold — *Various*

— WEEK 5 —

US45	Give Me Love (Give Me Peace On Earth) — *George Harrison*
USLP	Living In The Material World — *George Harrison*
UK45	Rubber Bullets — *10cc*
UKLP	Aladdin Sane — *David Bowie*

THE GRAPEVINE

■ Mick Jagger has been named in a paternity suit by Marsha Hunt, who claims he's the father of her daughter Karis.

■ The Sarstedt Brothers, Peter, Rick (better known as Eden Kane) and Clive, make their first appearance as a group at London's Croydon Fairfield Hall on June 20.

■ Murry Wilson, father of Beach Boys Brian, Carl and Dennis died on June 4, aged 55.

1973

BOWIE: 'NO MORE GIGS'

David Bowie's gigs at London's Hammersmith Odeon on July 2 and 3 marked the end of his career as a live entertainer.

Afterwards he announced: 'Those were my final gigs. That's it. Period. I don't want to do any more gigs, and all my forthcoming American dates have been cancelled. From now on, I'll be concentrating on various activities that have very little to do with rock and pop.'

After his hit with 'Space Oddity' in 1969, Bowie retired from rock music and ran an arts lab in Beckenham, South London for 18 months. He only returned to performing at the insistence of Mercury, then his record company, to record 'The Man Who Sold The World'.

A year ago, Bowie told NME: 'I can't envisage stopping gigging for the next year at least, because I'm having such a good

CHARTS

US 45	Will It Go Round In Circles *Billy Preston*
US LP	Living In The Material World *George Harrison*
UK 45	Skweeze Me Pleeze Me *Slade*
UK LP	Aladdin Sane *David Bowie*

——— WEEK 2 ———

US 45	Will It Go Round In cirlces *Billy Preston*
US LP	Living In The Material World *George Harrison*
UK 45	Skweeze Me Pleeze Me *Slade*
UK LP	Aladdin Sane *David Bowie*

——— WEEK 3 ———

US 45	Bad Bad Leroy Brown *Jim Croce*
US LP	Living In The Material World *George Harrison*
UK 45	Welcome Home *Peters And Lee*
UK LP	We Can Make It *Peters And Lee*

——— WEEK 4 ———

US 45	Bad Bad Leroy Brown *Jim Croce*
US LP	Chicago VI *Chicago*
UK 45	Welcome Home *Peters And Lee*
UK LP	Aladdin Sane *David Bowie*

Right: Ray Davies on stage at the White City Festival

Bowie – no more gigs for Zig

time doing it – I've never had such a good time.'

But now, it seems, things have changed.

VAN MORRISON HARD NOSES THE HIGHWAY

All of Van Morrison's upcoming UK gigs – staged to support his new album 'Hard Nose The Highway' – have been sell-outs.

Morrison recently gave his first press conference in over six years and claimed that he couldn't seriously accept the half legend, half myth persona bestowed on him by many.

'The only reason journalists call me this,' he said, 'is simply because they can't think of anything else to write – it's just a convenient label.'

His gigs include Birmingham Town Hall (July 22), London Rainbow (23-24), Bristol Colston Hall (25), Manchester Free Trade Hall (26) and Newcastle City Hall (27).

... AND RAY DAVIES STOPS TOO!

Emotional stress has been given as the reason behind the shock 'I quit!' announcement made by Ray Davies from the stage at London's White City Festival on July 15.

The Kinks' press secretary explained: 'One has to understand that Ray is in a very emotional and confused stated. Two and a half weeks ago, his wife Rasa left, together with Ray's two children – and he hasn't heard from her since.

'Ray is, naturally, a very worried man. He hasn't been eating since she left. He hasn't slept. It's a miracle he got through the gig. He feels that touring has contributed to the situation.

'And don't forget that Rasa had a nervous breakdown – so Ray knows all about nervous breakdowns. He's a grieving man and he just made an emotional announcement.'

THE GRAPEVINE

■ NME has become the biggest selling weekly music publication in the world, the latest official trade audit showing the paper's average weekly sale between January-June this year as 204,512.

■ Family have announced that they are to disband in the autumn.

■ It's reckoned that the recent US rock festival held at Watkins Glen raceway was the biggest of all time, the audience totalling 600,000; The Grateful Dead headlined.

STAR QUOTE
VAN MORRISON

'David Bowie's just doing what Phil May of the Pretty Things used to do. He's just wearing different clothes.'

Van Morrison who is, er..half legend, half myth

TOMMY GOES TO THE MOVIES

Pete Townshend's rock opera *Tommy* is to be made into a major feature film, it has been announced. The movie will be directed by Ken Russell and be produced by Track Records in association with the Robert Stigwood Organisation.

The Who will have starring roles in the film, which goes into production next January, on location in England and abroad. And an entirely new soundtrack will be recorded for the film later this year, with additional new material by Townshend.

The Who are currently completing work on their upcoming double-album, 'Quadrophenia', which they expect to complete anytime now, in readiness for autumn worldwide release.

Hear him – see him! Pete goes widescreen

HAWKS' GUERRILLA TACTICS

Hawkwind – IRA bomb scares led to dropping single

Hawkwind's 'Urban Guerrilla' single has been withdrawn from the UK market at the request of the group themselves – despite the fact that Hawkwind are currently undertaking a tour to promote the record, which is likely to be a chart entry.

At the group's suggestion, the B-side of 'Urban Guerrilla' will be the new single. Titled 'Brainbox Pollution', it will be out as soon as possible.

'Here's my impression of Rex Harrison'

STEVIE INJURED IN CAR CRASH

Stevie Wonder and his driver are reported as being in a 'satisfactory' condition after an accident on August 6, when their car ploughed into the back of a truck.

Doctors said that Wonder was under intensive care and being hospitalized in Salisbury, North Carolina, before being moved to nearby Winston for specialist treatment.

Both vehicles were completely wrecked in the smash.

THE GRAPEVINE

- Paul Williams, one of the original Temptations, was found shot dead on August 17. He was 34.

- Paul Kossoff has been busted for driving under the influence of drink or drugs; he's been fined £500 and ordered to undertake in-patient treatment at a London Hospital.

- David Bowie's 'Pin-Ups' album, which was recently completed in France, is now being mixed in London.

CHARTS

US45	The Morning After	Maureen McGovern
USLP	Chicago VI	Chicago
UK45	I'm The Leader Of The Gang	Gary Glitter
UKLP	We Can Make It	Peters And Lee
WEEK 2		
US45	The Morning After	Maureen McGovern
USLP	Chicago VI	Chicago
UK45	I'm The Leader Of The Gang	Gary Glitter
UKLP	We Can Make It	Peters And Lee
WEEK 3		
US45	Touch Me In The Morning	Diana Ross
USLP	A Passion Play	Jethro Tull
UK45	I'm The Leader Of The Gang	Gary Glitter
UKLP	We Can Make It	Peters And Lee
WEEK 4		
US45	Brother Louie	Stories
USLP	Chicago VI	Chicago
UK45	I'm The Leader of The Gang	Gary Glitter
UKLP	Now And Then	Carpenters

Rehabilitated, Etta James stages a welcome come-back

ETTA BETTA – YOU BETCHA!

Chess Records have just released Etta James' first album in two years. Titled 'Etta James', it was produced by Gabriel Mekler, former producer of Steppenwolf and others.

At a reception given for her at Mediasound Studios in New York, the singer – dressed in shocking pink – sang over the album's backing tracks and announced: 'I've been a bad girl but I'm better now.'

Etta, a confessed heroin addict for 14 years, has been participating in a methadone treatment course which she commenced last year. She has lost 75 lbs and is now looking back to her best.

A portion of the profits from the album will be donated to the Dr Eugene Silberman Methadone Maintenance Treatment Programme in New York City, and the Centre City 'Kick' Programme, in Los Angeles.

1973

THE GRAPEVINE

■ Deep Purple have settled on a new lead singer to replace Ian Gillan – he's 22 year-old David Coverdale, a complete unkown.

■ A sequel to the film *That'll Be The Day* will go into production in the new year; the movie has the working title of *Stardust* and will feature David Essex and Ringo Starr, re-creating the roles they played in the original movie.

LENNON RECORDING

John Lennon is currently in New York's Record Plant recording a song called 'Imagination', which is said to be a traditionally tough yet pretty original composition.

Spooky Tooth are working in the studio next door and came into Studio B when John's work was completed. Actress Julie Christie also came in with record producer Bob Ezrin, the former being greeted by Lennon with a 'Hello, Julie Christie'.

Ezrin appeared to be cut up when Lennon didn't recognise him and snapped: 'How come he says hello to Julie Christie? He probably knows me as the guy who borrowed his car for the night. Anyway, I'll match my last year's sales against his any-day!'

As John left the studio, he glanced at Julie Christie in her floppy T-shirt and jeans and grinned. 'You've changed a bit since Leeds,' he said, before bounding into a waiting limo.

MACCA IN AFRICA

Paul McCartney and the remnants of Wings – now down to Denny Laine and Linda McCartney – are soldiering on, recording their new album in Lagos, Nigeria.

Both Denny Seiwell and Henry McCulloch have departed due to reasons of musical policy, but McCartney denies that McCulloch and he had a fight that left the ex-Beatle with a black eye and injured pride.

He adds that, at present, there is no thought of adding new members to Wings to compensate for the resignations. 'Anyway,' says Paul, 'When we're recording, I could play the lot myself!'

MORE ROCK DEATHS

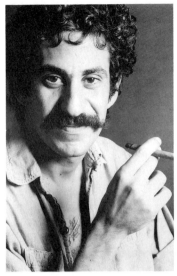

Gone, gone, gone, Jim Croce (left) and Gram Parsons (right)

Gram Parsons, ex-member of The Byrds and founder of The Flying Burrito Brothers, died in California on September 19. Parsons, 26, collapsed in a motel and was rushed to hospital in Uyya Valley, but was found to be dead on arrival. An initial post-mortem failed to reveal the cause of death and further tests are being made.

Jim Croce and his guitarist Maury Mulheisen were killed the very next day (20) when the small plane in which they were travelling from Louisiana to Texas crashed into a tree while attempting to take off.

The singer-songwriter had recently returned to America after his recent visit to Britain. Highly successful, he logged four Top 10 singles in the US charts before his death, including the recent No. 1 'Bad Bad Leroy Brown'.

The new Deep Purple line-up with David Coverdale (centre)

Macca – now in Lagos

CASSIDY MAKES QUICK GETAWAY

David Cassidy flew into London's Heathrow Airport on October 6 and gave a lightning press conference at the nearby Skyway Hotel.

Asked if he had any vices, Cassidy replied: 'Well I do bite my nails.'

He spoke about his latest album, which includes a version of 'Bali Hai' from *South Pacific*, 'I remember being very young and hearing my father humming that song in the next room' and the Peggy Lee classic 'Fever'.

Cassidy claimed: 'The album's like the story of my life. The songs are like vignettes in a way.' When questioned about drugs, Cassidy said: 'That's a past issue – I stated a long time ago that I took drugs when I was younger and I don't do them any more.'

He admitted that one friend had OD'd but concluded: 'I don't want to talk about that. He was a close friend, but it all happened years ago.'

STAR QUOTE

RAY DAVIES
of the Kinks

'I'm still only five years old. I know what food I like. I've got two pairs of shoes and, when they wear out, I replace them. I'm reasonably alright.'

CHARTS

US45	Half-Breed *Cher*
USLP	Brothers & Sisters *Allman Brothers*
UK45	Eye Level *Simon Park Orchestra*
UKLP	Goat's Head Soup *Rolling Stones*

WEEK 2

US45	Half-Breed *Cher*
USLP	Goat's Head Soup *Rolling Stones*
UK45	Eye Level *Simon Park Orchestra*
UKLP	Sladest *Slade*

WEEK 3

US45	Angie *Rolling Stones*
USLP	Goat's Head Soup *Rolling Stones*
UK45	Eye Level *Simon Park Orchestra*
UKLP	Sladest *Slade*

WEEK 4

US45	Midnight Train To Georgia *Gladys Knight & The Pips*
USLP	Goat's Head Soup *Rolling Stones*
UK45	Eye Level *Simon Park Orchestra*
UKLP	Hello *Status Quo*

ELVIS AND PRISCILLA CALL IT QUITS

Elvis and Priscilla Presley divorced in Santa Monica, California on 9 October. Elvis began proceedings in August on the grounds of irreconcilable differences after it was reported that Priscilla was living with karate instructor Mike Stone.

Elvis' lawyer stated: 'The reason for the divorce is that Elvis has been spending six months a year on the road, which put a tremendous strain on the marriage.'

THE GRAPEVINE

■ Rebop, Traffic's percussionist, has been jailed for a month for attacking two policemen; he was also fined £20($40) for biting a cab driver's ear.

■ Sopwith Camel, one of San Francisco's most notable bands in the Sixties, have reformed and already cut an album for Reprise.

■ Crosby, Stills, Nash & Young were re-united onstage during a recent Manassas concert at San Francisco's Winterland.

GOSPEL AND JAZZ LEGENDS DIE

Gospel singer and guitarist Sister Rosetta Tharpe died in Philadelphia on October 9 at the age of 57. She made her first record in 1938 and pioneered the development of gospel singing into worldwide popularity. Sister Rosetta had a leg amputated in 1970, but continued with her singing career and was planning a new album for Savoy Records at the time of her death.

The death of Gene Krupa has also been reported. The first of the showmen drummers, he was a victim of leukaemia, dying in New York, on October 16, at the age of 64.

BOWIE AND THE GNOME

The UK success of a rather elderly David Bowie recording called 'The Laughing Gnome' has provided a talking point. Recorded some six years ago for Deram, the single has remained in the catalogue ever since.

Amidst signing autograph books at Lou Reed's recent London Rainbow gig, Angie Bowie commented that she found the record 'gloriously nostalgic – rather like "White Christmas" ', while a flue-ridden Bowie staggered from his bed long enough to opine that he considered it to be 'a charming children's song'.

Bowie remembering Gnome life

LENNON'S 'MIND GAMES'

At one time I would have said that 'Mind Games' is a terrible album because it in no way reflects Lennon's capabilities. But, after four solo albums, each one lousier than the other, I'm no longer sure that Lennon is capable of anything other than leading a friendly corner-superstar existence, facing nothing more challenging than whether to watch *Sesame Street* on the living room or the bedroom TV set.

In conclusion, this album is not offensive, it is not inoffensive. It is simply nothing at all.

Coming shortly – The Return Of The Living Dead!

CHARTS

US45	Midnight Train To Georgia *Gladys Knight & The Pips*
USLP	Goat's Head Soup *Rolling Stones*
UK45	Day Dreamer/The Puppy Song *David Cassidy*
UKLP	Pin-Ups *David Bowie*

— WEEK 2 —

US45	Keep On Truckin' *Eddie Kendricks*
USLP	Goodbye Yellow Brick Road *Elton John*
UK45	Day Dreamer/The Puppy Song *David Cassidy*
UKLP	Pin-Ups *David Bowie*

— WEEK 3 —

US45	Keep On Truckin' *Eddie Kendricks*
USLP	Goodbye Yellow Brick Road *Elton John*
UK45	Let Me In *Osmonds*
UKLP	Pin-Ups *David Bowie*

— WEEK 4 —

US45	Photograph *Ringo Starr*
USLP	Goodbye Yellow Brick Road *Elton John*
UK45	I Love You Love Me Love *Gary Glitter*
UKLP	Pin-Ups *David Bowie*

BOWIE'S MILLIONS

David Bowie has now sold over one million RCA albums since he joined the label just under two years ago – the exact figure up to the beginning of November being 1,056,400. And, during the same period, he also sold over a million singles in Britain (1,024,068), plus a total of 120,000 eight track cartridges and cassettes.

To these must be added the sales of Bowie's 'Laughing Gnome' single, which are now in the region of 200,000.

General practice within the recording industry used for the purposes of gold record qualification calculates an album as being equal to six single units. On this basis Bowie has sold nearly eight and a half million units in Britain alone, in less than two years.

This easily makes him the biggest record seller in the country since the peak period of The Beatles. Meanwhile, British sales of 'Pin-Ups', Bowie's latest album, are fast approaching 200,000.

TRAGEDY HITS JERRY LEE AGAIN

Jerry Lee Lewis' son, Jerry Lee Lewis Jr (19), was killed in a car accident on November 13, while driving near Hernando, Mississippi. Just a few days before, he'd appeared as drummer with his father's band on the *Midnight Special* TV show.

The ill-fated Jerry Lee

Jerry Lee's brother died in an auto accident while the singer-pianist was still young, and in 1962, Steven Allen – Jerry Lee's other son – drowned in the family swimming pool.

Former Columbia University students Sha Na Na

FORMER SHAD ELECTROCUTED

Former Shadows bassist John Rostill was found dead in his Radlett, Hertfordshire studio on November 26. He had apparently been electrocuted while using his guitar to write new material.

A fine writer, he composed several songs for Olivia Newton-John, including 'Let Me Be There' and 'If You Love Me Let Me Know'.

Olivia Newton-John had hits with Rostill songs

THE GRAPEVINE

■ A split has caused a major upheaval in Sha Na Na, three members of the group quitting.

■ For his second album, Bruce Springsteen has reportedly moved his bed into the studio.

■ Two men have been charged with stealing the coffin containing the body of Gram Parsons; they claimed that they were merely carrying out Parsons' wish to be cremated in the desert.

DARIN DEAD AT 37

Bobby Darin, the singer who claimed he would be a legend at 25, died in Los Angeles' Cedars Of Lebanon hospital on December 20, at the age of 37. The end of a life-long battle against heart trouble came after a six-hour operation to replace two valves.

It was his second bout of open heart surgery within a short space of time. Said one friend: 'He was just too weak to recover.'

Perhaps best known for his early rock hits such as 'Splish Splash', 'Dream Lover' and his swinging version of 'Mack The Knife' (which sold two million copies), Darin later sold off all his possessions and moved to Big Sur on the Californian coast, where he lived in a trailer for a lengthy period.

In 1963 he collapsed from exhaustion and overwork and underwent major open-heart surgery in February 1971. In June, this year, he was married to Andrea Yeager, his companion for the past four years. However, the couple were divorced in November.

Darin's first wife was one-time teen-queen Sandra Dee, whom he divorced in 1966. He leaves a son, Dodd, now 12.

Tammy still stands by her man

SLADE CELEBRATE XMAS

Slade's 'Merry Xmas Everybody', which was released on December 7, has proved to be the band's fastest-selling single to date, registering a quarter of a million sales on the first day of release and providing Noddy Holder and Co with an instant UK No. 1.

The single was recorded at New York's Record Plant during Slade's US summer tour. Jim Lea claims that the tune to the song came to him while he was taking a shower in Memphis.

Slade luv Santa

'TOMMY' AT THE RAINBOW

Dress-rehearsal for those Rainbow chasers

Lou Reizner is to present another new version of The Who's *Tommy* at the London Rainbow on December 13 & 14. This time the cast features Roy Wood, Elkie Brooks, David Essex, Marsha Hunt, Jon Pertwee, Richie Havens, Graham Bell, Merry Clayton and Viv Stanshall.

The production will be broadcast in full on London's Capital Radio on December 26.

The Who completed their American tour in Washington on December 6, where they played a concert before an audience of 28,000. They suffered a mild setback at Montreal Forum on December 2, when the band and some friends were jailed overnight for wrecking hotel property.

CHARTS

US45	Top Of The World	*Carpenters*
USLP	Goodbye Yellow Brick Road	*Elton John*
UK45	I Love You Love Me Love	*Gary Glitter*
UKLP	Pin-Ups	*David Bowie*

WEEK 2

US45	Top Of The World	*Carpenters*
USLP	Goodbye Yellow Brick Road	*Elton John*
UK45	I Love You Love Me Love	*Gary Glitter*
UKLP	Pin-Ups	*David Bowie*

WEEK 3

US45	The Most Beautiful Girl	*Charlie Rich*
USLP	Goodbye Yellow Brick Road	*Elton John*
UK45	I Love You Love Me Love	*Gary Glitter*
UKLP	Pin-Ups	*David Bowie*

WEEK 4

US45	The Most Beautiful Girl	*Charlie Rich*
USLP	Goodbye Yellow Brick Road	*Elton John*
UK45	Merry Xmas Everybody	*Slade*
UKLP	Stranded	*Roxy Music*

WEEK 5

US45	Time In A Bottle	*Jim Croce*
USLP	Goodbye Yellow Brick Road	*Elton John*
UK45	Merry Xmas Everybody	*Slade*
UKLP	Goodbye Yellow Brick Road	*Elton John*

The original supergroup – Cream

Emerson, Lake and Palmer

SUPERGROUPS – AN IMPERFECT CONCEPT?

Maybe the first supergroup was Cream, the British trio of Eric Clapton, guitarist from The Yardbirds and John Mayall's Bluesbreakers, Jack Bruce on bass and vocals, also from one of the innumerable Bluesbreakers line-ups and before that The Graham Bond Organisation, where he had worked with drummer Ginger Baker.

In 1966, the trio of Clapton, Bruce and Baker decided to work together as Cream, and for just over two years, were hugely successful, until they announced their disbandment on the grounds that they had achieved what they set out to do, and wanted to explore fresh avenues.

A few months later, in early 1968, a new supergroup – to be known as Blind Faith – was announced, starring Clapton and Baker again, with the addition of singer/guitarist/keyboard player Steve Winwood, previously of Traffic and, before that, the star of The Spencer Davis Group, and bass and violin player Rick Grech from Leicester group Family.

Blind Faith's debut UK appearance was a mammoth free concert in London's Hyde Park attended by at least a quarter of a million people, preceding their debut album by a few weeks. It turned out to be their only UK gig. After a six week US tour around the release of the eponymous album came an ominous silence, broken less than a year after the group's formation by the announcement of its demise.

At the start of the 1970s, these sentiments were ignored as a plethora of supergroups emerged, particularly in the USA. Around the time Cream disbanded, Al Kooper, who had left Blood, Sweat & Tears – a group he founded from the ashes of The Blues Project – was offered the chance to become a record producer and to collaborate with other musicians with similar track records.

The first result of the latter was

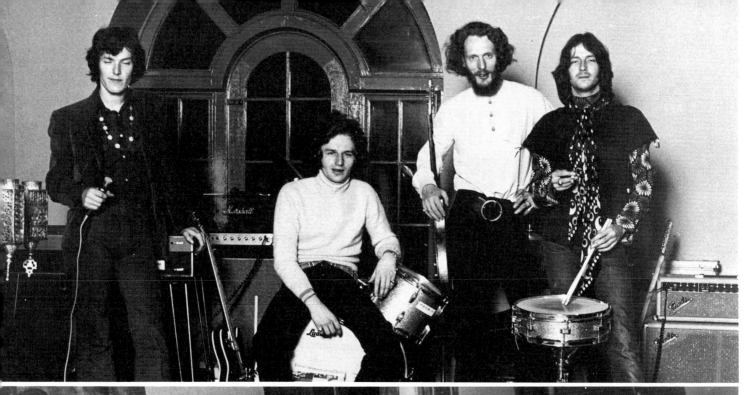

Cream spin-off – Blind Faith

Crosby, Stills, Nash and Young

'Supersession', an excellent album on which he worked with guitarists Mike Bloomfield (ex-Butterfield Blues Band and Electric Flag) and Stephen Stills (ex-Buffalo Springfield). The project led to a double album, 'The Live Adventures of Mike Bloomfield & Al Kooper', released in 1969.

However, Stephen Stills was already making plans to collaborate with David Crosby of The Byrds and – more surprisingly – with Graham Nash of British hitmakers The Hollies. In 1969, perhaps the most famous supergroup of them all, Crosby, Stills & Nash, was launched with a worthy debut album. Before long, the trio had expanded to a quartet with the addition of Stills's ex-Buffalo Springfield comrade, Neil Young.

What CSN had lacked was sufficient instrumental power to match their immense vocal talents, and Young's recruitment not only gave the quartet an additional distinctive vocalist and great songwriter, but also an equally distinctive co-lead guitarist to share instrumental solo duties with Stills.

However, certain elements of CSN&Y were not content only to be members of that group, and wanted other outlets for their talents, via solo projects and even perhaps collaborations with others. Predictably, Neil Young was the first to strike out on his own, followed by Stills, while Crosby & Nash remained as a duo as well as making solo albums. Twenty years later, CSN&Y are an on/off celebration,

still congregating (albeit infrequently) to record and tour.

Then there was (Keith) Emerson, (Greg) Lake & (Carl) Palmer, from respectively The Nice, King Crimson and Atomic Rooster. ELP went on to make probably more continuous hit albums than any other supergroup, before the inevitable desire to work outside the confines of the group made itself known. Amusingly enough, when a reunion took place in the 1980s, in which Palmer was not willing to be involved, his two ex-partners recruited drummer Cozy Powell to ensure that the name ELP was still accurate!

There have been innumerable attempts over the years to assemble latter day supergroups, most of them unsuccessful.

HIGH NOON FOR TEX

Tex Ritter, the singer who had a huge hit with 'High Noon', the theme from the Gary Cooper movie, died in Nashville on January 2.

An actor who originally made his name on radio, he appeared in more than 50 films, usually playing a singing cowboy. Last year he ran for the US senate but lost, incurring heavy debts.

But he'll always be remembered, not only for his music but also for his part in setting up the Country Music Foundation and Hall Of Fame, to which he was elected in 1964.

BOWIE HEADS FOR THE STATES

David Bowie leaves Britain in February to spend several months in New York preparing his stage revue, *The 1980 Floor Show*, the title provisionally chosen for his musical adaptation of George Orwell's *1984*, which he's hoping to premiere in London's West End later this year.

It's understood that the switch in title from 1984 to 1980 is intended to avoid any copyright problems which might arise.

Helping Bowie mount the show will be Rony Ingratsia, co-author with Andy Warhol of *Pork*, which played a season at London's Roundhouse in 1971. Meanwhile, Bowie is currently working at London's Olympic Studios on the album for the *1980 Floor Show* and tracks in production include 'Big Brother' and 'Are You Coming, Are You Coming?'

Bassist Trevor Bolder and keyboardist Mike Garson have been playing on the sessions, and recent visitors have included Pete Townshend, Mick Jagger, Ronnie Wood and Rod Stewart.

BAD COMPANY FOR FREE

All-star Company

The new-look Free has finally taken shape and, following a lengthy period of rehearsals, the band – to be known as Bad Company – are at present recording an album, to be issued by Atlantic.

The line-up comprises Paul Rodgers (vocals), Simon Kirke (drums), Boz Burrell (bass) and ex-Mott The Hoople guitarist Mick Ralphs.

Meanwhile, two former Free members, Paul Kossoff and Andy Fraser, have reportedly teamed-up with ex-Hendrix drummer Mitch Mitchell and have commenced rehearsals with a view to a spring tour.

ENERGY CRISIS HITS BRITISH ROCK

Victims of the power game – Steely Dan (above) and Chi Coltrane (left)

Because of the UK miners' strike and the ensuing energy crisis, which has resulted in nationwide power cuts, many American acts have withdrawn from British tours claiming that the situation is too risky.

These include The Allman Brothers, Steely Dan, Chi Coltrane and Joe Walsh. Some studios have suffered cancelled bookings as a result of the strike but at Abbey Road, engineers have continued working, thanks to the use of their own generators.

THE GRAPEVINE

■ Chicken Shack have disbanded after eight years; leader Stan Webb is joining Savoy Brown.

■ Dino Martin, son of Dean Martin, and once part of Dino, Desi & Billy, has been arrested after attempting to sell a machine-gun to an undercover government agent.

■ Bob Dylan, in the middle of his first US tour since 1965, has received a gold record for his 'Planet Waves' album.

DYLAN-BAND CONCERTS HAILED

Robbie Robertson and The Zim

Bob Dylan's tour with The Band ended in Los Angeles on February 14, when the singer played to a star-studded audience at the city's Forum. Jack Nicholson, Carole King, Neil Young and Ringo Starr were among those who stayed to cheer.

Dylan's recent concerts at New York's Madison Square Garden have been hailed by some as being among the greatest rock'n-'roll concerts of all-time, Dylan opening on acoustic guitar and rendering songs such as 'Most Likely You'll Go Your Way And I'll Go Mine', 'Lay Lady Lay', 'Just Like Tom Thumb's Blues', 'Rainy Day Women Nos 12 and 35', 'It Ain't Me Babe' and 'Ballad Of A Thin Man'.

He accompanied himself on piano for the last-named, returning after a Band set for an electric fling involving 'Like A Rolling Stone' and others.

He was forced back to encore on 'Maggie's Farm' and, finally, 'Blowin' In The Wind'.

The tour encompassed 39 shows in 21 cities.

Diarist Hunter

BIG MAC ROW

The strange case of the two Fleetwood Macs has turned into a major dispute between the original group and manager Clifford Davis, who recently launched a new band using the same name.

Davis contends that the group currently touring America as Fleetwood Mac is the only authentic Mac, even though none of its members has previously been connected with the group of that name. Their line-up is: Elmer Gantry (vocals), Paul Martinez (bass), David Wilkinson (piano), Craig Collinge (drums) and ex-Curved Air guitarist Kirby.

This outfit recently topped the bill at New York's Academy of Music and, on that particular evening, Gantry was ill with laryngitis, causing the remaining members to play a 43-minute instrumental set which was described by one critic as 'tedious, routine bluesy rock – all right for a street band but decidedly not for a headline act'.

CHARTS

US45	The Way We Were *Barbra Streisand*
USLP	You Don't Mess Around With Jim *Jim Croce*
UK45	Tiger Feet *Mud*
UKLP	The Singles, 1969-1973 *Carpenters*
	— WEEK 2 —
US45	Love's Theme *Love Unlimited Orchestra*
USLP	You Don't Mess Around With Jim *Jim Croce*
UK45	Tiger Feet *Mud*
UKLP	The Singles, 1969-1973 *Carpenters*
	— WEEK 3 —
US45	The Way We Were *Barbra Streisand*
USLP	Planet Waves *Bob Dylan*
UK45	Tiger Feet *Mud*
UKLP	The Singles, 1969-1973 *Carpenters*
	— WEEK 4 —
US45	The Way We Were *Barbra Streisand*
USLP	Planet Waves *Bob Dylan*
UK45	Devil Gate Drive *Suzi Quatro*
UKLP	The Singles, 1969-1973 *Carpenters*

BOWIE TOPS POLL

In the 1974 NME Reader's Poll, David Bowie has been voted Top Male singer in the World Section, while Diana Ross is the Best Female Singer spot.

Other winners include Yes (Top Group), Alice Cooper (Stage Band), 'Dark Side Of The Moon' by Pink Floyd (Album), 'Radar Love' by Golden Earring (Single), 'Yessongs' by Yes (Best Dressed Album), Golden Earring (Most Promising New Name), Stevie Wonder (Soul Act), Elton John and Bernie Taupin (Songwriters).

The explosive Keith Emerson

MARCH 1974

ELKIE GOES SOLO

Elkie Brooks is going solo and, as a result, Vinegar Joe have decided to disband, following their week-long tour of Yugoslavia later this month. Their last British date takes place at Cheltenham St Paul's College on March 9.

Elkie's manager, John Sherry, revealed that her decision to embark on a solo career was, to a large extent, sparked by her appearance in the London production of *Tommy* before Christmas, which aroused great interest. He added that she had since been approached about starring in a London West End musical, and for a leading part in a major TV play.

The male members of Vinegar Joe have not made any firm plans for the future, although it is understood that singer Robert Palmer is going to America to record solo.

SPECTOR – STILL ON DANGER LIST

Celebrated record-producer and composer Phil Spector is reportedly still in a serious condition in a Los Angeles hospital after suffering 'near-fatal' injuries in a car accident last month.

Spector was involved in a massive pile-up while driving out of town for a short vacation, and is understood to have sustained serious burns and severe head injuries, though exact details have still not been revealed. Even close friends in London and America have been unable to glean more information.

CSN&Y TO REFORM

Crosby, Stills, Nash & Young are to tour again. 'The first gig,' says Steve Stills, 'is on July 4, in Tampa, Florida, at a football stadium. We'll do about ten days on tour. I'm really looking forward to it.

'I know we can still sing well together, it's just down to deciding on arrangements and stuff.'

He revealed he's shelved an album called 'Stolen Stills' of which he says: 'It's all out-takes. It's songs that didn't make the two solo albums or the Manassas releases because we had too many songs of the same type. Some were roadies' favourites – things like that.'

CSN&Y – reunion at last. But rehearsals are needed to loosen the rust

THE GRAPEVINE

■ Stevie Wonder, who recently won five Grammy Awards, has announced plans to quit the music business in 1976 and work with handicapped children in Africa.

■ Sandy Denny is to rejoin Fairport Convention.

■ Jefferson Airplane are now touring under the name Jefferson Starship.

■ Nashville's Grand Ole Opry moved to a ritzy new home on March 16, after 33 years at the Ryman Auditorium.

CHRISSIE ON KISS BY KISS

The lyrics are pretty turgid but they've got good taste in rip-offs. 'Everybody says she's looking good – and the lady knows it's understood.' Yeah, John Winston was coming up with some real classics, huh? I dunno – I suppose even after eating a can of beans, every little fart is its own self-contained composition – but perhaps I'm being too kind.

Kiss is an essay in rock mannerisms, and stale ones at that – Chrissie Hynde.

Kiss – kissed off by Chrissie

YES-MEN SOLO ALBUMS

All five Yes members are likely to have solo albums on the market before the end of the year. Rick Wakeman already has two albums of his own on release but the other four – Jon Anderson, Chris Squire, Steve Howe and Alan White – will each be spending three months, this summer, working on individual projects.

A spokesman for the band revealed: 'Steve and Chris already have demo tracks on tape and plan to develop these further. Alan and Jon each have a lot of ideas which they want to put down on tape. And while these four are working, Rick, who has no future solo plans at present, will be busy producing the two bands he has taken under his wing – Warhorse and Wally.

'There is no question of a Yes split, neither is there any question of Rick taking his *Journey To The Centre Of Earth* show on tour. He would like to be able to do this, but it's only a pipedream, uneconomic and impractical.'

Yes – no split yet

Below: Shades of Eric

Bowie looking unscathed by the fall-out, radiates as usual

BOWIE'S 1980 PROJECT TOUR

David Bowie arrived in New York on Good Friday aboard the SS France and is now preparing for his major concert tour of the North Americas.

The tour opens at The Montreal Forum Concert Bowl on June 14 and runs for two months. The concert concept, described as a 'theatrical extravaganza', is based upon Bowie's RCA album 'Diamond Dogs', which will have a simultaneous release in Britain and America in May.

This forms the basis of what was to have been Bowie's '1980 Floor Show', freely based upon George Orwell's *1984* novel. But the intended London West End revue has now been translated into concert tour terms, replete with an adaptable and packable set provided by noted Broadway lighting man Jules Fisher, whose credits include *Pippin* and *Hair*.

Mike Garson (keyboards), Herbie Flowers (bass) and Tony Newman (drums) will be backing Bowie on the tour, while auditions are taking place for a guitarist.

The theme of the album and the show is the breakdown of society after the holocaust, when men are deformed from the effects of radiation.

CHARTS

US45	Hooked On A Feeling *Blue Swede*
USLP	Greatest Hits *John Denver*
UK45	Billy Don't Be A Hero *Paper Lace*
UKLP	The Singles, 1969-1973 *Carpenters*

WEEK 2

US45	Bennie & The Jets *Elton John*
USLP	Band On The Run *Paul McCartney & Wings*
UK45	Seasons In The Sun *Terry Jacks*
UKLP	The Singles, 1969-1973 *Carpenters*

WEEK 3

US45	TSOP (The Sound Of Philadelphia) *MFSB with The Three Degrees*
USLP	Band On The Run *Paul McCartney & Wings*
UK45	Seasons In The Sun *Terry Jacks*
UKLP	The Singles, 1969-1973 *Carpenters*

WEEK 4

US45	TSOP (The Sound of Philadelphia) *MFSB with The Three Degrees*
USLP	Chicago VII *Chicago*
UK45	The Cat Crept In *Mud*
UKLP	The Singles, 1969-1973 *Carpenters*

Below: Sha Na Na supply the latest rock casualty

ERIC'S BACK

Elton John and Pete Townshend were among those who attended a party held at The China Garden, in London's Berwick Street, to celebrate Eric Clapton's return to the fray.

Clapton has now flown to America to commence work on a new album. Carl Radle, who worked with Clapton in Derek & The Dominoes, will be playing with him on the sessions.

THE GRAPEVINE

■ Ex-Family members Roger Chapman and Charlie Whitney have completed their new album 'Streetwalkers'.

■ Vinnie Taylor, guitarist with Sha Na Na, has died of a drug overdose.

■ Also gone is Pam Morrison, Jim Morrison's widow; she was found dead in her Hollywood apartment on April 24.

■ The California Jam Festival on April 6, attracted 200,000 punters to hear ELP, Black Sabbath, Deep Purple and The Eagles.

1974

FAREWELL TO THE DUKE

Duke Ellington, one of the most influential jazz musicians of all time, died of cancer and pneumonia, in a New York hospital on May 24.

Composer of such classics as 'Mood Indigo', 'Sophisticated Lady', 'Satin Doll' and 'Solitude', he created a big band whose sound was never completely imitated.

In 1969, President Nixon honoured Ellington by inviting him to The White House for a party on the occasion of Duke's 70th birthday.

THE GRAPEVINE

■ Eno has been producing John Cale in London; both Cale and Eno – together with Nico – are to be the special guests of Kevin Ayers when he appears with his new band at the London Rainbow on June 1. The project was originally envisaged as a Velvet Underground reunion but Lou Reed was unable to take part.

■ Led Zeppelin have launched a new label – Swansong.

Cockney Rebel onstage

BOGERT SAYS BBA ARE FINISHED

Rumours concerning a split in Beck, Bogert & Appice, have been confirmed by bassist Tim Bogert.

Speaking in New York, he said that he expected to remain together with drummer Carmen Appice in a new band, but it was highly unlikely either of them would play with Jeff Beck again.

Bogert said that he hoped Robin Trower would join them, but Trower did not want to be tied down. No comment was available from Beck or his manager.

The band-less Beck

COCKNEY REBEL DEBUT TOUR

Cockney Rebel are to undertake their first-ever British tour – a six week schedule, starting on May 25 and running into July. Highlight of the itinerary is a Sunday gig at London's Victoria Palace on June 23.

Throughout the tour, Rebel will be promoting their second EMI album, 'The Psychomodo', set for release on June 2. It features nine Steve Harley compositions and is produced by Harley and Alan Parsons, engineer of Pink Floyd's 'Dark Side Of The Moon'.

Rebel will be supported by Bebop DeLuxe, the four-piece fronted by singer-guitarist Bill Nelson. Their debut album, 'Axe Victim', will be released in early July to coincide with tour dates.

GRAHAM BOND KILLED IN FALL

Graham Bond, a leading pioneer in the British R&B movement, died on May 8 when he fell in front of a train at London's Finsbury Park Station. He was identified from his fingerprints.

Bond first gained attention as a jazz saxist with the Don Rendell quintet, later fronting various Sixties bands as a gifted organist, his sidemen including Ginger Baker, Jack Bruce, John McLaughlin and Jon Hiseman. He formed his first band in 1963 and eventually progressed to the renowned Graham Bond Organization.

After its break-up, he concentrated on session work and writing before joining Ginger Baker's Airforce. Later still, he formed a new band with his wife Diana Stewart and Pete Brown and, when his marriage ended, formed yet another new group, called Magus, with singer Carolanne Pegg. Magus played a few gigs, then folded with financial problems.

Bond, who had quit drugs, was recently hospitalized but was planning a major comeback at the time of his death.

CHARTS

US45	The Loco-motion *Grand Funk Railroad*
USLP	The Sting *Soundtrack/Marvin Hamlisch*
UK45	Waterloo *Abba*
UKLP	The Singles, 1969-1973 *Carpenters*
WEEK 2	
US45	The Loco-motion *Grand Funk Railroad*
USLP	The Sting *Soundtrack/Marvin Hamlisch*
UK45	Waterloo *Abba*
UKLP	The Singles, 1969-1973 *Carpenters*
WEEK 3	
US45	The Streak *Ray Stevens*
USLP	The Sting *Soundtrack/Marvin Hamlisch*
UK45	Sugar Baby Love *Rubettes*
UKLP	The Singles, 1969-1973 *Carpenters*
WEEK 4	
US45	The Streak *Ray Stevens*
USLP	The Sting *Soundtrack/Marvin Hamlisch*
UK45	Sugar Baby Love *Rubettes*
UKLP	The Singles, 1969-1973 *Carpenters*

WAKEMAN QUITS YES

Rick Wakeman has quit Yes. Speculation has been rife for some time, and it reached a head in January, when Rick performed a solo concert at London's Royal Festival Hall, at which his current album, 'Journey To The Centre Of The Earth', was recorded.

But, until now, the question of Wakeman parting company from Yes has always been strenuously denied by the band. A few weeks ago, Wakeman criticized Yes' 'Topographic Oceans' double-album and the band's last

Rick Wakeman (centre) journeys to the centre of Crystal Palace next month

British tour, adding: 'Yes could last ten years or ten minutes. But if anybody did leave, the band would survive.'

Wakeman plays his first date since quitting Yes when he headlines the first of this year's Garden Parties at London's Crystal Palace on July 27, when he will once more present 'Journey To The Centre Of The Earth', supported by the 102-piece New World Symphony Orchestra.

REBEL RE-BOOK AFTER RIOT

Cockney Rebel are to play a return gig at Aylesbury's Friars on June 6, following the near-riot at the venue which greeted the opening night of their current UK tour, two weeks ago.

Over 2,500 people applied for 700 tickets, and a further 400

were turned away at the door.

Ticket demand has forced Rebel to switch to larger venues in Scarborough and Bristol – they now play Bristol Locarno on June 25 instead of Boobs, while a new Scarborough venue for their June 12 date is being finalized.

Cockney Rebel's Steve Harley

NME'S TOP ALBUMS

In the UK NME writers have compiled a list of the 99 best rock albums ever made, the Top 20 comprising (1) The Beatles, 'Sgt Pepper'; (2) Bob Dylan, 'Blonde On Blonde'; (3) Beach Boys, 'Pet Sounds'; (4) The Beatles, 'Revolver'; (5) Bob Dylan, 'Highway 61 Revisited'; (6) Jimi Hendrix, 'Electric Ladyland'; (7) Jimi Hendrix, 'Are You Experienced'; (8) The Beatles, 'Abbey Road'; (9) Rolling Stones, 'Sticky Fingers'; (10) The Band, 'Music From Big Pink'; (11) Rolling Stones, 'Let It Bleed'; (12) Derek & The Dominoes, 'Layla and Other Assorted Love Songs'; (13) Velvet Underground, 'The Velvet Underground and Nico'; (14) Chuck Berry, 'Golden Greats'; (15) The Beatles, 'Rubber Soul'; (16) The Who, 'Tommy'; (17) Simon & Garfunkel, 'Bridge Over Troubled Water'; (18) David Bowie, 'Hunky Dory'; (19) Rolling Stones, 'Beggars' Banquet'; (20) Cream, 'Disraeli Gears'.

STAR QUOTE

STEVE HARLEY

'Maybe in six months time, some perceptive journalist will say: "Didn't Steve Harley do this a year ago and didn't we say it was rubbish?"'

JUNE 1974

CHARTS

US45	The Streak / *Ray Stevens*
USLP	The Sting / *Soundtrack/Marvin Hamlisch*
UK45	Sugar Baby Love / *Rubettes*
UKLP	The Singles, 1969-1973 / *Carpenters*
WEEK 2	
US45	Band On The Run / *Paul McCartney & Wings*
USLP	The Sting / *Soundtrack/Marvin Hamlisch*
UK45	Sugar Baby Love / *Rubettes*
UKLP	The Singles, 1969-1973 / *Carpenters*
WEEK 3	
US45	Billy Don't Be A Hero / *Bo Donaldson & The Heywoods*
USLP	The Sting / *Soundtrack/Marvin Hamlisch*
UK45	The Streak / *Ray Stevens*
UKLP	Diamond Dogs / *David Bowie*
WEEK 4	
US45	Billy Don't Be A Hero / *Bo Donaldson & The Heywoods*
USLP	Sundown / *Gordon Lightfoot*
UK45	The Streak / *Ray Stevens*
UKLP	Diamond Dogs / *David Bowie*
WEEK 5	
US45	Sundown / *Gordon Lightfoot*
USLP	Sundown / *Gordon Lightfoot*
UK45	Always Yours / *Gary Glitter*
UKLP	Diamond Dogs / *David Bowie*

Geoff Britton and friend.

WINGS ADD DRUMMER

After several months without a drummer, Paul McCartney's Wings have announced the addition of Geoff Britton, who re-

places Denny Seiwell.

Wings' next single 'Band On The Run'/'Zoo Gang' gains a UK release on June 28.

JULY 1974

MAMA CASS ELLIOT DEAD

Cass Elliot, Mama Cass of The Mamas And The Papas, died in the early morning of July 29 in the London flat of Harry Nilsson, where she was living with her friend and road manager George Caldwell during her stay in the UK.

At a coroner's hearing, held the next day, it was established that she had died as a result of choking on a sandwich while in bed, and from inhaling her own vomit. Cass, who went solo in late 1968 but rejoined The Mamas And The Papas for an ill-fated reunion in 1971, had her biggest solo hit with 'Dream A Little Dream Of Me' in 1968.

She linked with Dave Mason for an album and tour during 1970, but in recent times had enjoyed considerable success on the nightclub circuit.

BLUESMAN DIES

Lightnin' Slim, who's been described as 'the king of the blues in Louisiana, a man who influenced everybody', died in Detroit of stomach cancer on July 27.

Born Otis Hicks in St Louis in 1913, he last toured Britain with the American Blues Legends package in 1973 and recorded for Big Bear during his stay.

ALAN PRICE BECOMES ALFIE AND DALTREY GETS LISZT

Price as Alfie

Daltrey as Liszt

Alan Price has landed the title role in a new major film, *Alfie Darling*, which goes before the cameras next month. It's planned as the sequel to the original *Alfie*, which starred Michael Caine.

Nat Cohen of EMI said that the film will have a budget of over half a million and will be shot at Elstree Studios and on location in France, the director being Ken Hughes, who also did the screenplay.

A spokesman said: 'We are not sure if it will have any musical content, but whatever music there is, Alan will write it.'

Roger Daltry of The Who has also been offered a title role in a movie, namely Ken Russell's upcoming film biography of composer Franz Liszt, which goes into production in the new year.

Russell, who has already filmed biographies of classical composers Tchaikovsky and Mahler, had originally planned to approach Mick Jagger to play Liszt. But he was so impressed with Daltrey's work in the movie version of *Tommy*, which he is currently directing, that he decided to offer the part to The Who singer.

STAR QUOTE

BRYAN FERRY

'Bowie's a nice guy but maybe a little misguided in some ways.'

CHARTS

US45	Rock The Boat *Hues Corporation*
USLP	Sundown *Gordon Lightfoot*
UK45	She *Charles Aznavour*
UKLP	Diamond Dogs *David Bowie*

— WEEK 2 —

US45	Rock Your Baby *George McCrae*
USLP	Caribou *Elton John*
UK45	She *Charles Aznavour*
UKLP	Band On The Run *Paul McCartney & Wings*

— WEEK 3 —

US45	Rock Your Baby *George McCrae*
USLP	Caribou *Elton John*
UK45	She *Charles Aznavour*
UKLP	Band On The Run *Paul McCartney & Wings*

— WEEK 4 —

US45	Annie's Song *John Denver*
USLP	Caribou *Elton John*
UK45	Rock Your Baby *George McCrae*
UKLP	Band On The Run *Paul McCartney & Wings*

THE GRAPEVINE

■ Tir Na Nog are to play their final gig in Dublin on July 27.

■ Vangelis Papathanassiou is said to be the hottest contender as Rick Wakeman's replacement with Yes.

■ Silverhead have broken up and singer Michael Des Barres is going ahead with a solo career, cutting an album for Purple Records with producer Gus Dudgeon.

SLADE IN FLAME FLICK

Slade's planned film *Flame* is a comedy drama in which the band play struggling rock musicians battling against the seedy elements of the pop business.

Shooting starts on July 29, with four weeks on location in London, two in the English Midlands and one in Spain. The movie will be directed by Richard Loncraine.

WYATT RETURNS

(l to r) Mike Oldfield, Nick Mason, Julie Tippett (Driscoll) – helping Wyatt

Robert Wyatt, the one-time Soft Machine drummer, makes his first major stage appearance since the accident which paralysed the lower half of his body when he leads a band at London's Theatre Royal on Sunday, September 8. Among the guest stars booked for the event are Mike Oldfield (whose new album 'Hergest Ridge' is released at the end of this month), trumpeter Mongezi Feza, sax-player Gary Windo, Pink Floyd's Nick Mason, ex-Egg keyboardist Dave Stewart, drummer Laurie Allen, and Fred Frith, who played viola on Wyatt's highly acclaimed 'Rock Bottom' solo album.

Julie Tippett, formerly Julie Driscoll, will appear in a solo spot. A Wyatt single gets released on September 1. Titled 'I'm A Believer', it's a reworking of the old Monkees hit.

CHARTS

US45	Annie's Song	John Denver
USLP	Caribou	Elton John
UK45	Rock Your Baby	George McCrae
UKLP	Band On The Run	Paul McCartney & Wings

— WEEK 2 —

US45	Feel Like Makin' Love	Roberta Flack
USLP	Back Home Again	John Denver
UK45	Rock Your Baby	George McCrae
UKLP	Band On The Run	Paul McCartney & Wings

— WEEK 3 —

US45	The Night Chicago Died	Paper Lace
USLP	461 Ocean Boulevard	Eric Clapton
UK45	When Will I See You Again	Three Degrees
UKLP	Band On The Run	Paul McCartney & Wings

— WEEK 4 —

US45	(You're) Having My Baby	Paul Anka
USLP	461 Ocean Boulevard	Eric Clapton
UK45	When Will I See You Again	Three Degrees
UKLP	Band On The Run	Paul McCartney & Wings

— WEEK 5 —

US45	(You're) Having My Baby	Paul Anka
USLP	461 Ocean Boulevard	Eric Clapton
UK45	When Will I See You Again	Three Degrees
UKLP	Band On The Run	Paul McCartney & Wings

THE GRAPEVINE

■ ELP's usual dynamic stage show became even more De Mille-like when a tornado hit their gig at New Jersey's Roosevelt Stadium. The equipment is still drying out.

■ Patrick Moraz has been named as Rick Wakeman's replacement with Yes.

■ Peter Wolf got spliced to Faye Dunaway on August 5.

■ John and Michelle Phillips, Sonny Bono and Lou Adler were among those who attended Mama Cass' funeral on August 2.

DYLAN RE-SIGNS

Bob Dylan has re-signed with CBS Records. The agreement was announced on August 2 at the label's annual convention, in Los Angeles, and is a five-year deal.

Although no figures were given, the contract is reportedly worth a minimum eight million dollars to Dylan. Since his previous deal with CBS expired, he has had two albums released on Island (in Britain) and Asylum (in the States), namely 'Planet Waves' and 'Before The Flood'.

The Zim is now due to start recording a new set for CBS before the month is out.

Moraz: replacing Rick

MAC ARE BACK

Fleetwood Mac have been granted a High Court injunction preventing anyone other than the original group – Mick Fleetwood, John McVie, Bob Welch and Christine McVie – from operating under the name The Fleetwood Mac.

The band now intend to sue their old manager Clifford Davis for damages arising from his formation of a bogus group. The Mac are at present in Los Angeles, where they have just completed an album for Warner Bros and are currently rehearsing in preparation for an American tour which is due to start on October 1 – 'to repair the damage done by the other band'.

BILL CHASE DIES IN CRASH

Trumpeter Bill Chase, 39, plus three other members of his group, Chase, died in a plane crash in Jackson, Minnesota on August 9.

Chase, who worked for the Maynard Ferguson, Stan Kenton and Woody Herman big bands before forming his own jazz-rock outfit, had a US Top 30 hit during 1971 with 'Get It On'. The other Chase members who died in the crash were Wally Yohn (keyboards), John Emma (guitar) and Walter Clark (drums).

The band were touring in support of their current Epic album 'Pure Music' at the time of the disaster.

1974

On his Todd

HEEP'S THAIN BADLY HURT

Uriah Heep's current American tour has been disrupted by an injury to bassist Gary Thain, who was rushed to hospital in Dallas after collapsing onstage during the band's September 15 gig at the Moodie Coliseum. He appeared to have suffered a severe shock and burns.

Said one onlooker: 'Gary leapt about three feet in the air and then collapsed unconscious on the floor.' The remainder of the tour is now in doubt.

RONSON LINKS WITH MOTT

It has been confirmed that guitarist Mick Ronson is joining Mott The Hoople, replacing Ariel Bender and making his live debut with the band in a European tour that runs from October 10 to November 2. His first UK appearance with Mott will be at London's Hammersmith Odeon on December 6.

Ronson has already recorded with Mott and is on the single 'Saturday Gigs' which CBS are to release in mid-October. Also scheduled for release at the same time is Mott's live album, recorded half at Broadway's Uris Theatre and half at the Hammersmith Odeon, although, of course, Ronson does not figure on this set.

The former Spiders From Mars leader will be performing some of his own material during Mott's stage act. He will also be involved in production and arrangements for the live show.

At the same time, he is also working on a new solo album and single, which RCA hope to issue during November. This indicates that Ronson will continue with his solo career whenever it does not interfere with Mott's commitments.

THE GRAPEVINE

■ All 18 members of Hawkwind's entourage, including the band themselves, were arrested in Indiana for alleged non-payment of US taxes.

■ Robert Fripp has disbanded King Crimson – but their new album 'Red' gets an October release.

■ The New York Dolls have also reportedly split after a brief two-album career.

■ Ringo Starr has announced that he's shortly to launch his own record label, Ring O Records.

Hawkwind blows no good for US taxman

CHARTS

US45	(You're) Having My Baby	*Paul Anka*
USLP	461 Ocean Boulevard	*Eric Clapton*
UK45	Love Me For A Reason	*Osmonds*
UKLP	Band On The Run	*Paul McCartney & Wings*

WEEK 2

US45	I Shot The Sheriff	*Eric Clapton*
USLP	Fulfillingness' First Finale	*Stevie Wonder*
UK45	Love Me For A Reason	*Osmonds*
UKLP	Band On The Run	*Paul McCartney & Wings*

WEEK 3

US45	Can't Get Enough Of Your Love Baby	*Barry White*
USLP	Fulfillingness' First Finale	*Stevie Wonder*
UK45	Kung Fu Fighting	*Carl Douglas*
UKLP	Hergest Ridge	*Mike Oldfield*

WEEK 4

US45	Rock Me Gently	*Andy Kim*
USLP	Bad Company	*Bad Company*
UK45	Kung Fu Fighting	*Carl Douglas*
UKLP	Hergest Ridge	*Mike Oldfield*

OLDFIELD SCORES VADIM FILM

Mike Oldfield, whose 'Tubular Bells' was used as the main theme for *The Exorcist*, has been commissioned to write the music for a new film by celebrated French director Roger Vadim. Literally translated, the title of the film is *The Murdered Young Woman*, and shooting is now nearing completion. Oldfield will pen the entire score and has already commenced work on it.

The multi-instrumentalist is now confirmed to play a London Royal Albert Hall gig on December 9. His 'Tubular Bells' and 'Hergest Ridge' works will be featured, both being performed in orchestrated form by the Royal Philharmonic Orchestra, conducted by David Bedford, while Oldfield himself will be featured on guitar.

During the new year he will make his debut UK tour with a band which, he claims, 'Will not consist merely of established superstars but of sympathetic and, quite possibly, unknown musicians whom I think will fit in with my ideas.'

ELVIS ON THE DEFENSIVE

Elvis Presley is the subject of rumours that he is either sick, messed up on drugs, dying or gay. He is currently the undisputed hot number as far as the US show biz scandal sheets are concerned and each week at least two dozen of them are offering hot poop on Elvis' alleged illegitimate kids or terminal cancer.

Not that he's been taking this lying down – during his last season at the Las Vegas Hilton, Presley's act became a marathon of denials and denunciations with songs fitted in between.

He launched into long diatribes against bellhops and head waiters who carried lies to the gutter press and showed the audience the badge and certificate the Federal Bureau of Narcotics gave him when they made Elvis an honorary nark in an attempt to prove that he'd never used drugs.

Priscilla Presley has even been pressed into service to produce a series of syndicated newspaper confessions to prove that Elvis' sexual tastes ran along conventional lines.

NICK DRAKE FOUND DEAD

Nick Drake, the U.K. singer-songwriter was found dead in bed at his parent's home in Tamworth, near Stratford-on-Avon, on October 25. A very private man who was hardly known even to the people at his record label, he spent a great deal of time in various mental hospitals after the release of 'Pink Moon' in 1972.

At the time of his death, resulting from an overdose of antidepressants, Drake, 26, was recording tracks for a new album with producer Joe Boyd.

'HAMMY' McCARTNEY

Though 'Junior's Farm' is Wings' 'official' UK single release this month, 'Walking In The Park With Eloise', an EMI release which purports to be by The Country Hams, is also by Wings.

Recorded in Nashville with help from country stars Chet Atkins and Floyd Cramer, the A-side features a song penned over 20 years ago by Paul's father.

INCREDIBLES – IT'S THE END

The Incredible String Band have broken up. They were lining up for a string of concerts in Britain and Ireland but, in the wake of various rumours, the band have announced: 'We realize that we have learned a lot and achieved much in our years as The Incredibles. That stage is over and now is the time for all of us to start a new phase.

'There were no hassles, no big emotional scenes, no financial or legal complications. So, with just a little nostalgia and a great deal of affection for each other and our public, we are all getting our new directions together.'

Incredible announcement

Lulu: Bond ballad

BEATLEMANIA YET AGAIN

Beatlemania ruled in New York once more when the show *Sgt Pepper's Lonely Hearts Club Band On The Road* opened at the city's Beacon Theatre. John Lennon was mobbed as he and girlfriend May Pang tried to make their way past the hordes being held back by the police, May Pang getting knocked to the ground.

Also there were Bianca Jagger with Andy Warhol, Ruby Keeler in a fabulous sable coat, Wayne County, Divine, Yoko Ono all in white satin and furs, Robert Stigwood, Elton John's manager John Reid and Atlantic Records' Ahmet Ertegun.

Playing the lead role of Billy Shears in the show is Ted Neely, while the role of his romantic counterpart, Strawberry Fields, is performed by Kay Cole. However, the show is stolen by Alaina Reed, whose costumes and stage presence were highly reminiscent of LaBelle's Nona Hendryx.

Lennon and May Pang were practically the last to leave, going on to a party which Alice Cooper attended with Cindy Lang. The Ronettes also showed up, Wayne County and Divine were photographed together and John Phillips and Genevieve Waite danced together.

But Wayne County proved a party pooper. When asked by Warhol to meet Bianca Jagger, he declined, saying 'My Mama told me not to have anything to do with those kind of people.'

Wright off

THE GRAPEVINE

■ Keef Hartley, who has been largely inactive since his last band broke up in early 1972, has formed a new outfit called Dog Soldier.

■ Gary Wright has quit Spooky Tooth.

■ Ivory Joe Hunter, the bluesman, died in Memphis on November 8, aged 63. Hunter, who wrote some 7,000 songs had hits with 'I Almost Lost My Mind' and 'Since I Met You Baby'.

Mud (above) and Peter 'Herman' Noone (right) among balding bubblegummers pleading they're 'Never Too Young To Rock'

MUD, GLITTERMEN IN ROCK MOVIE

Mud, The Glitter Band and The Rubettes are among the UK chart groups who have major roles in a new film titled *Never Too Young To Rock*, which has just gone into production.

Described as a high speed comedy with music, the cast also includes Peter Noone, Sally James (presenter of London Weekend Television's *Saturday Scene*) and Scott Fitzgerald. Producer is Denis Abey.

MOTT SCRAP TOUR

Mott The Hoople have now scrapped their entire British tour which was originally scheduled to open on November 10 and continue until December 12. The reason for calling off the jaunt is that Ian Hunter – whose collapse from physical exhaustion, while on a brief private trip to America to visit his US manager Fred Heller, caused the initial four dates to be cancelled – has not recovered and has been ordered to rest for two months.

Accordingly, he is staying in America to recuperate and is not expected to return to Britain until Christmas. In the interim, speculation has been growing on both sides of the Atlantic that Hunter's illness may lead to Mott breaking up.

One proffered reason for Hunter being in the States at the time of his collapse was that he was looking for a house in the USA because he has an American wife and is likely to be spending more time there.

MICK TAYLOR IN NEW BAND

Mick Taylor has left The Rolling Stones to join a new outfit being formed by Jack Bruce. News of Taylor's departure broke when it became apparent that he was not working with The Stones in a Munich studio.

Reports from Germany at first suggested he had been sacked, but Jagger quickly squashed these rumours in a statement saying: 'After five and a half years, Mick wishes a change of scene. While we're all sorry that he is going, we wish him great success and much happiness.'

Also in the new Bruce band are Carla Bley, keyboardist on the 'Escalator Over The Hill' album, and pianist Max Middleton, who was recently part of the Jeff Beck group. A drummer still has to be signed.

Taylor-made move

THE GRAPEVINE

■ Ravi Shankar was hospitalized in Chicago on December 2 after complaining about chest pains.

■ David Crosby and Graham Nash performed together in San Francisco at a benefit concert for the United Farm Workers and a whale protection project.

■ George Harrison was presented to President Ford at a recent White House shindig after the President's son attended a Harrison gig in Salt Lake City.'

LED ZEP GIGS

Led Zeppelin will definitely be playing spring gigs in the UK, claims Jimmy Page. These will follow the band's extensive US tour which opens on January 18 and continues into March.

Zeppelin have been out of the public eye for the greater part of the year and have been spending the past few months on their new film and album. It was because of these commitments that they were forced to withdraw from the UK Knebworth open-air concert during the summer.

The album, called 'Physical Graffitti', will be Atlantic's first release in January. Reporter Nick Kent, given a preview claims: 'It's 82 minutes and 30 seconds of inimitable heavy metal grandiosity for mass consumption. Whatever you do, set the volume switch to "loud" (on second thoughts make that "VERY loud") because Led Zeppelin are still, absolutely, the best mainstream metal band around.'

The film is a semi-documentary that includes in-concert sequences, shot on the band's last American tour – notably at New York's Madison Square Garden, plus several fantasy sequences filmed at various locations.

Ravi Shankar

HUNTER GOES SOLO

Ian Hunter, back in Britain earlier than expected, has quit Mott The Hoople and is now making a solo album with the aid of Mick Ronson. It's said that he's accepted a lucrative, six-figure deal (rumours suggest $750,000) with CBS that will 'set him up for life.'

It seems that Hunter's plans have come as a shock to the other members of Mott, who claim that they didn't know what was happening, though it seems a rift developed between Hunter and drummer Buffin over the recently released live album, while other sources suggest that some members of the band became unhappy about Ronson's Mott involvement.

Was 1974 just a Page missing from history?

CHARTS

US45	Kung Fu Fighting *Carl Douglas*
USLP	Greatest Hits *Elton John*
UK45	Gonna Make You A Star *David Essex*
UKLP	Elton John's Greatest Hits *Elton John*

─── WEEK 2 ───

US45	Kung Fu Fighting *Carl Douglas*
USLP	Greatest Hits *Elton John*
UK45	You're The First, The Last, My Everything *Barry White*
UKLP	Elton John's Greatest Hits *Elton John*

─── WEEK 3 ───

US45	Cat's In The Cradle *Harry Chapin*
USLP	Greatest Hits *Elton John*
UK45	Lonely This Christmas *Mud*
UKLP	Elton John's Greatest Hits *Elton John*

─── WEEK 4 ───

US45	Angie Baby *Helen Reddy*
USLP	Greatest Hits *Elton John*
UK45	Lonely This Christmas *Mud*
UKLP	Elton John's Greatest Hits *Elton John*

Hunter foxes Mott

E Street Band focal point Clarence Clemons blows, leader Bruce Springsteen testifies

SPRINGSTEEN – BORN TO RUN ... AND RUN

Although it took him virtually the entire decade to prove it, the ultimate rock star to emerge during the 1970s was Bruce Springsteen. From his initial arrival as the latest in a long line of "new Bob Dylans" (a critical epithet which many fail to artistically survive), Springsteen overcame the successive pressures of media hype, falling out with his manager, and becoming the most bootlegged artist of the decade, to become the biggest rock star of the 1980s.

Born on September 23rd, 1949, in Freehold, a small town with a population of around 10,000 situated twenty miles inland from the low-rent seaside resort of Asbury Park, the New Jersey equivalent of Southend (to a father and mother of respectively Irish and Italian ancestry, even though his surname is apparently of Dutch origin), Springsteen's youth was spent as the kid of a blue collar family. His earliest idol was Elvis Presley, and he grew up with a healthy respect for British groups like The Rolling Stones and The Animals, who invaded the US in the mid-1960s, as well as for the early American rock'n'rollers by whom they in turn had been inspired.

He was very conscious of the roots of rock music, and although it took several years before a substantial audience began to

understand where he was coming from, Springsteen remained a traditionalist at heart. His first notable group, The Castiles, passed an audition at a New York club with a respectful version of The Who's 'My Generation', and before long, via other bands like Earth and Child (later renamed Steel Mill), he began to assemble what would eventually become The E Street Band. After a 1971 group he joined, Dr. Zoom & His Sonic Boom fell apart after three gigs, Springsteen formed The Bruce Springsteen Band, a ten piece combo with a horn section and girl singers, but soon abbreviated it to the musicians who became the original E Street Band: keyboard players like David Sancious and Danny Federici, Gary Tallent on bass and Vini Lopez (drums), Steve Van Zandt (guitar) and himself as lead vocalist, guitarist and songwriter, with saxophonist Clarence Clemons who later became an important visual as well as musical member of the group.

In early 1972, Springsteen signed a management deal with aspiring record producer Mike Appel, who arranged an audition with CBS Records A&R man John Hammond, among whose previous discoveries in a long career had been blues legend Bessie Smith and Bob Dylan. Hammond could recognise Springsteen's potential, and despite Appel's abrasive approach, CBS signed

The respectable face of rock in the 1970s (and 1980s), The Boss

Springsteen – they had apparently thought he was a solo folk singer, so were surprised to discover that their new artist came with a backing band!

His first album, 'Greetings From Asbury Park, N.J.', was not an instant success, and only made the US chart over two years after it was first released in early 1973. It included two original Springsteen songs which were later successfully covered by Manfred Mann's Earth Band, who topped the US singles chart in 1976 with their million selling version of 'Blinded By The Light', while their version of 'Spirit In The Night' also made the US Top 40.

At the end of 1973 came Springsteen's second album, 'The Wild, The Innocent & The E Street Shuffle', a similar recipe with as little immediate success, although once again it featured a song which became a US hit after it was covered by a British group: '4th Of July, Asbury Park (Sandy)', a 1975 chart item by the Hollies. The album also included the early classic of Springsteen's live sets, 'Rosalita (Come Out Tonight)', but the ecstatic critical praise was not being translated into sales.

In 1974, rock critic Jon Landau enjoyed a Springsteen show, dubbing him "the future of rock'n'roll" in print. Springsteen invited Landau to help with production of his next album, 'Born To Run', which gave him the necessary breakthrough – the

anticipation for the new album (and liberal use of Landau's quote, which began to embarass Springsteen) finally took the first two albums into the US chart, and they were followed only weeks later by 'Born To Run', his first US Top 3 album whose title track also became a US Top 3 single. Springsteen was a star – but he began to feel that his management deal with Appel was inequitable.

Protracted legal negotiations prevented Springsteen from releasing a new album until nearly three years after 'Born To Run', but meanwhile his long and very exciting live shows had become a major target for bootleggers – dozens of high quality unauthorised live albums were released during this period. When his fourth album, 'Darkness At The Edge of Town', was finally released in 1978, it reached the Top 10 of the US album chart, but seemed to disappoint as many as had felt cheated by his first UK show – as a British radio personality remarked on the latter occasion, "They promised us Jesus Christ, but sent us Billy Graham'.

It was the 1980s before Bruce Springsteen's fifth album, 'The River', was released. A two record set, it became his first to top the US chart, and many still regard it as his most satisfying album to date. Although the 1970s were hardly Bruce Springsteen's happiest years as a musician, the decade laid the groundwork for his commercial domination of the 1980s.

ZEP ZAP WINDY CITY

They rioted just to get tickets for Led Zeppelin's latest US onslaught. In New York 60,000 tickets at Madison Square Gardens were snapped up in four hours after the crowd forced the box office to open a day early. In Boston they trashed the foyer and the mayor was so angry he cancelled the show.

It's nearly two years since 'Houses Of The Holy', and the new album, the double 'Physical Graffiti', isn't out in time for the start of their tour. But Led Zeppelin are the band everyone wants to see this time around.

'It's not only that we think we're the best group in the world – it's just that in our minds we're so much better than whoever is No. 2', boasts Robert Plant as he prepares for the first of three shows in Chicago. Not even the wrecked throat that traditionally haunts him at the start of the tour can dampen his spirits. But it's not just Robert's voice; Jimmy Page has a broken finger, sustained during rehearsals, when he trapped it in a door.

'It's the most important finger for a guitarist,' he says. 'It's the one that does all the leverage and most of the work. I'm still not really playing with it but I'm starting to master a three-fingered technique!' Their collective ailments get the better of them on the first night. They are depressed all next day. But on the second night the band turn in a blinder. After the third night everyone goes out partying. And out at Chicago's O'Hare Airport the super Starship, painted red white and blue with white stars and LED ZEPPELIN written along the side, waits patiently . . .

AVERAGE WHITE BAND PICK UP THE PIECES

The Average White Band are playing a benefit show for the widow of drummer Robbie MacIntosh at London's Marquee Club. Robbie's death was caused by snorting heroin laced with poison. According to bassist Alan Gorrie: 'Somebody gave him a nasty. It's as simple and stupid as that. It's easy to say "Stupid sod for taking it" when you read about it a thousand miles away. You always do that when it's someone you don't know. But when you're in the middle of it you see it as an accident . . . Oh well.'

THE GRAPEVINE

■ John Lennon has won access to the Department Of Immigration file on his pending deportation case.

■ Bob Dylan has released 'Blood On The Tracks', his first album back on CBS after his brief encounter with Asylum.

■ 17-year-old Elvis fan Areecia (Honeybee) Benson and her 19-year-old friend wrapped themselves up in brown paper and a packing case and had themselves delivered to Gracelands.

STAR QUOTE

IAN ANDERSON

JETHRO TULL

'I don't think it's very easy to make friends with musicians. We're all a bit paranoid. It soon becomes very heavy.'

The Average White Band

JUST A KISS AWAY

Klassic Kiss, all made up and breathing glam-rock fire into heavy metal. From left to right Ace Frehley guitar, Peter Criss drums, Paul Stanley guitar, Gene Simmons bass

The latest glam-rock band to totter out of New York on their stack heels are Kiss, four boys who conceal their identities behind a tray full of war-paint and flame-throwing antics.

The music is heavy metal, the lyrics are juvenile escapism shot through with blatant sexual fantasy. But there are two obvious deviations from the norm: they can actually play and they are deliberately steering away from the traditional glam'n'glitter clichés.

'That thing is dead and the participants are finished too,' growls bassist Gene Simmons. 'But we're getting a bigger response all the time. I don't want to sound malicious, but with people like The New York Dolls . . . well, you can't go on fooling audiences all the time. We can play. Before this came together we were practising for months in a loft to get it right.'

Simmons is getting better at flame-throwing too. The first time he tried it the fire rebounded from his dagger and set his hair alight. 'It wasn't until my roadie smothered me with his jacket that I knew what was happening. The crowd loved it though. They thought it was all part of the act.'

Their 110 dB sound on stage has the audiences bouncing off the walls, but Simmons insists it's a healthy attitude. 'It's not a negative vibe, like smashing seats. They get rid of their frustration with the music. Personally I'd be insulted if people didn't react immediately. Groups have tried that laid-back experimental trip too long.'

FEATS DON'T FAIL IN UK

Little Feat arrive in Britain for their first visit, headlining over The Doobie Brothers in Manchester and supporting them in London – where the audience makes it clear they should be headlining as well.

'The thing is,' says a Warner Brothers UK person, 'the American side didn't know the extent of Little Feat's following here, although we've tried to tell them often enough. . . . As it happens we've been trying to get them over here for the last two years. It's no surprise to us . . .'

Lowell George, the enigmatic force behind Little Feat's soul strut

BOWIE THE 'CRACKED ACTOR'

'Cracked Actor', a documentary on David Bowie by Alan Yentob screened by BBC Television, does the Thin White Duke no favours. 'Bowie is seen alternating neurotic, speedy exhilaration, irritation and moments of deadpan depression, spouting platitudes and attempts at self-revelation that indicate nothing so much as that he doesn't really have a self to reveal'. But he does have a new single to reveal – 'Young Americans'.

STAR QUOTE

TODD RUNDGREN

'A red polygon is only a red polygon if it knows it's a red polygon . . . I guess'

JOHN LENNON – LONG TIME IN NEW YORK CITY

John Lennon still faces deportation from America after three years of legal battles. Officially, a British drug conviction (for marijuana) disbars him from US residency. Unofficially, his political activities have made him a pain in President Richard Nixon's ass.

'It was getting to be a bug (pun intended) because I had to keep going to court and court cases got to be a way of life,' admits Lennon. 'I guess it showed in me work. Whatever happens to you happens in your work. So while on the surface I tried to make it appear as if I was making a game of it, trying not to take it seriously, there were periods of real paranoia.'

Lennon is also facing lawsuits from former manager Allen Klein, the other three Beatles and a photographer who claims he was hit in the Los Angeles Troubadour during Lennon's infamous 'lost weekend'.

Lennon faces lawsuits from his ex-Beatle mates, his manager and the US Government

But at least his personal life is on an even keel again. 'I just sort of came home, is what happened. I went out to get a newspaper or a coffee somewhere and it took a year . . . like Sinbad. I had a mad trip which I'm glad is over. It was a long year – maybe it was the seven-year crutch!'

CAN YOU HEAR ME ABOVE THE HYPE?

'*Tommy*' the movie premiered in New York to unprecedented ballyhoo. A planeload of celebrities flying in from Los Angeles suffered from culture shock when they were decanted into a subway station for the post-premiere party. Co-stars Elton John and Tina Turner joined The Who for celebrations which lasted three days and included two $50,000 parties to stretch the combined publicity resources of the film and rock industry.

Having worked painstakingly on the 'quintaphonic' soundtrack, Pete Townshend was upset by the sound problems on the opening night: 'How are they going to get the sound right in the 40 cinemas across the country equipped for quintaphonic sound if they can't get it right in New York?" He'd spent three hours trying to fix the delay between the front and back speakers.

The next day the caravan trekked back to Los Angeles to repeat the whole shebang.

Elton John the Pinball Wizard

GENESIS SAY BAA TO UK CRITICS

Genesis's '*Lamb Lies Down On Broadway*' live extravaganza has been going down better in America and Europe than Britain.

And singer Peter Gabriel believes he knows why: 'I think Europeans like the exaggeration and the sense of festival whereas the English are more reserved. In America I find it much healthier. There's room for different opinions and you don't have to justify yourself when you like a band.'

UK critics remain distrustful of Genesis's pomp rock music and art-rock motives. But Gabriel reckons they just don't understand: 'While it's fun to be pompous and sermonise it's still an illusion, a grand illusion. If you can retain your sense of humour and be cynical, it's better. I go right inside my lyrics and laugh at them at the same time.'

Which is why he can act out his Mick Jagger parody and sing 'It's only knock and knowall but I like it' at the climax of '*The Lamb Lies Down*'.

'Is there a man alive who hasn't performed his Jaggerisms in front of the mirror? I know I have.'

Peter Gabriel as Rael in The Lamb Lies Down On Broadway

THE GRAPEVINE

■ David Bowie has filed a lawsuit in London against MainMan and Tony Defries to annul his management contract. MainMan responded with a US injunction against Bowie's new album, 'Young Americans', which has been lifted on appeal.

■ LA police have busted Linda McCartney for 'six to eight' ounces of marijuana. Hubby Paul was not charged.

STEELY DAN – REINING IN THE YEARS

The brains behind Steely Dan – Walter Becker (left) and Donald Fagen

'I don't want to do a record unless it's fantastic and will really do something to people. I mean, I could make a few thousand dollars other ways – I'm a good hustler. I haven't done that much, but most of what I've done is real good and I don't ever want to do a lousy thing.'

Patti Smith, variously described as 'the female Jim Morrison' and 'Keith Richards' kid sister', has signed to Clive Davis' Arista label.

Best known in media circles for her poetry and contributions to *Rolling Stone*, *Creem*, *Crawdaddy* and the now-defunct *Rock* (where she was fired when her interview with Eric Clapton consisted of asking him to list his five favourite words), her band includes fellow rock journalist Lenny Kaye on guitar.

Her credentials are impeccable, including a period spent living at New York's Chelsea Hotel, the obligatory Paris sojourn and friendship with artist Robert Mapplethorpe.

APRIL 1975

THE GRAPEVINE

■ Bob Dylan, Neil Young, The Grateful Dead, Jefferson Starship, The Doobie Brothers and Santana played a benefit gig for SNACK (Students Need Athletics, Culture and Kicks) in San Francisco.

■ Al Green says he'll be dedicating more of his act to God after the incident in Miami last year when a girlfriend poured boiling grits over him in the bath and then shot herself.

CHARTS

US45	Lovin' You *Minnie Riperton*
USLP	Physical Graffiti *Led Zeppelin*
UK45	Bye Bye Baby *Bay City Rollers*
UKLP	Physical Graffiti *Led Zeppelin*

— WEEK 2 —

US45	Philadelphia Freedom *Elton John*
USLP	Physical Graffiti *Led Zeppelin*
UK45	Bye Bye Baby *Bay City Rollers*
UKLP	Physical Graffiti *Led Zeppelin*

— WEEK 3 —

US45	Philadelphia Freedom *Elton John*
USLP	Physical Graffiti *Led Zeppelin*
UK45	Bye Bye Baby *Bay City Rollers*
UKLP	Young Americans *David Bowie*

— WEEK 4 —

US45	Another Somebody Done Somebody Wrong *B.J. Thomas*
USLP	Physical Graffiti *Led Zeppelin*
UK45	Bye Bye Baby *Bay City Rollers*
UKLP	Once Upon A Star *Bay City Rollers*

Patti Smith: born in Chicago and brought up in New Jersey, she moved to New York in 1967 and began writing poetry which she performed to the backing of a rock and roll band

Walter Becker and Donald Fagen of Steely Dan are rock'n'roll's odd couple – a couple of disrespectful misfits who've stuck to their unconventional guns until it finally paid off.

Which it did when they finally got the chance to record their first album, 'Can't Buy A Thrill'. Since then, they've fallen in and out of favour with each successive album. 'Our music is somehow a little too cheesy at times and turns off the rock intelligentsia for the most part,' admits Fagen.

Their latest album, 'Katy Lied', has taken a while because of various technical hitches. They've also lost a couple of members along the way, which has curtailed their touring activities.

But Becker and Fagen explain that Steely Dan is not your conventional rock band. 'If you think of it more as a concept than a group of specific musicians, there's no way it will break up,' says Fagen. 'We have a bunch of satellite performers who are more or less interchangeable. Usually we pick musicians who we think will fit a particular song. We grew up listening to jazz musicians and they're always playing with different people . . . It makes it much more interesting.'

They're more evasive on defining the Steely Dan 'concept', however. 'All we can do is give clues because we're too close to it,' says Fagen. 'It's all on the record, you know.' 'Even if we could answer the question,' says Becker smiling, 'you know that we would lie. We would deliberately lead you off the scent.'

NEIL YOUNG – THE NEEDLE AND THE DAMAGE DONE

Neil Young tears it down

Three years ago, Neil Young was on the brink of superstardom, with his 'Harvest' album selling in huge quantities. But since then Neil has deliberately refused to play the chords of fame.

'It's odd, I don't know why. It was a subconscious move. I think "Tonight's The Night" is the most grand example of that resistance,' Neil agrees.

'Tonight's The Night' is a harrowing album. The title track is the story of Bruce Berry, Young's guitar roadie, who 'died, out on the mainline'. 'Lookout Joe' is the song they were working on when Crazy Horse rhythm guitarist Danny Whitten OD'd, and 'Tired Eyes' is about a dope-dealing vendetta that ends in bloodshed.

'These two cats had been a close part of our unit – our force and our energy. And they were both gone to junk – both of them OD'd,' sighs Neil. 'I don't think "Tonight's The Night" is a friendly album. It's real, that's all. I'm really proud of it. You've got to listen to it at night, which was when it was done.'

So is that it for Neil Young, Superstar? 'We gotta tear all that down,' he laughs. 'It's gone now. Now we can do whatever. It's open again, there's no illusions that someone can say what I'm going to do before I get there. That's how I have to feel. I don't want to feel like people expect me to be a certain way. If that's the way it is, then I quit.'

IGGY ON THE BRINK

'There are basically three kinds of people who "perform". there are those who do it naturally, those who desperately want to possess that ability but don't have that touch, and there are those who want to and don't give a damn either way. I'm part of the last category.'

Iggy Pop is coming up for the third time, and even Iggy knows that he can't afford to sink once more. The kamikaze panache of The Stooges has already claimed two victims. Sax player Steve McKay died from an overdose and bassist Dave Alexander is dead from alcohol poisoning.

'Yeah . . . I just know for a fact that if anyone is going to be next to go, it'll be me. I'm not afraid to die. I know that sounds like a dumb boast or something, but it's a fact. I've proved it enough times, for chrissakes.'

His good buddy David Bowie isn't much help at the moment; the pair were recently reduced to fisticuffs to settle an argument. But he does have the makings of a band. Guitarist and Stooges sur-

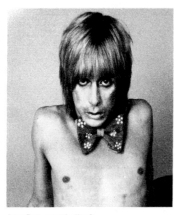

Iggy Pop: next in line?

vivor James Williamson is still on hand, and Hunt and Tony Sales are interested in taking on the rhythm section. 'If a guy walked into this room right now and handed me a cheque for a million dollars, I'd only spend it all on forming a band.'

THE GRAPEVINE

■ Pete Ham, a founder member of Badfinger, has been found dead, hanging in the garage of his house.

■ Van Morrison is planning to return to his native Ireland to settle after a six-year sojourn on the American West Coast.

■ Ten Years After have confirmed their demise after months of speculation.

■ Stevie Wonder played to 125,000 people at the Washington Monument for Human Kindness Day.

Van Morrison goes home

CHARTS

US45	He Don't Love You (Like I Love You)	*Tony Orlando & Dawn*
USLP	Chicago VIII	*Chicago*
UK45	Honey	*Bobby Goldsboro*
UKLP	Once Upon A Star	*Bay City Rollers*

WEEK 2

US45	He Don't Love You (Like I Love You)	*Tony Orlando & Dawn*
USLP	Chicago VIII	*Chicago*
UK45	Loving You	*Minnie Riperton*
UKLP	Once Upon A Star	*Bay City Rollers*

WEEK 3

US45	He Don't Love You (Like I Love You)	*Tony Orlando & Dawn*
USLP	That's The Way Of The World	*Earth, Wind & Fire*
UK45	Stand By Your Man	*Tammy Wynette*
UKLP	Once Upon A Star	*Bay City Rollers*

WEEK 4

US45	Shining Star	*Earth, Wind & Fire*
USLP	That's The Way Of The World	*Earth, Wind & Fire*
UK45	Stand By Your Man	*Tammy Wynette*
UKLP	Once Upon A Star	*Bay City Rollers*

WEEK 5

US45	Before The Next Teardrop Falls	*Freddy Fender*
USLP	That's The Way Of The World	*Earth, Wind & Fire*
UK45	Stand By Your Man	*Tammy Wynette*
UKLP	Once Upon A Star	*Bay City Rollers*

STONES REV UP WITH RON

The Rolling Stones unveiled their 1975 touring model – featuring Ron Wood – on the back of a truck cruising around Greenwich Village. Officially, Ron's just the guest guitarist for the tour. He's supposed to be touring with The Faces again in August.

But right from the opening show of the Stones' US tour at Louisiana State University, Baton Rouge, Ron looks like a permanent fixture. He's changed the musical shape of the band too. Mick Taylor's guitar solos are a thing of the past, to be replaced by a strong, funky, strutting twin guitar attack from Ron and his lookalike, Keith Richards.

The Stones have gone out with their most elaborate stage show yet. The stage is a six-petalled flower that unfolds at the start of the show to the gladiatorial strains of Aaron Copeland's 'Fan-

fare For The Common Man'.

Jagger makes full use of the 360 degrees in which to prance, preen and pose. There's even another toy for him during 'Star Star' – a giant hosepipe that rears up from the ground and ejaculates a stream of confetti over the audience. It's only rock'n'roll . . .

'Just sort of funny entertain-

ment,' says Jagger philosophically. 'Mass funny entertainment. There is a certain element in the form which is agreeable, especially performing it in these sports arenas. It's like an un-art event. I prefer that to, say, the Metropolitan Opera House.'

Jagger designed the stage with Charlie Watts. 'There's no obstructed view. The people at

The Stones roll out on the road again with two new members: Ron Wood on guitar and Mick Jagger's latest stage prop (not shown here). And they say this could be the last time

the back can see. They get a fantastic view because the sound is all hung from above. And it sounds better too, because it's directional sound.'

How about the rumours that this is the last Stones tour? 'They said it in 1969, and they said it again in 1972. Why do they say it? They don't have anything else to write.'

ELTON LIES BLEEDING

A week before his London Wembley Stadium gig in front of 80,000 people, Elton John was worried. 'I've never had a nervous rash before in my life. I came out in blotches all over the place.'

The blotches knew something Elton didn't, because on the night, he got it all wrong. The crowd didn't want to listen to an hour's worth of new and unfamiliar material. But that's what they got – the whole of the

scarcely released and definitely undigested 'Captain Fantastic And The Brown Dirt Cowboy' album.

Elton got it wrong right from the opening 'Love Lies Bleeding', miscalculating the atmosphere in

the wake of the heady nostalgia The Beach Boys had created as opening act. Midway through Elton's set, a steady stream of punters was heading for the exit. His grandiose gesture had misfired.

Elton John forgot to give his audience what they wanted at Wembley Stadium and introduced them to Captain Fantastic And The Brown Dirt Cowboy. The crowd made their excuses and left

THE GRAPEVINE

■ Alice Cooper took a tumble during his 'Welcome To My Nightmare' tour in Vancouver and broke six ribs.

■ Former Columbia Records head Clive Davis and Philly Soul bosses Kenny Gamble and Leon Huff are among ten record company executives indicted for payola in New Jersey.

■ Folksinger Tim Buckley has died of a heroin/morphine overdose in Santa Monica.

CHARTS

US45	Thank God I'm A Country Boy *John Denver*
USLP	Captain Fantastic & The Brown Dirt Cowboy *Elton John*
UK45	Whispering Grass *Windsor Davies & Don Estelle*
UKLP	Once Upon A Star *Bay City Rollers*
WEEK 2	
US45	Sister Golden Hair *America*
USLP	Captain Fantastic & The Brown Dirt Cowboy *Elton John*
UK45	Three Steps To Heaven *Showaddywaddy*
UKLP	Captain Fantastic & The Brown Dirt Cowboy *Elton John*
WEEK 3	
US45	Love Will Keep Us Together *Captain & Tenille*
USLP	Captain Fantastic & The Brown Dirty Cowbo *Elton John*
UK45	Whispering Grass *Windsor Davies & Don Estelle*
UKLP	Captain Fantastic & The Brown Dirt Cowboy *Elton John*
WEEK 4	
US45	Love Will Keep Us Together *Captain & Tenille*
USLP	Captain Fantastic & The Brown Dirt Cowboy *Elton John*
UK45	I'm Not In Love *10cc*
UKLP	Captain Fantastic & The Brown Dirt Cowboy *Elton John*

CLAPTON TELLS THE TRUTH

'Half way through the second Derek & The Dominoes album, we realised we'd hit our peak. We broke up and it took three years to pluck up enough courage to do "461 Ocean Boulevard."'

During those three years, Eric Clapton developed a heroin habit that threatened to destroy him. Pete Townshend got him cured – 'He gave me faith in myself again. I owe him that.'

And he's back on the road again, touring America. But wherever he goes, day or night, his 'minder', Mick Turner, stays three paces behind. Just in case.

Clapton back on the road again

BOB MARLEY – RASTAMAN VIBRATIONS

'Y'call me natty 'ead . . . greyat. Because who care what you think? Me no vex meself while you laugh. Laugh and make the world laugh mon, so me dig it, so me live.'

Bob Marley has come out of the Trenchtown ghetto of Kingston, Jamaica, to give reggae music inspiration and charisma.

London's Lyceum ballroom was the venue where a show by Bob Marley & The Wailers was recorded, and the resulting live album has become the catalyst to launch Marley's career as a superstar.

He's released three albums since Chris Blackwell signed him to Island Records, and each has rolled back the boundaries of re-

ggae. His own stature has grown faster than his dreadlocks, aided by Eric Clapton, who took Marley's song, 'I Shot The Sheriff', to the top of the US charts last year.

Live, Marley is a mesmeric character, driven by the hypnotic force of his music and the commitment to Rastafari that peppers his lyrics and conversation: 'Y'know, Jah appear to me in a vision – and every time he look just a bit older then me. Man, it's so sweet: it's me brother, me father, me mother, me creator, everything . . .'

But The Big Guy didn't tell Bob to be tolerant of everyone: 'Politicians, they are devils; devils who corrupt. They don't smoke 'erb, because when y'smoke, y'think alike, and them don't want that . . .'

But beyond the politics and the rasta, Marley has found a new twist to the oldest inspiration of all – 'No Woman, No Cry'.

PINK FLOYD – WELCOME TO THE MACHINE

Dave Gilmour of Pink Floyd who were dwarfed by a barrage of special effects at the Knebworth Festival

Two Spitfires – relics of the fighter plane that stood between Britain and the German Luftwaffe in 1941 – buzzed the 70,000 crowd at the start of Pink Floyd's Knebworth Festival show in the grounds of a stately home 20 miles north of London.

As the roar died away, Floyd took off for a two-hour journey around 'The Dark Side Of The Moon', 'Echoes' and bits of 'Wish You Were Here', the album EMI are anxiously waiting to release as the follow-up to 'Dark Side Of The Moon', which is now two years old.

As ever, the Floyd didn't stint on the special effects: quadrophonic sound, another plane (this time a model) swooping over the crowd and crashing in front of the stage, a 30ft circular screen showing Gerald Scarfe's paranoid animations and a gigantic mirror ball.

THE GRAPEVINE

■ Keith Richards has been charged with reckless driving and carrying a concealed weapon (a hunting knife) in Arkansas.

■ Three Dog Night's Chuck Negron has been arrested for cocaine possession in Kentucky.

■ 'Miami' Steve Van Zandt has left Southside Johnny to play guitar with Bruce Springsteen & The E Street Band.

■ US Immigration is backtracking as Lennon starts revealing details of the file against him.

THE WORST PART OF BREAKING UP

It's been a bad month for some of Britain's biggest bands. Rod Stewart has released his solo album, 'Atlantic Crossing', and it looks as if The Faces are finished. Ron Wood's looking set in The Rolling Stones and the rest of The Faces are squabbling with each other. Rod admits they're further away from each other than ever.

Peter Gabriel has quit Genesis after months of speculation. Says Gabriel: 'I need to absorb a wide variety of experiences. It's difficult to respond to intuition and

Rod Stewart looking for his Faces

impulse within a band.'

The Who aren't looking too healthy either. Pete Townshend has been notably acerbic in the wake of the movie version of 'Tommy', which prompted Roger Daltrey to unload his own grievances. Meanwhile Keith Moon has carried on blowing up hotel rooms, oblivious to it all.

And Led Zeppelin have cancelled their second US tour this year after Robert Plant and his wife were badly injured in a car crash in Greece.

SPRINGSTEEN – READY TO RUN

The rock event of the summer in New York has been ten shows at The Bottom Line by Bruce Springsteen & The E Street Band. Every show was sold out in advance and around 600 people lined up for the 50 standing tickets available each night.

Bruce is the emerging talent of the year, a fact that his new album, 'Born To Run', will confirm. There are comparisons with Dylan and Van Morrison, but Bruce has a presence all his own, performing for two hours with much mumbled 'street style' rapping, whispered introductions and a slick stage image.

He played just two songs from the new album, one of them the awesome title track. And all of it was familiar to the crowd – most of whom seemed to come from Asbury Park to judge from the whoops every time he mentioned New Jersey or 'The Shore'.

BOWIE LEANING TO THE RIGHT

Out on the set of *The Man Who Fell To Earth*, David Bowie is feeling none too enamoured with the rock'n'roll world he's left behind: 'Rock'n'roll is dead – a toothless old woman. It's embarrassing.'

And his own latest album, 'Young Americans', isn't exempted. 'I tried to do a little stretch of how it feels musically in America, which is sort of . . . relentless plastic soul, really.'

If the present is bad, the future looks even worse. And so does Bowie's solution. 'Dictatorship. There will be a political figure in the not too distant future, who'll sweep this part of the world like early rock'n'roll.'

'The best thing that can happen is for an extreme right-wing government to be elected. It will do something at least to cause commotion in people. They'll either accept the dictatorship or get rid of it.'

STAR QUOTE

ROGER DALTREY

'Pete was being held back by two roadies . . . he was spitting at me and hitting me with his guitar . . . I was forced to lay one on him.'

CHARTS

US45	One Of These Nights	*Eagles*
USLP	One Of These Nights	*Eagles*
UK45	Barbados	*Typically Tropical*
UKLP	Venus And Mars	*Wings*
WEEK 2		
US45	Jive Talkin'	*Bee Gees*
USLP	One Of These Nights	*Eagles*
UK45	Barbados	*Typically Tropical*
UKLP	Venus And Mars	*Wings*
WEEK 3		
US45	Jive Talkin'	*Bee Gees*
USLP	One Of These Nights	*Eagles*
UK45	I Can't Give You Anything	*Stylistics*
UKLP	Best Of The Stylistics	*Stylistics*
WEEK 4		
US45	Fallin' In Love	*Hamilton, Joe Frank & Reynolds*
USLP	One Of These Nights	*Eagles*
UK45	I Can't Give You Anything	*Stylistics*
UKLP	Best Of The Stylistics	*Stylistics*
WEEK 5		
US45	Get Down Tonight	*K.C. & The Sunshine Band*
USLP	One Of These Nights	*Eagles*
UK45	Sailing	*Rod Stewart*
UKLP	Best Of The Stylistics	*Stylistics*

THE GRAPEVINE

■ Alice Cooper is being sued by Warner Brothers, for failing to make enough 'commercially successful' albums.

■ CBS has released Dylan's 'Basement Tapes'; tracks recorded with The Band in 1967 and previously only available on bootleg.

■ Lou Reed has pulled out of a European tour, and Back Street Crawler cancelled a concert when Paul Kossoff was taken 'seriously ill' with kidney failure.

Bruce Springsteen: standing room only

STARSHIP BOLDLY GO . . .

Three years ago, Jefferson Airplane played their last concert - typically, it was a free one. Jefferson Starship isn't so much of an institution, it's really more of an evolution.

As the Airplane disintegrated, Grace Slick and Paul Kantner tried to pretend it wasn't happening by making albums together and then helping each other out on their solo albums. After a while they got bored with that, put a band together, called it Jefferson Starship and went out for test flights.

Their first album ('Dragonfly') sold nearly half a million copies. And the song that got them noticed most was 'Caroline', sung by Marty Balin, who'd baled out of Airplane but was lured aboard Starship for a couple of songs.

For their new album, 'Red Octopus', which has just dislodged Elton John's 'Captain Fantastic' from its marathon run at the top of the US album charts, Marty is back on the payroll full-time.

Kantner says the band works on 'anarchistic democracy. There's never total agreement on things.'

'Trouble is, that same reason separated the Airplane,' adds Grace. 'But I think Starship people appreciate the difference . . . or are at least amused by it.'

CHARTS

US45 Rhinestone Cowboy
Glen Campbell

USLP Red Octopus
Jefferson Starship

UK45 Sailing
Rod Stewart

UKLP Atlantic Crossing
Rod Stewart

───── WEEK 2 ─────

US45 Rhinestone Cowboy
Glen Campbell

USLP The Heat Is On
Isley Brothers

UK45 Sailing
Rod Stewart

UKLP Atlantic Crossing
Rod Stewart

───── WEEK 3 ─────

US45 Fame
David Bowie

USLP Between The Lines
Janis Ian

UK45 Sailing
Rod Stewart

UKLP Atlantic Crossing
Rod Stewart

───── WEEK 4 ─────

US45 I'm Sorry
John Denver

USLP Between The Lines
Janis Ian

UK45 Moonlighting
Leo Sayer

UKLP Atlantic Crossing
Rod Stewart

BLAND ON THE RUN

Paul McCartney's reputation has been up and down like a yo-yo since he started his solo career. Just when he though he'd got everybody on his side with the genial 'Band On The Run', he scared half of them away again with 'Venus And Mars'.

Multi-millionaire he may be, but he's no tax exile. He's currently taking his two-hour show around the same venues that the Beatles played to screaming hordes in '63.

The difference is that this time you can hear what he's playing. And while the songs tend towards the cloyingly comfortable there's enough rockers like

THE GRAPEVINE

■ Gregg Allman and Cher got married – for four days.

■ Elvis Presley said he's coming to Britain next year; and promptly checked into the Memphis Baptist Memorial Hospital midway through a Las Vegas residency.

■ Members of Black Oak Arkansas, sleeping in their carbon monoxide-filled tour bus, narrowly escaped asphyxiation.

■ Jackie Wilson collapsed on stage in Cherry Hill, New Jersey, and has lapsed into a coma.

'Jet', 'Lady Madonna' and "Hi Hi Hi' to remind you of the mercurial talents of his bachelor days.

Paul McCartney, Linda McCartney and Denny Laine. The gold albums roll in though the quality varies. And Wings are playing the same halls as The Beatles

MAN-MACHINE MUSIC

Kraftwerk means 'power plant' and the German band of that name describes its music as *menschmachine* or people-machine. They are four men in sober suits and short-cropped hair whose single, 'Autobahn', has been a major hit across Europe.

In the United States, people say that it won't go beyond the Top 30, but their synthesised, robotic rock is making such a wideranging impact that it's spreading beyond the charts.

'I think the synthesiser is more sensitive than a traditional instrument like a guitar,' explains Ralf Hulter.

Kraftwerk refer to their studio as a laboratory and make their music on banks of synthesisers and computers: 'The whole complex of equipment we use can be regarded as one machine,' adds co-leader Florian Schneider.

They met up at a musical academy in 1970 and have been 'working on the music building equipment' ever since.

WHO'S IN LOVE AGAIN?

After a bout of full, frank and acrimonious exchanges of views via the press, all is sweetness and light in The Who once more. The band are boisterously touring Britain in the wake of their 'Who By Numbers' album.

'There's absolutely no excuses any more,' says Pete Townshend. 'You're there on stage to enjoy yourself and if you don't then you might as well stop because that's how close we were to splitting.'

Roger Daltrey admits he was only able to communicate his feelings through the press. 'Pete read what I'd said and realised that all was far from well. I thought Pete had got thoroughly disillusioned with what he was doing. That's all in the past now. The 'Oo'v have become a challenge again and Pete's guitar playing is unbelievable.'

Keith Moon only ever heard the rumours, but it was enough to make him consider taking a day job to ensure his supply of drinking money. 'Perhaps it's because we hardly see each other socially. I mean, I wouldn't pick 'em as friends . . . but I wouldn't pick any one else as musicians to play with.'

If the new album reveals a more intricate side to Townshend's writing, on stage the band are still the same bundle of intense and unpredictable energy. Their shows seldom run smoothly.

'That doesn't mean we don't give a shit,' says Daltrey. 'We do. But life's too short to worry about missing a beat or forgetting the lyrics. The only thing that really matters is the 'Oo'v.'

CHARTS

US45	Fame	David Bowie
USLP	Wish You Were Here	Pink Floyd
UK45	Hold Me Close	David Essex
UKLP	Atlantic Crossing	Rod Stewart

—— WEEK 2 ——

US45	Bad Blood	Neil Sedaka
USLP	Wish You Were Here	Pink Floyd
UK45	Hold Me Close	David Essex
UKLP	Atlantic Crossing	Rod Stewart

—— WEEK 3 ——

US45	Bad Blood	Neil Sedaka
USLP	Windsong	John Denver
UK45	Hold Me Close	David Essex
UKLP	Atlantic Crossing	Rod Stewart

—— WEEK 4 ——

US45	Bad Blood	Neil Sedaka
USLP	Windsong	John Denver
UK45	I Only Have Eyes For You	Art Garfunkel
UKLP	Wish You Were Here	Pink Floyd

THE GRAPEVINE

- John Lennon has won his four-year battle to stay in America and Yoko celebrated his 35th birthday by giving birth to son Sean.

- Paul Simon has released 'Still Crazy After All These Years' and reunited with Art Garfunkel on 'Saturday Night Live'.

- Drummer Al Jackson (who backed Otis Redding, Sam & Dave, and Booker T) has been shot dead in Memphis. His wife has been arrested.

THE LONG AND SHORT OF BOC

STAR QUOTE

ERIC CLAPTON

'When "Layla" was finished we were so chuffed. We couldn't believe it was so good. We knew it was great, but nobody else seemed to. In the end we were right. We were just too far ahead.'

Blue Oyster Cult attribute their music to the "primal paranoia" in the air

The heaviest band in America right now is Blue Oyster Cult. Their live album, 'On Your Feet Or On Your Knees', was widely panned by the critics, but it's their most successful so far. The reasons aren't hard to find.

On stage, Blue Oyster Cult are explosive operators out to dazzle, and by the time they've finished everyone's on their feet; no-one's on their knees.

Their formula works in the heat of the moment, because they don't have hits as such; just a balanced, destructive blitz. BOC are redefining heavy metal.

Offstage it doesn't always look like it. Tough punk Eric Bloom is positively diminutive. 'I often have to apologise to fans for not fulfilling my reputation. But how can we be our size and serious about it?'

RHYTHM & BOOZE

Those good ole Southern boys Lynyrd Skynyrd ain't looking so good in the Hamburg dressing room. Singer Ronnie Van Zant has bust his fist and guitarist Gary Rossington has two slashed wrists.

And this is only the first night of their European tour!

As manager Peter Rudge says, 'They didn't have to fight before the opening of the tour. It's stupid.'

Stupid or not, Skynyrd played the gig. And then it was back to the bar . . .

Ronnie Van Zant: Southern comforts

CHARTS

Dylan: singing for Hurricane Carter

BORN TO SURVIVE THE HYPE

A couple of months ago, Bruce Springsteen was the future of rock'n'roll, his reputation increasing with every gig and his growing army of fans waiting impatiently for his third album, 'Born To Run'.

Suddenly, he's a household name, his picture on the front of *Time* and *Newsweek* in the same week and the hype machine in overdrive. CBS have decided to hurl him into the superstar arena, hailing him as 'the new Dylan'.

Bruce is worried. 'They made the mistake. They came out with the big hype. I mean, how can they expect people to swallow something like that? I was trying to tell these guys at the record company "Wait a second, gimme a break!"

'I was in this big shadow right from the start and I'm just getting over this Dylan thing, then phooweee – "I have seen the future of rock'n'roll and it's name is Bruce Springsteen." John Landau's piece meant a lot to me, but it was like they took it out of context and blew it up. I called up the company and told them to get that quote out.'

But the hype won't let go as easily as that. He's just made his first trip to Britain where he found the theatre billboards proclaiming 'Finally London is ready for Bruce Springsteen'. That was a hype he couldn't live up to, and for the second concert he'd made CBS take the posters down.

Springsteen: running for cover

NEW YORK SUBWAY?

Down in the New York underground scene, something's stirring: a thriving club scene centred around venues like CBGB's, Max's Kansas city and the Bottom Line which present acts like Television, The Heartbreakers (featuring ex-New York Doll Johnny Thunders), Talking Heads, The Ramones, Blondie, The Shirts and Patti Smith, the only one of them with a recording contract so far.

At the moment, the record companies don't know what to make of this outburst of nervous energy; they've been lulled into complacency by their mega-buck superstars. But the noise is getting too loud to be ignored.

RON WOOD

(temporarily back in The Faces)

'If Rod's gonna leave the band, then Rod's gonna leave the band. We wouldn't necessarily know about it.'

IS IT ROLLING, BOB?

While 'the new Dylan' is gathering all the publicity with the release of the legendary 'Basement Tapes', the old Dylan is embarking on an idiosyncratic tour with a selection of old and new friends under the title The Rolling Thunder Review.

Among the friends – Joan Baez, Ronnie Blakely, Bobby Neuwirth, Ramblin' Jack Elliott, Allen Ginsberg, Bette Midler, Eric Andersen, Mick Ronson and Patti Smith. Most of this unlikely crowd piled on to a bus and headed to Plymouth, Massachussetts, to begin a series of small-scale shows.

In typical Dylan fashion, they've decided to make a film at the same time to record anything that moves . . . and a lot of things that don't.

Just to give the whole adventure a focus, there's a campaigning Dylan single called 'Hurricane', in defence of boxer Hurricane Carter, imprisoned after allegedly being framed for murder.

GRAPEVINE

■ The Who have started their US tour in traditional style: John Entwistle was arrested for disorderly conduct at a party in Houston and spent the night in jail.

■ Elton John flew 120 of his mates to Los Angeles to admire his sequined Dodgers outfit onstage at his Dodgers Stadium shows.

■ The Sex Pistols played their first show at London's St Martin's College of Art.

LITTLE FEAT STILL SHUFFLING

Lowell George isn't a star – he's a musician. A stocky, bearded man in jeans and scuffed suede boots, he fronts Little Feat. Greatly admired by musicians and critics, they just can't seem to crack the commercial market.

Their last album, 'Feats Don't Fail Me Now', was their first to reach the Top 40. They're looking to improve on that with 'The Last Record Album' which has been getting the usual rave reviews.

Trouble is, Lowell George can't seem to be bothered with the glitzy end of it. He's not even impressed with half the big stars

who came to see the band recently at a show in Vance, California.

'It cracked me up that these people should be concerned enough about us to go to Vance, California. I was impressed pretty much, despite myself!'

And the business aspect really turns him off. 'I'd rather sit down and try to write a good song. I guess I'm a real negative factor for many of the people who have to deal with the band. But I've realised that none of the people in this business see any reason why you should do it other than to make money.

Little Feat: not starstruck

'I will cancel a show – and have – if we're supposed to be opening for a band I despise. The logic behind why you do it is something that a lot of people forget too early on. I want to try and hold on to it . . .'

CHARTS

US45	That's The Way (I Like It)	*K.C. & The Sunshine Band*
USLP	Still Crazy After All These Years	*Paul Simon*
UK45	Bohemian Rhapsody	*Queen*
UKLP	Perry Como's 40 Greatest Hits	*Perry Como*

— WEEK 2 —

US45	Fly, Robin, Fly	*Silver Convention*
USLP	Chicago IX-Greatest Hits	*Chicago*
UK45	Bohemian Rhapsody	*Queen*
UKLP	Perry Como's 40 Greatest Hits	*Perry Como*

— WEEK 3 —

US45	Fly, Robin, Fly	*Silver Convention*
USLP	Chicago IX-Greatest Hits	*Chicago*
UK45	Bohemian Rhapsody	*Queen*
UKLP	Perry Como's 40 Greatest Hits	*Perry Como*

— WEEK 4 —

US45	Let's Do It Again	*Staple Singers*
USLP	Chicago IX-Greatest Hits	*Chicago*
UK45	Bohemian Rhapsody	*Queen*
UKLP	A Night At The Opera	*Queen*

FACES FINALLY SPLIT

The long-running Faces-to-split saga is finally over. Rumours have been circulating for the past 18 months, and when Ron Wood left for the Stones earlier this

Maggie may, Faces won't

year, everyone thought that was that.

Rod recorded his own

'Atlantic Crossing' album which has become a big hit, although Faces keyboard player Ian McLagan doesn't think much of it. 'It's sterile and unemotional. "Sailing" is pandering to the crowds. Deep down, Rod hasn't changed at all, but he's into all that Hollywood thing.'

Yet this autumn Rod unfurled himself from Britt Ekland's arms and got back with The Faces for a US tour. But the rumours kept on growing. Finally, just before Christmas, Rod announced that he could 'no longer work in a situation where Ron Wood seems to be permanently on loan to The Rolling Stones'.

He will form his own band while The Faces decide what to do next. There's even talk of a Small Faces reunion. And Ron Wood can always go back to the Stones.

THE GRAPEVINE

- Middle America was stunned when John Denver confessed that he's smoked marijuana.
- Keith Moon, having bought a cop uniform, has taken to frisking Who audiences for illicit substances.
- Led Zeppelin played a club gig to 350 people in Jersey, where Robert Plant is recovering from car-crash injuries.
- Ex-Uriah Heep bassist Greg Thain (27) has died after being rushed to hospital with respiratory failure.

THE COST OF ROYALTY

A night at the opera? More like four months. But then Queen had to get the sound of their new album absolutely right.

'We wanted to experiment with sound. Sometimes we used three studios simultaneously,' says singer Freddie Mercury, '"Bohemian Rhapsody" took bloody ages to record but we've had all the freedom we wanted and we've been able to go to greater extremes.'

BORN TO BE WILD

If the Sound of the late Sixties was psychedelia, then the Sound Of The Seventies was arguably Heavy Metal, initially a musical sub-genre which expanded to become one of the mainstream sounds of the early 1990s. However, its detractors might suggest that the elitism and innovation which typified its late Sixties genesis (a well-chosen word) had deteriorated into the mundanity of the lowest common denominator by the end of the next decade, and has spiralled downwards ever since.

Like other sub-genres (punk rock is a good example), fans of hard rock (the alternative description for Heavy Metal) are loyal to their favourites and remain faithful even after their heroes have been rejected in favour of a new five minute wonder by the world at large. How else could a band like Hawkwind (a 'space/rock' group formed in 1969) survive more than two decades with so few hit records? Heavy metal acts are hugely popular with on-tour merchandisers for a similar reason – their fans are often comparatively affluent, and will buy sweat shirts, caps, posters, patches, badges and even overpriced satin tour jackets featuring the name of their heroes.

The prototype Heavy Metal band was Led Zeppelin, a quartet which remains the bench mark by which all other Metal bands are measured, despite the fact that they broke up in 1980, when thunderous drummer John Bonham reputedly drank himself to death. Formed from the ashes of The Yardbirds by lead guitarist Jimmy Page in 1968, Zeppelin's muscular R&B-rooted rock was performed with both power and subtlety – Robert Plant was the archetypal Metal vocalist, with shoulder-length blond hair, bare chest and a voice which could whisper as well as scream. Unlike most Metal megastars since, in the case of Zeppelin your average rock fan was able to name every member of the group. Of their ten original albums, the most significant are arguably their untitled fourth (also known as the "Runes" album) from 1971, which included the sublime but ultimately over-exposed 'Stairway to Heaven', and 1975's 'Physical Graffiti', a double album of breathtaking power. The group were afflicted with misfortune, particularly Plant, who was seriously injured in a car crash, and whose young son died in a tragic accident – some cynics saw this as karmic revenge for Page's heavily publicised interest in black magic.

Black magic also became a staple of Heavy Metal, although the term 'heavy metal thunder' was allegedly first used by William Burroughs in a novel, then used by American R&B band Steppenwolf in their clasic hit, 'Born To Be Wild'. While the Sixties forerunners of heavy metal acts tended to be major stars, like Cream and the Jimi Hendrix Experience, and to be initially associated with the UK rather than the US, latterday metal acts tended to be too extreme, either in volume or lyrical content, for hit single success, thus Metal became the preserve of the album (and in some cases, the double or triple album). For most of the 1970s, British Metal bands ruled the world, like Deep Purple (very loud but talented) and Black Sabbath, who were even louder and wrote simplistic but nevertheless unsettling lyrics. Their name invoked black magic, although their connections with it were ersatz compared to those of early Seventies

Steppenwolf

Jimmy Page

Blue Oyster Cult

Genesis

Def Leppard

Deep Purple

contemporaries Black Widow, who actually claimed friendship with a modern day black magic priest.

Cream included Eric Clapton, who was regarded favourably by 1970s Metal fans as one of the pioneers of the style, although he has displayed far broader musical talents than its narrow confines could embrace, and similarly, mega-acts like Genesis, Pink Floyd and Jethro Tull were regarded for a while as honorary metallurgists, although none of them was especially loud or outrageous. Real Metal bands tended to become cult acts, like Grand Funk Railroad, whose claim to be the loudest band in the world was disputed by Blue Cheer (neither act was consistently successful) and Blue Oyster Cult, an ambitious quintet managed by two erstwhile rock critics. Grand Funk (as they were later known) were occasionally commercial (by mistake?), Mountain, who were fronted by corpulent guitar terrorist Leslie West (nee Weinstein), ran out of steam when bass player/producer Felix Pappalardi's hearing was destroyed by over-exposure to excessive onstage volume, and BOC's classic '(Don't Fear) The Reaper' was reminiscent of The Byrds. No common ground bar appearance, attitude and volume linked Metal bands, although Canadian power trio Rush favoured the "swords & sorcery/wizards & witchcraft" lyrical approach sometimes adopted by Led Zeppelin and another comparatively mellow group enjoyed by Metal fans during the Seventies, Yes.

In the late 1970s, as punk rock was drowning in its own saliva, several UK bands emerged and were dubbed leaders of the New Wave of British Heavy Metal (or NWOBHM, as it became popularly known). With names like Def Leppard and Iron Maiden, they re-established British domination along with AC/DC, a quintet from Australia, most of whom had emigrated as children from Scotland. Their original vocalist Bon Scott supposedly drank himself to death, while lead guitarist Angus Young wore a short-trousered schoolboy's uniform and was occasionally prone to displaying his naked posterior to audiences who regarded such antics as acceptable due to the thunderous music made by the group. Sheffield quintet Def Leppard sold millions of albums, mainly in the US where they became stadium superstars, while Iron Maiden remarkably topped the UK singles chart in the first week of 1991 by releasing a brand new record, 'Bring Your Daughter To The Slaughter' (which ran into more than a lttle trouble on account of its 'sexist' lyric), on December 26, 1990, a day when no other singles were released.

Most of these acts which started in the 1970s enjoyed their most consistent successes in the Eighties and were still strongly in contention at the start of the 1990s, although the same was unfortunately not true of the biggest of them all (in more ways than one), Meat Loaf. An operatic vocalist/actor with a Billy Bunter shape, he sang songs written by Jim Steinman, a lover of Wagnerian music and Gothic lyrics. The first result was 'Bat Out Of Hell', which spent nearly ten years in the UK album chart without ever rising above No.9. Various follow-up albums briefly charted, but 'Bat' inevitably overshadowed them. Inconsistency was the drawback for Heavy Metal in the 1970s, and two decades on, it still remains a problem.

AEROSMITH WALK THIS WAY

After three years on the road, Aerosmith are the second hottest act in America after Springsteen. Singer Steven Tyler reckons he takes a plane virtually every day, and has to moisturise his face three times daily to prevent in-flight skin dryness.

But it does have its compensations, 'I'll tell you what's fun. It's finding the right stewardess and having her take you to the back of the plane . . . It's the greatest . . . Just the thought that you might get caught. That's the extent of our fun on the road. Waiting for it to happen. Waiting for it not to happen.'

So what's the secret of Aeros-mith's success? 'I think we're really rocking out and nobody else is doing that. People are getting dressed up for a masquerade, doing this, doing that . . . but nobody's really going on and rocking out.'

And the downside? 'It might be a little more fun if things weren't so hectic. If we had more time to cut albums . . .

'I feel like an old shoe. Sometimes I'll be looking at the audience and I'll just stop dead in the middle of a song. I'll look out at them and think, what is this? There's one thing that keeps me doing it though – I really love it. I believe in it.'

THE GRAPEVINE

■ Keith Moon has taken up US residency to avoid paying British taxes.

■ Elvis Presley is reported to be 'distressed' over his weight problems.

■ New albums this month from: Bob Dylan ('Desire'), David Bowie ('Station To Station') and Peter Frampton ('Frampton Comes Alive').

■ Beatles roadie Mal Evans has been shot dead by police after a gun battle at his LA home.

The Who's Keith Moon (left) seen sharing a drink with Ron Wood

TELEVISION IN FOCUS

'There must be 400 bands in New York right now,' says Television's leader/singer/guitarist Tom Verlaine. 'I don't think we're like any of them.'

Television have become the focus of the New York new wave, now that Patti Smith is gaining national prominence with her debut album. But record companies still regard the quartet with suspicion.

Island Records tried to interest Eno in producing the band but Tom would have none of it. 'He's an intellectual and I really don't think we are. I just want a commercial sound.'

This uncompromising stance has already caused bassist Richard Hell to quit. Verlaine wants to get signed so that he can get ahead. 'I don't want to be some little underground sensation. I think there's a big audience out there for us.'

LOU REED DEFIANT

Lou Reed may be churning out vinyl like it's going out of fashion but he's not winning many friends in the process. Last year's 'Metal Machine Music' was greeted with derision and the latest, 'Coney Island Baby', isn't faring much better.

He's defiant about it. 'I was never that interested in the other albums. I mean, they're OK but they weren't Lou Reed albums. Or if they were, I was on automatic pilot. But this one is the way we all wanted it, so if people don't like it they're definitely not liking my kind of album.'

THE LAMB STANDS UP AGAIN

Genesis haven't bothered to recruit a replacement for Peter Gabriel – they've just brought Phil Collins out from behind the drumkit to handle the vocals on their new album, 'Trick Of The Tail'.

Casual fans might find it difficult to notice the difference. Collins' voice is unnervingly like Gabriel's. But critics have found the new album more accessible than the complex 'Lamb Lies Down On Broadway'.

'I think there was less friction between vocals and instrumentals,' explains Mike Rutherford. 'Peter's going has made us more of a band.'

They've also nailed the misconception that Gabriel wrote all Genesis' material. Rutherford and Tony Banks now have their contributions individually credited instead of being under the group banner. And they've already got a pile of material pre-

Genesis: spot the missing Gabriel

pared for another album.

But first they'll be going on the road, adding ex-Yes and King Crimson drummer Bill Bruford, so that Collins can divide his time between drumming and singing.

Freddie Mercury tinkles his ivories

QUEEN WILL ROCK YOU

Finally, New York is ready for Queen. Four sell-out shows at the Beacon Theatre have created the kind of impact that has already conquered Britain and Europe.

Their spectacular stage show combines the theatrically outrageous with a camp humour which blunts any accusations of pretentiousness.

Freddie Mercury's wardrobe defies description. On stage he opts for a white satin jump suit slashed to the navel . . . until he changes into a similar black number slashed even further down. He saves his flowing satin Zandra Rhodes top for the encore.

But beyond the lights, dry ice, flashpots and stage props, Queen demonstrate a musical ability that outshines the visual excesses.

'We're riding on the crest of a wave and things are opening up for us here,' exclaims a delighted Freddie.

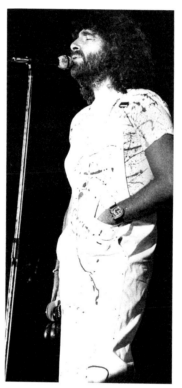
Kevin Godley of 10cc

Florence Ballard, a Supreme alone

LOADED PISTOLS

A chair flies through the air, hitting the PA system with a noise that's indistinguishable from the sound emanating from it.

The chair was thrown by singer Johnny Rotten during The Sex Pistols' London Marquee gig. But it's impossible to tell whether he'd thrown it in anger or excitement.

The Pistols have played less than a dozen gigs so far, but they've already built up a fanatical teenage following.

They play Small Faces numbers, early Kinks B-sides, a couple of Stooges tracks, and only a handful of their own songs.

'Actually we're not into music,' says one of the group afterwards. 'We're into chaos.'

1976

THE SPECTRE OVER SPECTOR

'How could they hate me? I made records like 'River Deep Mountain High', 'Da Doo Ron Ron', 'Be My Baby'. How could they hate anybody whose records are overflowing with so much love, and not only love but honesty? . . . and so much pure fuckin' talent!'

It's been ten years since Phil Spector vanished from public view, reportedly emotionally destroyed by the failure of Ike & Tina Turner's 'River Deep Mountain High' to climb above 93 in the US Top Hundred, despite reaching the Top Three in the British charts and being hailed worldwide as a masterpiece.

He returned to salvage The Beatles' ill-fated 'Let It Be' album and has produced George Harrison's 'All Things Must Pass', plus several John Lennon albums. But his genius is hard to work with and most record companies are easily scared off by his eccentric behaviour.

Yet Spector's self-belief remains inviolate: 'There's nobody in the world who can make better records than I can. Anytime I'm ready I'm tomorrow's headlines . . . And I'm ready now!'

Wings' Jimmy McCulloch: fingered

BOWIE – STRIPPED DOWN TO BASICS

For the first time in David Bowie's career it's impossible to predict what audience he's going to attract for his latest world tour. The success of 'Fame' has opened him up to both the Top 40 and the disco crowd.

The audience at the 17,000-capacity Vancouver Coliseum for the opening date of the tour have scarcely had time to digest the contents of the just-released 'Station To Station' album. And the 'support act' of non-stop Kraftwerk tapes, plus a screening of the 1927 surrealist film *Un Chien Andalou* are not calculated to put them at ease.

But there are few such complications once the show gets underway. The staging is as stripped-down as the presentation. There are no distracting visuals; not even any coloured lights.

Gone are the props, the costumes and the other theatrics on which Bowie has built his reputation. Instead, he's gone back to basics and for 90 minutes he plays the front man for a hot rock'n'roll band.

Soul survivor Bobby Womack

THE GRAPEVINE

■ Former MC5 guitarist Wayne Karmer is facing five years in prison after pleading guilty to cocaine dealing.

■ Gregg Allman has been subpoenad by a Federal Grand Jury in Georgia, investigating a multi-million dollar drug ring.

■ The Who's Keith Moon collapsed on stage at the Boston Gardens – two more shows were cancelled.

■ Wings' US tour has been delayed three weeks as guitarist Jimmy McCulloch has broken a finger.

CHARTS

US45	Love Machine (Part One) *Miracles*
USLP	Desire *Bob Dylan*
UK45	I Love To Love *Tina Charles*
UKLP	The Very Best Of *Slim Whitman*

— WEEK 2 —

US45	December 1963 (Oh What A Night) *Four Seasons*
USLP	Greatest Hits 1971-1975 *Eagles*
UK45	I Love To Love *Tina Charles*
UKLP	The Very Best Of *Slim Whitman*

— WEEK 3 —

US45	December 1963 (Oh What A Night) *Four Seasons*
USLP	Greatest Hits 1971-1975 *Eagles*
UK45	I Love To Love *Tina Charles*
UKLP	Desire *Bob Dylan*

— WEEK 4 —

US45	December 1963 (Oh What A Night) *Four Seasons*
USLP	Greatest Hits 1971-1975 *Eagles*
UK45	Save Your Kisses For Me *Brotherhood Of Man*
UKLP	Blue For You *Status Quo*

ELO FIND ELDORADO

Would you believe 20,000 people clapping along to an un-accompanied cello solo? It's a nightly occurrence in America where Electric Light Orchestra are barnstorming their way across the country.

'People back home in Britain don't realize what's happening,' says ELO leader Jeff Lynne. 'Even my own mum thinks I'm making it up!' Roll over Beethoven and tell Jeff's mum the news!

Jeff cites Lennon & McCartney as his main influence. The hype says they're picking up where 'I Am The Walrus' left off and the stage show is what the Beatles might have produced if they'd taken 'Sgt Pepper' out on the road.

Despite the techno-flash, ELO have resisted the temptations of self-indulgence. The set is action-packed songs jammed together in a steadily mounting crescendo that American audiences find irresistible.

Lynne is still a little overawed by the process that turns his home-written songs into tracks on mega-selling albums.

'The first time I heard an orchestra record one of my songs it was like an orgasm. I got there and there were 30 musicians tuning up. I had to tell them what I wanted them to play. It was a great feeling.'

GIMME GIMME GIMME, MONEY MONEY MONEY

Ever since Abba won the 1974 Eurovision Song Contest with a song called 'Waterloo' they've been dominating the European, American, Australian and Asian charts with a succession of pure pop hits.

Abba are a phenomenon: the first Swedish pop group to achieve international success, they are currently Sweden's second biggest export behind

Volvo. Songwriters Bjorn Ulvaeus and Benny Anderson and their partners Agnetha and Amrifrid have come up with a formula that no continent appears able to resist.

Their music is skilfully put together with infinite patience and technology. The lyrics remain banal, but it makes them easy to understand in Hong Kong or the Phillipines.

S T A R QUOTE

IAN STEWART
Rolling Stones original member.

'You can squawk about money, but the money The Stones have made hasn't done them much good. It's really gotten them into some trouble. They can't even live in their own country now.'

THE GRAPEVINE

■ Former Free and Back Street Crawler guitarist Paul Kossoff has died of heart failure on a London-New York flight aged 26. He had been suffering heart and drug problems for years.

■ Folk singer Phil Ochs hanged himself at his sister's house in Queens, New York.

■ Stevie Wonder has re-signed to Motown for a reported $13 million advance.

CHARTS

US45	Disco Lady / Johnnie Taylor
USLP	Greatest Hits 1971-1975 / Eagles
UK45	Save Your Kisses For Me / Brotherhood Of Man
UKLP	Blue For You / Status Quo

— WEEK 2 —

US45	Disco Lady / Johnnie Taylor
USLP	Frampton Comes Alive! / Peter Frampton
UK45	Save Your Kisses For Me / Brotherhood Of Man
UKLP	Their Greatest Hits / Eagles

— WEEK 3 —

US45	Disco Lady / Johnnie Taylor
USLP	Greatest Hits 1971-1975 / Eagles
UK45	Save Your Kisses For Me / Brotherhood Of Man
UKLP	Rock Follies / TV Cast

— WEEK 4 —

US45	Disco Lady / Johnnie Taylor
USLP	At The Speed Of Sound / Wings
UK45	Save Your Kisses For Me / Brotherhood Of Man
UKLP	Rock Follies / TV Cast

WHITE DOPES ON PUNK

Nobody hires The Tubes as a support band since Led Zeppelin were unable to follow their stunt of throwing giant amphetamine tablets at a 60,000 crowd in San Francisco.

The Tubes specialize in warp-rock theatrics. Singer Fee Waybill splits his persona into a weird and wonderful assortment of characters, climaxing the band's staggering show as the ultimate glamster, Quay Lewd, singing The Tubes' finest anthem, 'White Punks On Dope'.

Despite selling out every-where, The Tubes lose money. But it hasn't stopped them so far. 'I may grow tits for the next tour,' confides Waybill.

1976

BERNIE TAUPIN: THE WRITE STUFF

Bernie Taupin is 'The One Who Writes The Words For Elton John'. That's the title of his newly published illustrated book of lyrics. He's happy to let Elton take all the glory. Royalties provide their own compensation, particularly when you consider that Elton John albums accounted for 2 per cent of all world record sales last year.

'If we actually sat down together and attempted to write songs in the orthodox manner – sweating out inspiration over ashtrays full of cigarette ends – we'd probably drive each other nuts,' says Taupin.

Instead, he knocks out his lyrics in solitary splendour and passes them on to Elton, who puts them into musical shape.

It's a speedy process but never slapdash. 'Elton and I are very aware of our success and we've tried not to be complacent about it. We both want to retain our popularity and therefore we both work hard at our respective jobs.'

Taupin: lyrics and flares

LOFGREN BOUNCES BACK

Nils Lofgren is one of the few young artists who genuinely understands the true spirit of rock'n' roll. Which is strange considering how straight his upbringing was. Trained as a classical musician, he took no interest in rock music until his mid-teens.

Seeing Hendrix in concert clinched it. Lofgren formed a band called Grin and spent time in Neil Young's Crazy Horse before setting out on his own.

His second solo album, 'Cry Tough', has cracked the US and UK charts, and his current UK tour has inspired Nils to his finest playing yet.

'I'm into playing rock'n' roll whenever and wherever I can,' he says, doodling on an acoustic guitar in his hotel room. 'We leave a lot of space in the songs for improvisation, and I don't just mean the guitar solos. I'm up for playing and travelling as far as I can.'

THE GRAPEVINE

■ Four Brunswick Records execs have been indicted for payola.

■ Arista President Clive Davis has pleaded guilty to failing to declare $8,800 income back in 1972. A further charge has been dropped.

■ Keith Richards was arrested after crashing his Bentley during the Stones UK tour. Various substances from the wreckage were confiscated by police.

■ Yardbirds singer Keith Relf was fatally electrocuted while playing his guitar at home.

NO PARTICULAR THING TO SAY

Chuck Berry's habit of using unrehearsed pick-up musicians on British tours is frustrating in the extreme. This time around he doesn't even know who he's going to be playing with.

So doesn't he ever feel the urge to get up with a really good band and jam? 'What?' Question repeated. 'It's up to the promoter'.

Is he aware of his influence on rock'n'roll? 'I wouldn't know about that. I just do what I do. Writing, doing my thing.'

Sometimes legends are a letdown.

STAR QUOTE

KEITH RICHARDS

'I only really listen to black groups these days. I ain't too interested in white bands who rip off white bands who ripped off black bands.'

Keith Richards lets rip

LISTEN TO THE NEW MUSIC

A year ago, Doobie Brothers singer/guitarist Tom Johnston bowed out of the band midway through a US tour. 'He was ill from different things,' says colleague Pat Simmons. 'He had an ulcer. He was run down, spaced out, doped out . . .'

As Johnston had written the best known Doobies songs – 'Listen To The Music', 'China Groove' and 'Long Train Coming' – his collapse could have been a mortal blow for the band.

They reacted by recruiting Steely Dan keyboard player Mike

The Doobie Brothers get down and boogie their way out of adversity

McDonald and carrying on the tour.

Johnston is back for the new album, 'Taking It To The Streets' – but only just. He's written one song and doesn't even make the group shot on the back cover. But the rest of the band have broadened out to take up the slack.

'Audiences are more inclined to listen to us now,' says Simmons, smiling.

WINWOOD PASSES GO

You don't see too much of Steve Winwood these days since Traffic got jammed. Last time he played live was with salsa band The Fania All-Stars. Now he's resurfaced via Japanese percussive genius Stomu Yamashta's 'Go' album, and a series of European dates.

This East-West fusion project also features former Tangerine Dream synthesist Klaus Schulz, ex-Santana drummer Michael Shrieve, nearly ex-Roxy Music guitarist Phil Manzanera and former Return To Forever guitarist Al DiMeola.

Winwood is making slow but steady progress on his own solo album. 'I try not to be narrow-minded, but I don't know whether that's good or not,' he says.

ROD – NO REGRETS

'The name of the game is to get people there,' says Rod Stewart, 'but you never know whether you've done it or not. Especially when you've lived with an album for three or four months.'

. Rod certainly did it with 'Atlantic Crossing', last year's hit album. And 'A Night On The Town' looks set to go even better. But the recriminations that followed at the end of last year's break up of The Faces have left a bitter taste that Rod still has to overcome.

Rod, – in Britain to form a new band, – remains unrepen-

Rod Stewart: never look back

tant: 'The river dried up with The Faces. I'd heard some things by other people and I suddenly realized I could be doing a lot better if I was to branch out. And then I met my producer Tom Dowd . . .'

STAR QUOTE

TOM WAITS

'I once worked in a jewellery store and when I quit I took a gold watch. I figured they weren't gonna give me one 'cause I'd only been with them six months.'

THE GRAPEVINE

■ As Wings tour America, Capitol have released Beatles' 'Rock'n'Roll Music' compilation.

■ Roxy Music have confirmed a trial separation.

■ S/M advertisement for Rolling Stones 'Black And Blue' album has caused outrage in America.

■ Ramones' debut album released.

■ ZZ Top tour USA with a 2,000lb buffalo, two turkey vultures and four rattlesnakes on a stage shaped like Texas.

Sharp-dressed ZZ Top

SAYIN' IT LOUD ...

The Ohio Players and War bear little relation to each other musically, but they have enough similarities – both are black and flash with a rare artistic and financial freedom – to make a dynamite package tour that's peeling the scales off European eyes.

The Players are more easily definable, growing up with Sixties soul and taking it a stage further. They're the leaders of the convoy along the highway of modern black music. Any white interest is unsolicited but welcome.

War are camped over in the middle ground, attracting an equal number of blacks and whites and unconcerned about moving off in any particular direction.

Both bands use a barrage of lights and effects to put across their energetic brands of funk, ostentatiously reaching out to pull the audience right in there with them. They can do it because they've never let go of their roots. They understand their audiences as well as they understand their music and they funk with both feet firmly on the ground.

War and a funky piece

FRAMPTON SHOWS THE WAY

'Frampton Comes Alive' has sold three million copies since it came out in the spring, so it's not surprising that Peter Frampton is the hottest touring act in America this summer.

This is the third time Frampton has been a 'star', and he's still only 26. He started in the UK with The Herd back in the last Sixties, then formed Humble Pie with Steve Marriott (ex-Small Faces) in the early Seventies. Despite the fame, neither band made any money and by the time he'd disbanded the ill-fated Frampton's Camel, he was a quarter of a million dollars in debt.

These days he can earn nearly that in a weekend, selling out stadiums on his own.

The reasons for his success aren't hard to find; pretty, clean, spacey music, equally pretty looks and an astute management and record company.

Frampton plays guitar with rare melody and fluidity, with very little trace of the blues – something unusual for a rock guitarist. 'Eric Clapton turned me on incredibly but I tried not to listen too much because everyone else was copying him. The guitarists who intrigue me most are the old jazzers like Django Reinhardt.

'People have been saying some ridiculous things – the new Elton John and all this shit. I'm not, but it's quite possible.'

THE GRAPEVINE

- After two platinum and nine gold albums, Deep Purple have disbanded.
- The Allman Brothers have split up after Gregg 'fingered' roadie Scooter Herring during a police drugs probe.
- Bruce Springsteen is sueing manager Mike Appel for fraud and breach of trust.
- Stevie Wonder's still holding back on his new LP but has released a T-shirt proclaiming 'Stevie's Nearly Ready'.

Dolly Parton: plastic surgery?

FLEETWOOD MAC'S 'BAD B-MOVIE' WINS AN OSCAR

Fleetwood Mac released their eponymous album nearly a year ago. It became their first US Top 10 LP, had a good run and dropped out. Meantime the band went out on the road for five months solid, and for the past three months the album has been back in the Top 5.

It's spawned two hit singles – 'Over My Head' and 'Rhiannon' – and sold two million copies so far. In Britain it's done only five thousand.

But then the Fleetwood Mac Britain knew and loved in the mid-Sixties bears little relation to the current outfit. At the start of the Seventies, guitarist Peter Green went AWOL in New Orleans. The other guitarist,

Stevie Nicks can give up being a waitress now that 'Fleetwood Mac' has sold two million copies

Jeremy Spencer, joined the Children Of God cult. Mick Fleetwood describes the period as 'a bad B-movie'.

The arrival of Lindsey Buckingham and Stevie Nicks just before they started recording 'Fleetwood Mac' proved the turning point.

'It felt right. It was very quick,' says Fleetwood. 'I think it's wrong to start analysing the whys and wherefores. That was it.'

It certainly was. And Stevie Nicks could quit her job as a waitress.

THE GRAPEVINE

■ The Rolling Stones played Britain's Knebworth Festival to 150,000 people with 10cc, Todd Rundgren and Lynyrd Skynryd.

■ The Clash have made their first appearance in London

■ Cliff Richard has embarked on a 25-date sell-out tour of Russia.

■ Blues singer Jimmy Reed, whose songs were covered by The Rolling Stones, The Who and The Yardbirds, has died in San Francisco immediately after a three-night club engagement.

RAMONES LEAVE HOME

'We may not be the brightest guys in the world,' says Dee Dee Ramone. 'But I don't think I'm no mutant weed, either.'

At the band's soundcheck at London's Roundhouse, he's yelling at the English roadcrew about the lack of power emanating from his stack. The Ramones' ideal is to play with their amps juiced to maximum. Their fingers bleed so that your ears can.

Not everyone's a fan. Glasgow politician James Dempsey is trying to get the track, 'Now I Wanna Sniff Some Glue', banned. Twenty Scottish kids have died from glue sniffing in recent years.

But the publicity is guaranteed to have the opposite effect. And as Ramones manager, Danny Fields, says: 'Why should the song be banned? War films aren't banned on the grounds that they advocate violence.'

STAR QUOTE

RON WOOD

'I mean, I suppose most of the time I'm honest. That's not too bad really is it? 'Cause basically it's too easy to be a bastard in this business.'

AUGUST 1976

TED NUGENT'S STRANGLEHOLD

'Wasn't I great? Wasn't that the best show you ever saw?' enthuses modest Ted Nugent backstage in Amarillo, Texas.

Nugent hails from Detroit, where he saw off the likes of Wayne Kramer (MC5) and Mike Pinero (Iron Butterfly) in a series of guitar duels.

He's scathing about drugs and alcohol, only eats what he shoots, and preserves his energy for playing his guitar at ear-splitting volume – and sex. 'Some chicks think I'm crazy when I'm on top of them, I don't want to hurt them. I just do everything like that.'

Nugent: ear-splitting meat eater

No silver lining for Jeff

CALIFORNIA DREAMING

The Runaways cheek to cheek. They just wanna be your Cherry Bomb

If you're looking for the ultimate image of Southern California then look no further than The Runaways – five 16-year-old honeys epitomising the wacked-out nuttiness of Hollywood rock 'n' roll.

But wait a minute. These chicks are blasting out the kind of raucous rock you'd find in a South London pub any night of the week. That's because they are the creation of two of Hollywood's most notorious Anglophiles.

Rodney Bingenheimer and Kim Fowley are the Hollywood hustlers who've put The Runaways together. The girls cut their (baby) teeth in Rodney's English disco, and producer Kim Fowley directed the girls' career to a recording contract with Phonogram and takes a composer's credit on seven of the ten tracks on their first album.

Naturally, the girls have their own influences. Lead guitarist Lita Ford (actually she's 17 but she won't tell if you won't) goes all the way back to Led Zeppelin and Black Sabbath's first albums. Bassist Jackie Fox passionately believes in Kiss and Aerosmith. And you just have to glance at guitarist Joan Jett's Suzi Quatro cut and singer Cherie Currie's Ziggy quiff to know where they're coming from.

The Runaways bring a new vehemence to the generation gap. 'We're putting our feelings into music in a way that no 30-year-old man could. They can sing about teenagers and sneaking out at night. But they don't really know,' says Cherie.

'I mean, 30-year-old guys don't have to sneak past their mothers to go out at night,' adds Joan Jett helpfully.

WHO ARE YOU CALLING PUNK, PUNK?

Patti Smith may be a punk. The Ramones may be punk, even Springsteen might sometimes be a punk. But they ain't punk rock; not the punk rock that's alive and kicking in the UK.

At the Screen on the Green cinema in North London – because no regular rock venue would have them – The Sex Pistols, The Clash and The Buzzcocks play nasty music for nasty kids.

For a while, record company execs might flash on a déjà-vu of the sixties as mutant misfits dance under freaky lights while films are projected onscreen. But the atmosphere is fuelled by amyl-nitrate, not hallucinogenics. This is definitely not the summer of love.

The Clash are exceedingly rough and scarcely ready musically. But singer/guitarist Joe Strummer has a vehemence that rises above their deficiencies.

In comparison, The Sex Pistols have the clean, tight sound of punk veterans. Within 30 seconds they've wiped out all the mock decadence that preceeded them with a sneering dose of realism. They are energetic, charismatic, arrogant and uncouth. Any minute now, record companies are going to have to deal with them.

The Clash: exceedingly rough and scarcely ready but very willing

SONGS IN THE KEY OF MONEY

Stevie Wonder's 'Songs In The Key Of Life' is finally out after the longest sell-in in the history of the record industry.

Pre-sold to dealers four times already this year, it's been a double-album, a triple album and now it's back down to a double with a 'free' EP of four extra songs

Its tortuous history is inextricably linked with Wonder's resigning to Motown (after ostentatiously being seen in the company of other record label executives) for $13 million – the largest advance ever secured by an artist.

Motown needed Wonder's signature: they've recently lost the services of The Four Tops, Gladys Knight, Martha Reeves, Ashford & Simpson, The Detroit Spinners, four of The Jackson Five and songwriters Holland, Dozier & Holland.

And the word is that Motown were determined to exploit every trick in the book to recoup as much of their advance as possible. It seems to be working – 'Songs In The Key Of Life' has worldwide advance orders of more than one million.

But what about the album itself? Like any double album it's self-indulgent, and there's scarcely a track that couldn't have been prudently edited. But Wonder's music has expanded enormously and his stylistic range pays full dividends.

George Harrison gets those subconscious sue me sue you blues

Pass the sick bag Patti

THE GRAPEVINE

■ The Sex Pistols have signed to EMI Records. 'Here at last is a group with a bit of guts for younger people to identify with,' says a spokesman.

■ George Harrison has been found guilty of 'subconsciously' plagiarising The Chiffons' 'He's So Fine' for 'My Sweet Lord'.

■ Ike & Tina Turner have split up after 19 years.

■ Victoria Spivey, blues singer, has died, aged 70.

STAR QUOTE

PATTI SMITH

'Every man I've ever screwed has thrown up on me at least once.'

CLINTON'S GAININ' ON YA!

'There's a lot of chocolate cities around. We got Newark. We got Gary. Somebody told me we got LA. And we're working on Atlanta. But you're the capital and I love ya. God bless Chocolate City and its vanilla suburbs!'

That's how George Clinton tells it to his audience in Washington DC, where 80 per cent of the population is black. 'They still call it the White House but that's a temporary condition too. Gainin' on ya!' he cackles.

George Clinton raps and sometimes sings. He's got a band called Parliament. He's also got a band of equal freaky funkiness

known as Funkadelic. George mainly writes and raps and whips it all together. He's the producer.

Let him explain. 'Parliament is more vocal, more disco with horns, and a bit more conservative. Funkadelic is more guitars, no horns, more free-form feelings and more wild. Sometimes there's a criss-cross but generally Funkadelic gets more pussy than Parliament.'

Then there's Bootsy's Rubber Band, put together by Bootsy Collins who used to be James Brown's guitarist, which is the root of where this whole Parliafunkedelicbootsyment thang got started. Except that was then and this is now. And George and Bootsy are playing all kinds of games that are turning white folks' perception of black music on its head. And some black folks too.

George Clinton: funk bench spokesman

LED ZEPPELIN'S COMMUNICATION BREAKDOWN

Robert Plant and Jimmy Page climbing the stairway to self-indulgence

CHARTS

US45	Rock'n Me *Steve Miller Band*
USLP	Songs In The Key Of Life *Stevie Wonder*
UK45	If You Leave Me Now *Chicago*
UKLP	Songs In The Key Of Life *Stevie Wonder*

———— WEEK 2 ————

US45	Tonight's The Night *Rod Stewart*
USLP	Songs In The Key Of Life *Stevie Wonder*
UK45	If You Leave Me Now *Chicago*
UKLP	Songs In The Key Of Life *Stevie Wonder*

———— WEEK 3 ————

US45	Tonight's The Night *Rod Stewart*
USLP	Songs In The Key Of Life *Stevie Wonder*
UK45	If You Leave Me Now *Chicago*
UKLP	Songs In The Key Of Life *Stevie Wonder*

———— WEEK 4 ————

US45	Tonight's The Night *Rod Stewart*
USLP	Songs In The Key Of Life *Stevie Wonder*
UK45	If You Leave Me Now *Chicago*
UKLP	20 Golden Greats *Glen Campbell*

Led Zeppelin manager Peter Grant has described *The Song Remains The Same* as 'the most expensive home movie ever made'. Maybe it should have stayed that way.

What seemed like a good idea at the time – capturing Zeppelin's live show on film – has been ruined by turning it into an orgy of self-indulgence.

The live material is slickly filmed, but Zeppelin have never been the most visual of rock bands. You have to be there.

The film falls most flat on its expensive face in the fantasy sequences. They are so banal and infantile one has to wonder why nobody dared to point out the folly of it all.

They don't even leave the music alone. The soundtrack sounds heavily doctored, and the best performance of the film, 'Since I've Been Loving You', is inexplicably absent from the double album.

Even Jimmy Page is not rushing to the film's defence. 'It's not a great film. Just a reasonably honest statement of where we were at that particular time.'

THE DAMNED SAY IT WITH FLOWERS

Other British punk bands may be grabbing the limelight, but The Damned are the first to get a record out.

'New Rose', released by the newly formed independent Stiff Records ('Today's Sound Today')

opens with singer Dave Vanian asking coyly 'Is she really going out with him?' before the thunder of Rat Scabies' drumkit paves the way for guitarist Brian James' power chords and Captain Sensible's heavy bass line.

Captain Sensible is so called because he's 'so bleedin' stoopid', according to Scabies, whose own name comes from his constant itching. The rat hanging down the front of his drumkit is, alas, only plastic.

Brian James does his best to look like former New York Doll Johnny Thunders and Dave Vanian, who resembles a runaway from the Adams Family, used to be a gravedigger.

What else do you wanna know?

MARVIN GETS IT ON

'I Want You' is Marvin Gaye's first album for more than two years and seems trapped in the shadow of the superb 'Let's Get It On' which established his reputation for being more than just a Motown stooge with a flair for interpreting ready-made hits.

He hasn't visited Britain since the mid Sixties, but any doubts that he might have lost his following there have been laid to rest by the audience acclaim at his concert at London's Royal Albert Hall.

From the moment an admirer leapt on stage during 'Trouble Man' and ran off with Marvin's bow-tie, the show was constantly interrupted by adoring fans invading the stage to grab a piece of the star, or an item of clothing.

Those who preferred to listen were enthralled by his Seventies material. He remains a truly great singer, if a somewhat vulnerable artist.

Sex Pistols manager Malcolm McLaren trying hard to feel cheated

THE GRAPEVINE

■ George Harrison has switched his Dark Horse label from A&M to Warners.

■ Lol Creme and Kevin Godley have left 10cc to pursue their own projects; Eric Stewart and Graham Gouldman are to carry on as 10cc with new members.

■ Jerry Lee Lewis has been arrested (again) after causing a disturbance outside Elvis Presley's Graceland home.

■ Bread have re-formed with their original line-up.

FROM ANARCHY TO CHAOS

Catapulted into the eye of a media hurricane after their infamous two-minute television interview, The Sex Pistols' debut UK tour has collapsed in ruins around them.

Within days, 12 out of 16 halls cancelled. In the town of Derby, town councillors insisted that The Pistols perform a private show so they could evaluate the band's threat to the nation's moral fibre. The group refused and another gig bit the dust.

At one of the few remaining dates (Leeds University), students were outnumbered by journalists eagerly awaiting another outrage to report. Sadly for them – and the punks who'd turned up – the gig was a dumb, castrated apology of a show that even Johnny Rotten's sneers couldn't enliven.

EMI Records are still considering their position. A statement from Chairman Sir John Read talks of making 'value judgements' within the 'contemporary limits of decency and good taste'. Meanwhile, EMI continue to press, distribute and collect the proceeds of 'Anarchy In The UK'.

Joe Strummer letting them know

THE GRAPEVINE

- Rick Wakeman has rejoined Yes.
- An inflatable pig being photographed for the cover of the Pink Floyd's 'Animals' broke loose and floated into the London Airport flightpath.
- Bob Marley, his wife and manager were shot and wounded at the singer's Kingston, Jamaica, home during the country's general election campaign.
- Former Deep Purple guitarist Tommy Bolin has died of a drug overdose in Miami.

Flying pig over Battersea

CHARTS

US45	Tonight's The Night *Rod Stewart*
USLP	Songs In The Key Of Life *Stevie Wonder*
UK45	Under The Moon Of Love *Showaddywaddy*
UKLP	20 Golden Greats *Glen Campbell*

— WEEK 2 —

US45	Tonight's The Night *Rod Stewart*
USLP	Songs In The Key Of Life *Stevie Wonder*
UK45	Under The Moon Of Love *Showaddywaddy*
UKLP	20 Golden Greats *Glen Campbell*

— WEEK 3 —

US45	Tonight's The Night *Rod Stewart*
USLP	Songs In The Key Of Life *Stevie Wonder*
UK45	Under The Moon Of Love *Showaddywaddy*
UKLP	20 Golden Greats *Glen Campbell*

— WEEK 4 —

US45	Tonight's The Night *Rod Stewart*
USLP	Songs In The Key Of Life *Stevie Wonder*
UK45	When A Child Is Born *Johnny Mathis*
UKLP	Arrival *Abba*

JACKSON BROWNE'S GREAT PRETENDER

Nobody epitomizes the Seventies singer/songwriter better than Jackson Browne. He writes songs about the fundamental themes with a perception that puts him on a different level from his contemporaries.

Browne started work on his latest album, 'The Pretender', at the beginning of March. On March 25 his wife, to whom he'd been married less than six months, committed suicide. He stopped work on the album, starting again in May. In September he worked every waking hour to complete it, apart from one brief spell when he took his son on a camping holiday.

'"The Pretender" is just about being totally lost,' says Browne. 'He's a character in a story, and the poor fucker's so confused he thinks that maybe if he got a job the world would fall into place, and he might be actually happy watching the *Tonight* show.'

THE BAND'S LAST WALTZ

The Band have bowed out after 16 years on the road with a star-studded spectacular that left scarcely a dry eye at The Winterland, San Francisco.

Lead guitarist Robbie Robertson wanted 'a party with our friends . . . like a New Orleans funeral.' He got it.

Ronnie Hawkins, Dr John, Paul Butterfield, Muddy Waters, Eric Clapton, Neil Young, Joni Mitchell, Van Morrison and Bob Dylan joined The Band for a song or two each.

Five thousand people paid $25 to be wined, dined and entertained in the hall, which has been festooned with decorations. Promoter Bill Graham cheerfully lost $40,000 on the evening.

And to make sure it was all preserved for posterity, six camera crews, under the direction of Martin Scorsese, filmed 'The Last Waltz', as the evening was called.

Dylan's farewell to The Band

DISCO FEVER WITH THE BEE GEES

As rock music has grown older, its audience has become more attuned to the occasional renaissance – a once big act, which had fallen on difficult times commercially, rising from its shallow unmarked grave for a further jouste at the fickle public. It happens, and more often than might be imagined, but one of the greatest Lazarus acts in the modern history of popular music involved The Bee Gees, the trio of brothers born in the Isle of Man who first came to fame in Australia before returning to Britain to become major stars of the late 1960s.

Big brother Barry Gibb and his twin younger siblings, Maurice and Robin, had discovered at an early age the unique vocal harmonic similarities enjoyed by close relatives and, coupled with a desire to entertain inherited from their bandleader father, had performed in local talent contests in the North of England even before the family emigrated to Australia in 1958.

Having arrived in their new surroundings, the trio became known as the Bee Gees (short for 'brothers Gibb') and appeared on television, becoming local celebrities during the first half of the 1960s before deciding to return to Britain and try their luck in a major market.

The First Coming

Soon after they arrived in England in early 1967, the group were signed for management by Australian born showbiz mogul Robert Stigwood, and before the year was out, had scored four hits in both Britain and America including 'Massachusetts', which topped the UK chart. They were almost instantly

The brothers Gibb

Stigwood and Travolta at 'Grease' launch

The Bee Gees in 'Sergeant Pepper'

international pop stars as several more hits in 1968, including another UK No. 1, 'I've Gotta Get A Message To You', emphasized. However, after releasing their first US chart topper, 'How Can You Mend A Broken Heart', in 1971, things began to go wrong and by 1972, the group, rocked by personnel changes and fraternal disagreements, seemed to have run out of steam, before Stigwood, a steadying influence, restored stability.

Return to the Charts

By 1975, the trio's talents had brought them back to prominence with another big international hit, 'Jive Talkin'', which became their second US No. 1 and also reached the UK top five. It seemed a short term revival in Britain, although in America – where it was followed by another big hit, 'Nights On Broadway – The Bee Gees appeared to have successfully reinvented themselves as hotshot songwriters and performers of disco music, which was newly established as a major force.

Hit Film

In 1976 Robert Stigwood purchased the rights to a yet unnamed movie to be scripted by British writer Nik Cohn after reading an article by Cohn in a New York magazine entitled 'Tribal Right of the New Saturday Night', about the lives of discothéque afficionados in New York. The movie was eventually to become one of the most successful ever made centred around popular music and was sensationally to revive the career of the Bee Gees.

Record Album

Two key elements in *Saturday Night Fever's* triumph were the casting of John Travolta in the starring role, and the use of The Bee Gees as the main contributors to the film's soundtrack. The group actually performed six self-composed

Travolta and Finola Hughes, 'Stayin' Alive'

'Saturday Night Fever'

songs used in the movie, one of which was also additionally performed by another group, Tavares, and they also wrote another song, 'If I Can't Have You', which was performed for the film by another artist signed to Stigwood's RSO label, Yvonne Elliman.

Both choices proved to be inspired – Travolta became a superstar and The Bee Gees topped the charts with all six of the songs which they had performed in the movie, five of them in succession 'Jive Talkin', 'You Should Be Dancing', 'How Deep Is Your Love' and 'Stayin' Alive'.

Stayin' on top

When 'Stayin' Alive' fell off the peak, its place was taken by '(Love Is) Thicker Than Water' by Andy Gibb, (youngest brother of the Bee Gees family), before 'Night Fever' became the sixth chart-topper in the film. That was replaced by Yvonne Elliman's 'If I Can't Have You', which made seven No. 1s on one soundtrack, a record which is hard to believe.

Four more singles from the movie entered the chart and the *Saturday Night Fever* album became the biggest selling soundtrack disc of all time, topping the US album chart for 24 weeks and its British equivalent for a mere 18, and selling considerably more than one million units.

They win again

The Bee Gees remained on the crest of the 'SNF' wave until 1980, but then – pop fashion being ultimately unpredictable – once more fell from favour for much of the 1980s, especially in Britain. Just when everyone had more or less forgotten them, out of the blue came another UK chart-topper, 'You Win Again', in 1987.

Subsequently, they seem to have disappeared again, but on the strength of their past achievements, it would take a gambler to predict that their absence will be permanent.

Kool And The Gang

K.C. of the Sunshine Band

JANUARY

1977

Apocalyptic looking Stranglers

PIGS ON THE WHINGE

The phenomenal success of Pink Floyd's 'Dark Side Of The Moon' – still in the charts four years after its release – hasn't made them a happier band.

As they prepare to release their new 'Animals' LP, drummer Nick Mason admits that the pressure of recording 'Wish You Were Here', the follow-up to 'Dark Side Of The Moon', nearly caused the band to split up. 'I really did find the time in the studio extremely horrible,' he says.

And bassist Roger Waters found the last tour 'very unpleasant, un-nerving and upsetting . . . The quality of life is full of stress and pain in most of the people I meet and in myself.'

PISTOLS FIRED ONCE

After nearly a month of pious procrastination, EMI have terminated their contract with The Sex Pistols. The straw that broke the camel's back was the group's widely publicized 'drunken and abusive' behaviour at London Airport en route for Holland for gigs in Amsterdam.

But the Pistols can console themselves with a £50,000 pay-off, and if the hysterical publicity surrounding them has made it impossible for them to play any concerts in the UK, there's no shortage of offers from Europe where they will be playing a 24-date tour throughout February.

It's not just record companies who are having trouble coming to terms with punk. The Who's Pete Townshend was involved in a 'tired and emotional' altercation with The Sex Pistols at London's Speakeasy Club. The man who wrote 'Hope I die before I get old' told drummer Paul Cook: 'I don't need to know what you're about' after lunging at a photographer who tried to take a picture of the pair of them.

'He thinks he's past it,' said Cook later. 'But he ain't. He's still great.' Guitarist Steve Jones agreed. 'He was really a great geezer even though he was, like, paralytic.'

Pink Floyd's Roger Waters showing the stress and pain of mega-stardom

The Bay City Rollers riding the wave of tartan teen hysteria

AMERICA LOVES THE ROLLERS

Bay City Roller-mania has come to America. The cute Scottish pop quintet, who've caused teenybopper hysteria wherever they appeared in the UK last year, have been greeted with the same reaction on their first US tour.

At New York's Palladium more than 30 teen and pre-teen girls fainted at their show. The banner-carrying fans were mostly dressed in tartan, displaying a visual identification which other teenybopper bands have never been able to achieve. 'What could the girls do to identify with the Osmonds?' asked one teen magazine. 'Dress up like Mormons?'

The Bay City Rollers' first two albums have already gone gold and the 'latest, 'Dedication', has sold 350,000 in four months.

Singer Les McKeown is feeling the strain: 'Psychologically it can be a real drag, all the travelling, never getting out of the hotel. But I think it'll mature eventually and they'll just scream at the end of numbers instead of all the way through.'

THE GRAPEVINE

- Keith Richards has been fined £750 for possession of cocaine found in his car during the Stones' UK tour last May.

- Original Fleetwood Mac guitarist Peter Green has been admitted to a mental hospital after trying to shoot a messenger delivering a royalty cheque.

- Patti Smith fell off stage in Florida and has broken her neck.

- Blues guitarist Freddie King, has died of heart failure in Dallas, Texas, aged 42.

MORE THAN A FEELING

From out of Boston – Boston. Their album, released last September, is the fastest-selling debut in history. It went platinum within three months and is now heading for two and a half million US sales.

Tom Scholz – a Massachussetts Institute of Technology graduate who has applied his scientific expertise to the art of rock 'n' roll – is the brains behind this five-piece band. The result is an album of technical perfection influenced by 'a lotta English groups' from The Yardbirds to Queen.

The band were signed to Epic on the strength of a set of demos that were not dissimilar from the finished album, such was Scholz's sophisticated studio technique.

Radio leapt all over their first single, 'More Than A Feeling', and the rest was simply a matter of getting the records into the shops fast enough.

The studious, self-assured Scholz denies accusations that he's a depersonalized rock star. 'Technology had nothing to do with it. "More Than A Feeling" hasn't sold just because it's a good production. I get off playing rock!'

HALL & OATES SWING INTO STYLE

Hall & Oates: blue-eyed soul

Sweet soul musicians and brainiac hard rockers Daryl Hall & John Oates have cracked it with their fifth album, 'Bigger Than Both Of Us', which has yielded their first No. 1 single, 'Rich Girl'.

Nobody's ever doubted the potential of the New York duo who learnt their craft at Gamble & Huff's Sigma Studio, the Philly Sound factory. But packaging their white soul has been more of a problem.

Three albums on Atlantic in the early Seventies with producers as diverse as Arif Mardin and Todd Rundgren achieved nothing but one minor hit with 'She's Gone'.

But a switch to RCA and a more straightforward blend of rock and R&B has been more productive, starting with 'Sara Smile' which reached No. 4.

But there's an ostentation about Hall & Oates that sits uneasily with their music. The latest album has the casually bare-chested duo writing a song together at a table whose designer gets a sleeve credit.

You can rock my soul but you can't ruffle my hairdo . . .

FEBRUARY 1977

CHARTS

US45	Torn Between Two Lovers — *Mary MacGregor*
USLP	Hotel California — *Eagles*
UK45	Don't Give Up On Us — *David Soul*
UKLP	Red River Valley — *Slim Whitman*
WEEK 2	
US45	Torn Between Two Lovers — *Mary MacGregor*
USLP	A Star Is Born — *Barbra Streisand/Kris Kristofferson*
UK45	Don't Cry For Me Argentina — *Julie Covington*
UKLP	Red River Valley — *Slim Whitman*
WEEK 3	
US45	Blinded By The Light — *Manfred Mann's Earth Band*
USLP	A Star Is Born — *Barbra Streisand/Kris Kristofferson*
UK45	Don't Cry For Me Argentina — *Julie Covington*
UKLP	Evita — *Various*
WEEK 4	
US45	New Kid In Town — *Eagles*
USLP	A Star is Born — *Barbra Streisand/Kris Kristofferson*
UK45	When I Need You — *Leo Sayer*
UKLP	20 Golden Greats — *Shadows*

THE GRAPEVINE

■ Led Zeppelin's eagerly awaited US tour – their first since Robert Plant's serious car crash – has been postponed at the last minute after he went down with tonsillitis.

■ Sex Pistols bassist Glen Matlock leaves – his replacement is Sid Vicious.

■ Fleetwood Mac have released their new album 'Rumours'.

■ Debut albums have been released by Blondie, The Damned, Television and Peter Gabriel.

STAR QUOTE

TODD RUNDGREN

'I was driving along in my car one day and this deep voice boomed out of the radio: "Rundgren, your next album will be called Ra. So now we're on this neo-Egyptian trip, a false Sphinx with smoke coming out of it, the works."'

KEITH RICHARDS' TORONTO BUST

Keith Richards' rock 'n' roll lifestyle is catching up with him – in the courts. Just a month after being fined £750 in the UK for possessing cocaine, the Royal Canadian Mounted Police raided his Toronto hotel room and seized 22 grams of heroin and 5 grams of cocaine.

Richards had arrived in Toronto to join the rest of The Stones completing their upcoming live album.

He's been charged with 'intent to traffic', which carries a life sentence. And although he's out on bail, the odds are mounting up against his chances of staying free and The Stones' chances of being able to tour America again.

The Damned: First British punk band to release an album

PISTOLS FIRED TWICE

The Sex Pistols' first contract with EMI lasted three months. Their second with A&M lasted a week.

In one of the most extraordinary turnabouts by any record company, A&M – who signed the group in a blaze of publicity outside Buckingham Palace – reneged on the deal almost before the ink had dried.

A&M would give no reason for their change of heart, but speculation has centred on reports of the group going on a drunken rampage through A&M's offices, complaints from other A&M acts, and a scuffle at London's Speakeasy Club.

Whatever the reasons, 25,000 copies of the band's eagerly-awaited debut single, 'God Save The Queen', have been scrapped. And The Pistols have received another pay-off – this time £75,000, making £125,000 in all this year for very little work indeed.

'But it's not very satisfying to us,' moans manager Malcolm McLaren. 'We want to get back into action.'

THE WHO SEE THE LIGHT

John 'Wiggy' Wolff, the man behind The Who's spectacular lights and laser show, had his own exhibition at London's Royal Academy this month.

Regarded as one of the world's foremost innovators of laser-beam technology, Wolff demonstrated his £250,000 ($500,000) worth of equipment, all paid for by The Who – which makes them the UK's biggest laser owners.

'They're as dangerous as a truck – it depends what you do with them,' says Wolff, who explains that his lasers are very different from the metal-cutting variety. He also takes elaborate precautions to prevent the beam getting anywhere near the eyes of a Who audience.

But that doesn't stop petty bureaucrats giving him a hard time. They tried to stop him at London's Wembley Arena, claiming reflections off the girders would blind the crowd.

'I had to point out to them that the girders hadn't been cleaned in forty years, and nothing was going to reflect off that gunge!' laughs Wolff.

THE GRAPEVINE

- Sara Lowndes Dylan is sueing Bob for divorce.

- The Ramones' 'Carbona Not Glue' track from 'Leave Home' has been cut from the UK version.

- Margaret Trudeau, wife of Canadian Prime Minister Pierre, attended The Rolling Stones' Toronto club shows.

- The Clash have signed to CBS and released their first single, 'White Riot'.

- Fleetwood Mac's 'Rumours' has gone platinum after a month.

GRAHAM PARKER'S HEAT TREATMENT

Graham Parker: a mod, a hippy and now surrounded by Rumours

Graham Parker ain't no punk. In fact he used to be a hippy, 'but a sneering one'.

But he has all the energy of punk and his second album, 'Heat Treatment', recorded in two tight weeks, is a superb example of his sweat 'n' sneakers rock 'n' roll that typifies the London pub and club scene.

'I saw The Damned once and I didn't like them,' Parker admits. 'They were the kind of band I used to watch when I was eating brown rice. They had this huge rush of energy but no tenderness. I prefer Gladys Knight & The Pips, because they move me.'

Before he was a hippy, Graham Parker was an Otis Redding-fixated mod which explains some of the aggression in his music and lyrics.

As the title track of the new album puts it: 'Out in the jungle there's a war going down/You wind up eating all the friends you've found.'

And as he himself says: 'I know what it's like to be woken up by a copper at two in the morning.'

Mirror mirror on the wall . . .

CHARTS

US45	Evergreen	Barbra Streisand
USLP	A Star Is Born	Barbra Streisand/Kris Kristofferson
UK45	When I Need You	Leo Sayer
UKLP	20 Golden Greats	Shadows
	WEEK 2	
US45	Evergreen	Barbra Streisand
USLP	A Star Is Born	Barbra Streisand/Kris Kristofferson
UK45	Chanson D'Amour	Manhattan Transfer
UKLP	20 Golden Greats	Shadows
	WEEK 3	
US45	Evergreen	Barbra Streisand
USLP	A Star Is Born	Barbra Streisand/Kris Kristofferson
UK45	Chanson D'Amour	Manhattan Transfer
UKLP	20 Golden Greats	Shadows
	WEEK 4	
US45	Rich Girl	Daryl Hall & John Oates
USLP	Hotel California	Eagles
UK45	Knowing Me, Knowing You	Abba
UKLP	20 Golden Greats	Shadows

TOWER BLOCK ROCK

No compromise, just commitment – live hostilities from the Clash

'It ain't punk. It ain't new wave. It's the next step, and the logical progression for groups to move. Call it what you want – all the terms stink. Just call it rock 'n' roll' – Mick Jones, guitarist.

'I ain't gonna fuck myself up like I seen those other guys fuck themselves up. Keeping all their money for themselves and getting into their heads, and thinking they're the greatest. I've planned what I'm gonna do with my money if it happens. Secret plans' – Joe Strummer, vocals/ guitar.

The Clash are not just a band. They are a commitment. Bassist and former South London skinhead Paul Simenon knew what he was doing when he named them. One of the first bands he saw was The Sex Pistols. He is a pure Seventies child.

Their no-compromise attitude has got them an uncompromising deal with CBS and an equally uncompromising debut album.

But it's also cost them a drummer, and finding the right replacement – musically and personally – is proving a problem. Particularly when there's gigs to be played. Or, as Mick Jones calls them, 'the hostilities'.

'I don't believe in guitar heroes,' he says. 'If I walk out to the front of the stage it's because I wanna reach the audience. I don't want them to suck my guitar off.'

THE SPLITS THAT BIND FLEETWOOD MAC

'Being in Fleetwood Mac is more like being in group therapy!'

So says drummer and leader Mick Fleetwood, and he should know. Just as the band achieved breakthrough with their 'Fleetwood Mac' album, they went into an emotional tailspin.

Long-standing singer/pianist Christine McVie split from bassist/husband John mid-way through an American tour.

Lindsey Buckingham and Stevie Nicks stopped sharing a room soon after. And then Mick Fleetwood's own marriage broke up, although he has since salvaged it.

Scarcely the right atmosphere in which to record 'Rumours', the follow-up to their four-million selling album.

'It turned out to be the reverse,' says Mick. 'Because it all came out in the music. Things never got bitchy. Sure, the atmosphere was confused – to say the least – but it wasn't destructive. We could all relate to each other's desperation.'

CHARTS

US45	Rich Girl *Daryl Hall & John Oates*
USLP	Rumours *Fleetwood Mac*
UK45	Knowing Me, Knowing You *Abba*
UKLP	20 Golden Greats *Shadows*

——— W E E K 2 ———

US45	Dancing Queen *Abba*
USLP	Rumours *Fleetwood Mac*
UK45	Knowing Me, Knowing You *Abba*
UKLP	Portrait Of Sinatra *Frank Sinatra*

——— W E E K 3 ———

US45	Don't Give Up On Us *David Soul*
USLP	Hotel California *Eagles*
UK45	Knowing Me, Knowing You *Abba*
UKLP	Arrival *Abba*

——— W E E K 4 ———

US45	Don't Leave Me This Way *Thelma Houston*
USLP	Hotel California *Eagles*
UK45	Knowing Me, Knowing You *Abba*
UKLP	Arrival *Abba*

——— W E E K 5 ———

US45	Southern Nights *Glen Campbell*
USLP	Hotel California *Eagles*
UK45	Knowing Me, Knowing You *Abba*
UKLP	Arrival *Abba*

THE GRAPEVINE

■ Bruce Springsteen's ex-manager Mike Appel has won an injunction against The Boss's recording, pending the outcome of their dispute.

■ Studio 54, an exclusive disco, has opened in New York.

■ The Damned have become the first British punk band to play New York.

■ New albums: Iggy Pop ('The Idiot'), The Beach Boys ('Love You'), The Stranglers ('Rattus Norvegicus') and ELP ('Works').

Muddy's mojo working

MUDDY WATERS – HARD AGAIN

Muddy Waters was nearly 50 when The Rolling Stones started picking up on his records. He's just turned 62, and has come up with an album that can still teach his students a thing or two.

The aptly titled 'Hard Again' finds Muddy getting back to the Fifties style he perfected in the tough Chicago clubs. And the man responsible for getting that sound out of him again is Johnny Winter.

Muddy's respect for Winter knows no bounds. 'I figured this was my greatest chance, man, of all my days, to get with somebody who's still got it, got that early Fifties sound. This is one of the best records I've made in a long time.'

STAR QUOTE

DENNIS WILSON

'There'd be many times when I'd look at my brother and think to myself, maybe he won't ever pull it together again. Brian went through a lot of bad times. Drugs didn't help.'

VIRGIN SAVES THE SEX PISTOLS

After weeks of speculation, The Sex Pistols have signed their third record deal in less than six months. Virgin are the brave label to take them on, and their new single, 'God Save The Queen' is out at the end of the month – just in time for the Queen's Silver Jubilee celebrations across the UK.

Advance orders are described as 'massive', but Virgin's marketing campaign has already been restricted by TV's refusal to run an ad for the record. And the chances of daytime radio play look slim.

Live gigs are a problem too, thanks to squeamish promoters. And other bands such as The Stranglers are being deemed 'unsuitable' at several provincial venues around the UK.

Not without some cause either. A Clash/Jam show at London's Rainbow Theatre resulted in 200 trashed seats, although there was little other damage. In fact, as riots go, it was an orderly one.

STEVE MILLER TAKES THE MONEY AND RUNS

When you finally get a hit after six years of trying, leaving a two-and-a-half year gap before you release another album scarcely makes sense – unless you're Steve Miller.

Exhausted by touring, Miller came off the road, took up farming and secured a better record deal before going back into the studio.

The next album, 'Fly Like an Eagle', spawned three hit singles – 'Take The Money And Run', 'Fly Like An Eagle' and 'Rock 'n' Me' – and is approaching four million sales. Miller has stripped his late Sixties San Francisco psychedelia down to a pure pop R&B sound that's a natural for the charts.

Not surprisingly his new album, 'Book Of Dreams', sticks closely to the formula. 'I feel I have a pretty good understanding of what a lot of people will like,' he says. 'I know how to make records, produce records, sing lots of parts and make this little thing that's music. I'm a craftsman.'

STAR QUOTE

JOHNNY RAMONE
The Ramones

'We usually wear out our audience before we wear out ourselves. And we're getting faster every day. Our first album sounds real slow now.'

CHARTS

US45	Hotel California	Eagles
USLP	Hotel California	Eagles
UK45	Free	Deniece Williams
UKLP	Arrival	Abba
— WEEK 2 —		
US45	When I Need You	Leo Sayer
USLP	Hotel California	Eagles
UK45	Free	Deniece Williams
UKLP	Arrival	Abba
— WEEK 3 —		
US45	Sir Duke	Stevie Wonder
USLP	Rumours	Fleetwood Mac
UK45	Free	Deniece Williams
UKLP	Arrival	Abba
— WEEK 4 —		
US45	Sir Duke	Stevie Wonder
USLP	Rumours	Fleetwood Mac
UK45	I Don't Want To Talk About It	Rod Stewart
UKLP	Hotel California	Eagles

Linda keeps her clothes on

SHARP DRESSED PUNKS

The Jam fly the flag just like the Who did back in the '60s

'We're the black sheep of the new wave,' asserts Paul Weller, singer and guitarist with The Jam.

For a start, their mohair suits and tight playing owe more to the Sixties beat groups than the new wave. They're not afraid of their influences either. Otis Redding is Weller's favourite singer. Bassist Bruce Foxton admits to listening to Bad Company and Thin Lizzy, while drummer Rick Buckler even confesses to owning a couple of Genesis albums.

The Jam have been together a couple of years, starting off covering Chuck Berry and progressing to Mersey Beat and soul. Even now they include 'Midnight Hour', 'Sweet Soul Music' and The Who's 'So Sad About Us' in their set.

'I didn't want to work,' says Weller. 'I didn't want to become Mister Normal.

'For the first time in years I realized that there was a younger audience there, young bands playing to young people. It was something we'd been looking for in a long time.'

Their first single, 'In The City', is the perfect response: a genuine late Seventies teen anthem.

THE GRAPEVINE

■ Led Zeppelin have broken their own world record for the largest audience at a single-act gig – 76,000 at Michigan's Pontiac Silverdome.

■ Bruce Springsteen has settled out of court with former manager Mike Appel who gets a million dollars. Springsteen gets his freedom.

■ ELP have started a US tour with a 72-piece orchestra.

■ Linda Ronstadt has turned down a nude modelling offer from *Hustler*.

VAN MORRISON – EXPECT THE UNEXPECTED

Van Morrison's first album for three years is rightly called 'A Period Of Transition'. After nearly a decade's exile in California, Van the Man is resident in his native Ireland once more.

The album too is back to his R&B roots; he sounds more like a singer with a club band than a singer/songwriter with a backing band. It's unpredictable, which is not what a lot of his fans want.

But the normally reclusive Van is unrepentant: 'People begin to get a preconceived idea about a particular artist and that can work against you . . . most definitely. I think I need to break a lot of that expectancy down.

'Quite recently I dug out all my old blues records, and there's something about that music that still turns me on. But you see, I was in that singer/songwriter phase . . . progression . . . what have you . . . I ain't knockin' it,

but I realized I was missing out on all the many other things I can do and, more important, enjoy doing.

'The moment you start to think you're one thing, you're not.'

'BANNED' SEX PISTOLS SINGLE IN THE CHARTS

Despite a blanket airplay ban across the UK, The Sex Pistols' 'God Save The Queen' single has reached No. 1, even though several chain stores are refusing to stock the record.

Chart shows are mentioning the single without playing it, although one station is pretending it doesn't exist.

The Pistols attempted to get round their concert ban by hiring a boat and sailing down the River Thames, playing at their own private party. But when they arrived back, the police were waiting for them. Eleven people were arrested, several more beaten up.

Within a week The Pistols became everybody's whipping boys – literally. Johnny Rotten was slashed by a razor outside a North London pub and needed stitches. And Paul Cook was attacked at a tube station by a gang who identified him as a Sex Pistol. He too needed stitches in hospital.

Boomtown Rats looking for No 1

DODGING THE RAT TRAP

Irish punks – some kind of joke? No, The Boomtown Rats actually.

Led by Bob Geldof, who's been described as 'a Jagger for the New Depression', they've broken out of Ireland by being abnormal – giving away raw liver as prizes at their gigs, letting live rats out into the audience, showing blue movies at their gigs and, when promoters got scared, hiring a truck and playing in the streets.

'We've definitely come from

the R&B thing, but we've swung off it,' declares Geldof. Their demo was good enough to secure a deal and they've already recorded an album. But they're waiting until they're better known before releasing it.

'We want a credibility that definitely comes from people who see the band,' says Geldof. 'If people come to see you because you've been hyped and you're not what they expected, they get disappointed.'

THE GRAPEVINE

■ The UK's punk gig ban is spreading, with The Damned, The Stranglers and The Jam all having dates cancelled.

■ Two members of The Clash were arrested after painting their names on a London wall.

■ Alice Cooper's boa constrictor died when it was bitten by its rat dinner.

■ Stevie Wonder has played his first show for a year and a half - to students at UCLA.

Alice looking for rat poison

WAITING FOR WINWOOD

At 15, Steve Winwood was a precocious pop star with The Spencer Davis Group. Since then he's been a rock star in Traffic and a superstar in Blind Faith. But it's taken him a while to summon up the confidence to record his first solo album.

'I had a lot of material ready and waiting, but I couldn't force myself any further. I couldn't see any reason, any real justification for doing it,' says Winwood.

He brought in his Traffic buddy and lyricist Jim Capaldi on four of the six tracks. Which makes you wonder why he broke up Traffic in the first place?

'There wasn't the cohesion to keep it together, and there were various personal problems which are best forgotten. I wasn't committed any more, and I felt that we'd achieved as much as we could with that version of the group.'

Winwood's impetus has slowed since he moved into the country. Even he admits that he's lost that sense of desperation that 'makes strong music'. Some of it also comes from rejecting the rock-star-making machinery.

'There was a time when I was ambitious in that sense, but not now. It can mess you up. I somehow doubt it did anyone any good in the long run.'

THE GRAPEVINE

■ The Sex Pistols have rush-released their new single, 'Pretty Vacant', but despite the assistance of airplay and TV it's failed to emulate 'God Save The Queen'.

■ 19-year-old Patrick Coultry has been stabbed to death at a Dublin punk gig.

■ Local councils are continuing to ban many punk gigs around the UK in response to random outbreaks of violence.

■ The Who have bought Shepperton Film Studios.

LED ZEPPELIN JINXED

Led Zeppelin's ill-fated US tour has collapsed in tragedy and violence.

The tragedy happened in England where Robert Plant's five-year-old son Karac died suddenly, while being treated for a stomach ailment. Plant immediately flew home from New Orleans, and the rest of the tour was cancelled.

The violence happened backstage at the group's previous show at the Oakland Coliseum. John Bonham, manager Peter Grant and two other Zeppelin employees were involved in a fight with two of promoter Bill Graham's security staff, one of whom was seriously beaten.

Police have charged all four with assault and Graham, America's top promoter, says he 'can never in all conscience book the band again.'

The tour – the first following Robert Plant's recovery from injuries received in a car accident nearly two years ago – was postponed when Plant went down with 'flu just before the first date. Chicago concerts were also postponed when Jimmy Page became ill.

With Bonham and Grant facing arrest if they return to America, and Plant grieving for his son, it's uncertain when or whether Zeppelin will return to complete the tour.

Manchester's Buzzcocks, part of the Roxy scene immortalized in vital vinyl

A DIFFERENT ROXY MUSIC

The birthplace of the London punk scene was the seedy Roxy Club, and its birth pangs have been captured for posterity on a live album called 'The Roxy London WC2 (Jan-Apr 77)' which was recorded documentary-style over four days in early April. Hi fi it ain't, but enough nostalgic punks(!) have bought it to push it into the UK Top 20.

The club still books punk acts, but most of the 'elite' bands have shunned it, or grown out of it.

STAR QUOTE

STEVE HARLEY

'I set out to be a winner. I don't want to lose. I spent four years in a hospital but I never expected favours from anyone. I don't give sympathy because I don't expect it. Nice guys don't make it.'

Steve Harley looking for favours

ELVIS IS DEAD . . .

The King of Rock 'n' Roll is dead.

Elvis Presley was found lying on his bathroom floor at his Memphis home in the early hours of August 16 and, despite efforts to resuscitate him, was pronounced dead at Memphis Baptist Memorial Hospital.

Within hours, thousands of people gathered outside the gates of Graceland and the scene was set for the biggest media event of the decade. 75,000 people were present for his funeral two days later, when he was laid to rest in a white marble mausoleum near his mother.

Speculation over the cause of Presley's heart-attack is rife. His health had been deteriorating for the past four years. He was hospitalized five times for intestinal

Elvis Aaron Presley. Born January 8, 1935. Died August 16, 1977

problems, eye trouble, recurrent 'flu and fatigue. No amount of skilful tailoring could disguise the fact that he was overweight, and there were incessant rumours of drug abuse.

But none of this matters to his millions of fans. Within a week, the second biggest selling artist of all time was back in the singles and album charts around the world as fans rushed out to buy whatever they could.

However, it is believed that RCA will not be releasing an 'instant' memorial album.

As President Jimmy Carter says, 'Elvis Presley's death deprives our country of a part of itself.'

CHARTS

US45	I Just Want To Be Your Everything *Andy Gibb*
USLP	Rumours *Fleetwood Mac*
UK45	I Feel Love *Donna Summer*
UKLP	The Johnny Mathis Collection *Johnny Mathis*

— WEEK 2 —

US45	I Just Want To Be Your Everything *Andy Gibb*
USLP	Rumours *Fleetwood Mac*
UK45	I Feel Love *Donna Summer*
UKLP	The Johnny Mathis Collection *Johnny Mathis*

— WEEK 3 —

US45	Best Of My Love *Emotions*
USLP	Rumours *Fleetwood Mac*
UK45	I Feel Love *Donna Summer*
UKLP	Going For The One *Yes*

— WEEK 4 —

US45	Best Of My Love *Emotions*
USLP	Rumours *Fleetwood Mac*
UK45	Angelo *Brotherhood Of Man*
UKLP	Going For The One *Yes*

STAR QUOTE

JOHNNY ROTTEN

'Turn the other cheek too often and you get a razor through it.'

. . . LONG LIVE ELVIS !

Most singer/songwriters write about love and romance. Not Elvis Costello.

'The only two things that matter to me, the only motivation points for me writing all these songs, are revenge and guilt,' he claims. 'Those are the only two emotions I know about. Love? I dunno what it means really, and it doesn't exist in my songs.'

Elvis Costello has just released his debut album, 'My Aim Is True', on the bubbling UK indie label Stiff Records. But that doesn't mean he's feeling talkative. He refuses to give any details about his background (Liverpool) or his past career as a member of country/rock combo Flip City and as a folk singer.

His demo was the first that Stiff bosses Dave Robinson and Jake Riviera listened to when they set up shop. They were so impressed they had to listen to a week's worth of dross before they could believe they weren't dreaming.

Elvis hates trendies, won't allow other guitar players on stage with him, keeps a 'black book' of enemies and scrutinizes guest lists to cross off 'undesirables'.

Despite his motivation, his musical passion is country music - particularly George Jones and Gram Parsons.

'Parsons had it all sussed – he did his best work and then he died. I'm never going to stick around long enough to churn out a bunch of mediocre crap like all those guys from the Sixties. I don't intend to be around to watch my artistic decline.'

Elvis Costello takes aim

1977

US45	Best Of My Love *Emotions*
USLP	Rumours *Fleetwood Mac*
UK45	Way Down *Elvis Presley*
UKLP	Moody Blue *Elvis Presley*

—— W E E K 2 ——

US45	Best Of My Love *Emotions*
USLP	Rumours *Fleetwood Mac*
UK45	Magic Fly *Space*
UKLP	Oxygene *Jean Michel Jarre*

—— W E E K 3 ——

US45	Best Of My Love *Emotions*
USLP	Rumours *Fleetwood Mac*
UK45	Magic Fly *Space*
UKLP	Oxygene *Jean Michel Jarre*

—— W E E K 4 ——

US45	Best Of My Love *Emotions*
USLP	Rumours *Fleetwood Mac*
UK45	Magic Fly *Space*
UKLP	20 Golden Greats *Diana Ross & The Supremes*

THE BOYS ARE BACK IN TOWN

Phil Lynott (left) of Thin Lizzy: all the ego a rock star needs

A black Irishman, a Roman Catholic with a decidedly irreligious lifestyle, a bass-playing poet in a rock 'n' roll band called Thin Lizzy – that's Phil Lynott.

A couple of years ago, Thin Lizzy were considered hapless losers. But with the new wave sweeping aside the old guard, Thin Lizzy have come into their own. Their image may be slightly *passé*, but they possess that vital chemistry that marks all great bands.

Their 'Jailbreak' album and hard-assed rockin' stage show have cracked it for them in the UK. And they'd be doing better in America right now if Lynott hadn't gone down with hepatitis mid-way through a tour that was successfully breaking the album there too.

The songs Phil's written for the new album, 'Bad Reputation', were composed while he was recuperating. They are 'more mellow', but his vanity remains undaunted.

'The main thing that pushes me to write songs is to share my personal experiences. Plus the sheer ego of thinking my life is so important it should be shared!' he grins.

RANDY NEWMAN – GUNNING FOR SHORT PEOPLE

Randy Newman is a master of black comedy. Such a master that he frequently gets misunderstood. His last album, 'Good Ole Boys', was labelled 'racialist' in *Rolling Stone* magazine.

While his songs have successfully been covered by a wide variety of artists, his own records have been less successful. Despite praise from the likes of Dylan and McCartney, Newman remains a cult hero – not least because of his prolonged bouts of inactivity.

He's currently putting the vocals on his new album, 'Little Criminals'.

'There's one about a child murderer,' Newman deadpans. 'That's fairly optimistic. Maybe. There's one called "Jolly Coppers On Parade" which isn't an absolutely anti-police song. Maybe it's even a fascist song. I didn't notice at the time.

'There's also this one about me as a cowboy called "Rider In The Rain". I think it's ridiculous. The Eagles are on there. That's what's good about it. There's also this song "Short People". It's purely a joke. I like other ones on the album better but the audiences go for that one.'

Wonder if short people will get the joke?

MARC BOLAN KILLED IN CAR CRASH

- Bob Marley had part of his right big toe removed in a 'routine' operation in Miami. The toe had failed to heal after a football accident.

- Guitarist Jimmy McCulloch has left Wings.

- 110,000 hippies fought back against the new wave, attending a Grateful Dead/New Riders Of The Purple Sage/Marshall Tucker Band concert at Old Bridge, New Jersey.

Marc Bolan, the pixie in T. Rex who spanned psychedelia and glam rock and was on the verge of a solo comeback, has been killed in a car accident.

He was a passenger in the yellow Mini being driven by his girlfriend, singer Gloria Jones, when the car spun off a wet road on Barnes Common, south-west London, and crashed into a tree. Bolan was killed instantly, and Gloria was rushed to hospital with a broken jaw.

Bolan scored a string of UK hits in the early Seventies with such songs as 'Hot Love', and 'Get It On', but failed to repeat the success in America where he became a tax exile.

He'd just started his British comeback, touring with The Damned and filming a TV series.

STAR QUOTE

SOUTHSIDE JOHNNY

'Rock 'n' roll should be made by truck drivers from Tupelo, Mississippi, not studio musicians with an album commitment to fulfil.'

Song titles on Randy Newman's 'Little Criminals' album include 'Sigmund Freud's Impersonation of Albert Einstein in America', 'Texas Girl at the Funeral Of Her Father' and 'Kathleen (Catholicism Made Easy)'. Rock and roll huh?

PETER GABRIEL'S RE-GENESIS

'I was going to take a bet that I wouldn't be back on the road within a couple of years of leaving Genesis,' smiles Peter Gabriel. 'I kept on with the songwriting, but I wasn't interested in performing.

'Then once the songs came out, I got back into recording and started enjoying it. And here I am on the road again!'

Gabriel is playing his first solo shows since quitting Genesis, who were on the brink of major success after nearly a decade of hard graft. Speculation continues to surround his departure, but in essence he simply wanted to make his music in a different way.

His debut solo album has yielded a hit single, 'Solsbury Hill'. And now he's touring the UK with a show that's essentially musical rather than visual.

'It would have been quite easy for me to develop a visual show, but I felt I needed to try and base it on my music and my performance.'

Which is why his show doesn't include any Genesis numbers but does feature covers of The Kinks' 'All Day And All Of The Night' and Marvin Gaye's 'I Heard It Through The Grapevine' and 'Ain't That Peculiar'.

'I'm not that interested in being a mythical superstar,' he explains. 'I would like to be a successful one, but the opportunity to live out that image doesn't appeal to me.'

Peter Gabriel has climbed Solsbury Hill leaving Genesis far behind him

NO MORE HEROES?

'In 1977, rock has become very much a gladiatorial sport,' avers Jean-Jacques Burnel, bass player of The Stranglers, the most successful chart band of the British new wave.

And yet The Stranglers' punk credentials are shaky to say the least. It's not just their ages which are closer to the old wave than the new. There's a strain of chauvinism and macho bravado about songs like 'Bring On The Nubiles' that sits uncomfortably with what the new wave is supposed to be about.

And then there's their private army of minders and hangers on, the Finchley Boys, whose gang mentality is definitely suspect.

The Stranglers are the perfect band for supplying reassurance to the nightmare of adolescent insecurity. Which goes a long way to explaining their huge popularity in Britain.

'We're up there singing "No More Heroes" and in front of us thousands of kids are going crazy,' muses singer Hugh Cornwell. 'It's almost as if we're perpetuating the very myth we set out to destroy.'

ROCK 'N' ROLL WITH THE MODERN LOVERS

Jonathan Richman certainly has the rock critics in a spin. Three of them are pacing the back of London's Hammersmith Odeon earnestly debating his status as a new wave messiah. Meanwhile, the object of their attention is crawling round the stage on all fours singing 'I'm A Little Dinosaur'!

The first 'Modern Lovers' album contained two Seventies rock classics – 'Roadrunner' and 'Pablo Picasso'. But subsequent albums have revealed a twee, naïve charm that's harder to take seriously.

At the Hammersmith Odeon, the boy from Boston sings 'Ice Cream Man', repeating the last verse five times to increasingly rapturous applause.

Lynyrd Skynyrd RIP

THE GRAPEVINE

■ Lynyrd Skynyrd have been wiped out by an air-crash in Mississippi which killed singer Ronnie Van Zant, guitarist Steve Gaines and his sister, backing singer Cassie and critically injured three others.

■ Guitarist Steve Hackett has quit Genesis on the eve of their live double 'Seconds Out'. The remaining three pledge to continue.

■ Damned drummer Rat Scabies has quit the band.

1977

CHARTS

US45	You Light Up My Life	*Debby Boone*
USLP	Rumours	*Fleetwood Mac*
UK45	Yes Sir I Can Boogie	*Baccara*
UKLP	20 Golden Greats	*Diana Ross & The Supremes*

— WEEK 2 —

US45	You Light Up My LIfe	*Debby Boone*
USLP	Rumours	*Fleetwood Mac*
UK45	Name Of The Game	*Abba*
UKLP	The Sound Of Bread	*Bread*

— WEEK 3 —

US45	You Light Up My Life	*Debby Boone*
USLP	Rumours	*Fleetwood Mac*
UK45	Name Of The Game	*Abba*
UKLP	The Sound Of Bread	*Bread*

— WEEK 4 —

US45	You Light Up My Life	*Debby Boone*
USLP	Rumours	*Fleetwood Mac*
UK45	Rockin' All Over The World	*Status Quo*
UKLP	The Sound Of Bread	*Bread*

Jazz-rock giants Weather Report

BOWIE IST EIN BERLINER

David Bowie has retreated from the excesses of his 'Station To Station' tour and *The Man Who Fell To Earth* movie to Berlin – scarcely an auspicious choice for someone whose recent utterances have shown a disturbing flirtation with fascism.

But he went to Berlin to experience the claustrophobic isolation of a city surrounded by barbed wire. And at the Hansa Studio – 20 yards from the Berlin Wall – he has recorded two albums that signal a dramatic shift in his musical style: 'Low' and 'Heroes'.

'The initial period of living in Berlin produced "Low",' explains Bowie. 'The first side of "Low" was all about me. "Always Crashing In The Same Car" and all that self-pitying crap. But side two was more of a musical observation – my reaction to seeing the Eastern bloc, how West Berlin survives in the middle of it, which is something I couldn't express in words. It required textures instead.

'It's also a reaction to that dull greeny-grey limelight of American rock and its repercussions; pulling myself out of it and getting to Europe and saying: "For God's sake re-evaluate why you wanted to get into this in the first place. Did you really want to clown around in LA?

'"Find some people you don't understand and a place you don't want to be and just put yourself into it. Force yourself to buy some groceries . . .".'

THE GRAPEVINE

■ Ozzy Osbourne has quit Black Sabbath, who have decided to carry on without him.

■ Elton John announced his 'retirement' during a concert.

■ Veteran Scottish rocker Alex Harvey has also retired.

■ *The Last Waltz*, Martin Scorsese's film of The Band's farewell concert, has been premiered in New York.

■ The Sex Pistols have released their debut album, 'Never Mind The Bollocks, Here's The Sex Pistols'.

BOB SEGER – GETTING OUT OF DETROIT

Bob Seger is the greatest local success story in the history of rock 'n' roll. He is massive in Michigan, his home state. In Detroit he plays to audiences of 90,000 and his albums outsell The Stones, Zeppelin, anyone you care to mention.

Outside Michigan his progress has been slower, mainly because record companies have found it difficult to market his albums of steaming rockers and gritty ballads about the pangs of life on the road.

But his 'Live Bullet' double album, recorded in front of a partisan Detroit crowd finally caught Seger's power and energy. And one of his finest rockers, the breakneck 'Get Out Of Denver', has been adopted by more than one British new wave band.

WEATHER OUTLOOK FINE

Joe Zawinul and Wayne Shorter, both in their mid-forties are the leaders of the most successful jazz group of the Seventies. Weather Report sell enough albums to get into the charts these days, but they're still willing to take chances.

They were both in Miles Davis' epoch-making band of the late Sixties that produced 'In A Silent Way' and 'Bitches Brew' and pulled jazz into the new decade.

'Jazz had become so boring,' says Zawinul. 'Sly Stone and Jimi Hendrix had this other quality, an attitude that jazz unfortunately didn't have. Now we're reaching the people on the streets. Not the critics but the people. And we don't play down to the people, ever.'

JOHNNY WINTER'S WOES

The world's whitest blues player is finally getting it together – after eight years of heavy rock, drug addiction and suicidal depression.

Johnny Winter is a Texas albino who played the blues as sweet as any black guitarist. But just as he was starting to make it in New York, he began to be compared with Cream and Hendrix instead of Muddy Waters and Otis Rush. He got waylaid into heavy metal and heavy drugs, but never stopped playing the blues. In fact, he played them better because he was in such mental anguish.

'I thought of myself as the best white blues player around. In my own mind I was sure of that. But I never thought of myself as Jimi Hendrix or Cream. I loved them both but I wasn't trying to compete,' he says.

It took nine months to get the monkey off his back, and what completed his cure was producing and playing on Muddy Waters' 'Hard Again' album.

He's also toured with Muddy, although he has to keep a wary eye on the road these days. 'I won't stay out there more than six weeks at a time. I couldn't handle it.'

HOLIDAYS IN THE UK

The Sex Pistols have ended 1977 in the same way they ended 1976 – in a blaze of controversy.

London's Capital Radio got the ball rolling by banning the group's 'Holidays In The Sun' single because the lyrics likened Belsen to a holiday camp. EMI then got in on the act, suggesting a track on the 'Never Mind The Bollocks' album might be an infringement of copyright.

Nottingham police had a go at taking a local shop to court for displaying the album, claiming that the word 'bollocks' was indecent. Two expensive attorneys and a few star witnesses later, the case was dismissed.

A week later, Sid Vicious and his American girlfriend Nancy Spungen were arrested following the discovery of 'certain substances' in their London hotel room. Police were called after complaints of a 'disturbance'.

But at least the band have been able to get round the unofficial ban that prevents them from playing in the UK. They lined up a series of 'secret' gigs over the Christmas period – including one on Christmas day – that passed off without incident.

But they've now got problems in the States. They were denied a visa to visit New York for a TV show two days before they were due to fly.

Ian Dury salutes the perverse

CHARTS		
US45	You Light Up My Life	*Debby Boone*
USLP	Rumours	*Fleetwood Mac*
UK45	Mull Of Kintyre	*Wings*
UKLP	The Sound Of Bread	*Bread*
WEEK 2		
US45	You Light Up My Life	*Debby Boone*
USLP	Simple Dreams	*Linda Ronstadt*
UK45	Mull Of Kintyre	*Wings*
UKLP	The Sound Of Bread	*Bread*
WEEK 3		
US45	You Light Up My Life	*Debby Boone*
USLP	Simple Dreams	*Linda Ronstadt*
UK45	Mull Of Kintyre	*Wings*
UKLP	Disco Fever	*Various*
WEEK 4		
US45	How Deep Is Your Love	*Bee Gees*
USLP	Simple Dreams	*Linda Ronstadt*
UK45	Mull Of Kintyre	*Wings*
UKLP	Disco Fever	*Various*
WEEK 5		
US45	How Deep Is Your Love	*Bee Gees*
USLP	Simple Dreams	*Linda Ronstadt*
UK45	Mull Of Kintyre	*Wings*
UKLP	Disco Fever	*Various*

Macca mulling in Kintyre

THE GRAPEVINE

■ The Who have played a 'secret' gig in London for their *Kids Are Alright* film rockumentary.

■ Elvis Costello, banned from singing 'Radio Radio' on *Saturday*

Night Live in the US because of its caustic comments on the radio industry, sang it anyway.

■ Wings' 'Mull Of Kintyre' has topped the UK Xmas charts to become the biggest selling British single in history.

■ Jazz instrumentalist Rahsaan Roland Kirk has died, aged 41.

BUZZCOCKS – POP PUNKS

The Buzzcocks played their first gig supporting The Sex Pistols, a month after they'd formed in June '76. But it's taken them a lot longer to get signed.

'If we'd come from London, we'd have been signed a year ago, and we wouldn't be in the position we are now,' asserts Pete Shelley who, like the rest of the band, hails from Manchester.

Their first single, 'Orgasm Addict', wasn't so much banned as simply never played on the radio. And their London gigs have been few and far between. Even so, they were included in the legendary 'Roxy' compilation.

The Buzzcocks play love songs. The love may be bitter, vitriolic and vengeful, but it's still love.

'There's bitterness in our songs, yeah,' concedes Shelley. 'But there's hope in them too.'

Buzzcocks: no radio orgasms

JANUARY

1978

PIANO MAN GROWS UP

Billy Joel's latest press release calls him a '28-year-old former punk'. Previous descriptions include a 'poor man's Elton John', but he's neither.

Billy Joel played on the Shangri Las' 'Leader Of The Pack' and became a songwriter. He grafted and got his first hit in 1973 with 'Piano Man'. That made him a singer-songwriter and he's still grafting, on the road and in the studio.

His songs have developed a cool, cosmopolitan, urban feel, although he's not afraid to bite the hand that buys him on his latest album, 'Turnstiles', mocking hip radicalism, the decadence of modern luxury and nostalgia.

'Nostalgia's unhealthy. I don't remember the young days to be all that great. Yeah, we had fun but we live now.'

SEX PISTOLS SPLIT

At the beginning of the month, The Sex Pistols started their first US tour. At the end of the month the group are in tatters – Johnny Rotten back home in disgust having been fired, Sid Vicious rushed to hospital in Los Angeles having been carried unconscious off a plane, and Steve Jones and Paul Cook down in Brazil making a video with train robber and celebrated British fugitive Ronnie Biggs.

The Pistols' US tour quickly turned into a fiasco with the media looking for any excuse, and the FBI just looking. Sid Vicious's behaviour became increasingly unpredictable. They were banned by American Airlines and the Holiday Inn chain. And they'd stopped talking to each other.

The final break-up occurred

<table>
<tr><td>

STAR QUOTE
JOHNNY ROTTEN

'Love is 2 minutes and 50 seconds of squelching noises.'

</td></tr>
</table>

over manager Malcolm McLaren's plan to fly the band to Brazil and hook up with Ronnie Biggs – which was one publicity stunt too many for Rotten. At a showdown in San Francisco, McLaren accused Rotten of 'behaving like a constructive cissy rather than a destructive lunatic'.

Rotten stormed out and flew back to England via New York, Vicious flew back via an OD, and Cook and Jones went with the stunt. The only sure thing is that this may be the end of The Sex Pistols, but it isn't the end of the story.

BANSHEES HOLD OUT

Siouxsie & The Banshees are the last great unsigned UK punk band. They were in the audience at the earliest Sex Pistols' gigs and formed their band soon after. They even had Sid Vicious as a drummer to start with.

But while their contemporaries have taken the first reasonable record company bait that was offered, Siouxsie & The Banshees have held out, preferring to sell out gigs rather than their souls.

Their Teutonic style and occasional flirtations with Nazi regalia have stirred up strong feelings – which are perhaps calculated, because they themselves give away no feelings of exhilaration, exhaustion or even frustration on stage.

They play sound, rather than music. 'We go out of our way not to be musicians. We don't rehearse til our fingers bleed. We can play rock'n'roll but we ignore it. We're out on a limb. It's dangerous but it excites us, makes it worth while.'

<table>
<tr><td>

THE GRAPEVINE

■ EMI have censored The Buzzcocks 'Oh Shit', the B-side of 'What Do I Get' single, but they OK'd Tom Robinsons's 'Glad To Be Gay'.

■ Thin Lizzy guitarist Brian Robertson, who damaged his left hand in a brawl a year ago has split open his right hand on a flick knife in a pub.

■ Original Fleetwood Mac guitarist Peter Green has played his first gig since quitting a decade ago.

</td></tr>
</table>

CHARTS

US45	How Deep Is Your Love	*Bee Gees*
USLP	Rumours	*Fleetwood Mac*
UK45	Mull Of Kintyre	*Wings*
UKLP	Disco Fever	*Various*
	— WEEK 2 —	
US45	Baby Come Back	*Player*
USLP	Saturday Night Fever	*Soundtrack*
UK45	Mull Of Kintyre	*Wings*
UKLP	Disco Fever	*Various*
	— WEEK 3 —	
US45	Baby Come Back	*Player*
USLP	Saturday Night Fever	*Soundtrack*
UK45	Mull Of Kintyre	*Wings*
UKLP	Rumours	*Fleetwood Mac*
	— WEEK 4 —	
US45	Baby Come Back	*Player*
USLP	Saturday Night Fever	*Soundtrack*
UK45	Mull Of Kintyre	*Wings*
UKLP	Rumours	*Fleetwood Mac*

Brian Robertson (left) with Scott Gorham

HEAD CASES!

X-OFFENDERS

'The name of this band is Talking Heads.' And the name of the singer who always introduces the band that way on stage is David Byrne.

Talking Heads are without precedent. They take the basic rock ingredients – guitar, bass, keyboards and drums – and come up with a crackling new syntax.

'There are certain things I feel need to be done in terms of music and performance,' declares Byrne. 'and what these things amount to is that what the world doesn't need is another posturing clown yammering away about his baby.'

'Our premise is that we are trying to present something that's convincing; music that we believe in. It can get a little complicated that way . . .'

Their first single, 'Love Goes To A Building On Fire', sounds like a cross between a Cossack dance and a child's riddle, - but try getting it out of your head – and their debut album reveals more of the same.

As keyboard player Jerry Harrison puts it: 'We're not trying to be bigger than life, we're trying to be about life.'

THE GRAPEVINE

- The Damned have broken up and announced a farewell UK tour.
- UK punk fanzine *Sniffing Glue* has given up in sympathy.
- Bob Dylan has released his documentary film of the Rolling Thunder tour called *Renaldo and Clara* and set off on a world tour.
- Sid Vicious and girlfriend Nancy Spungen have been arrested on drug charges at New York's Chelsea Hotel.

CHARTS

US45	Stayin' Alive	Bee Gees
USLP	Saturday Night Fever	Soundtrack
UK45	Uptown Top Ranking	Althia & Donna
UKLP	Rumours	Fleetwood Mac
	WEEK 2	
US45	Stayin' Alive	Bee Gees
USLP	Saturday Night Fever	Soundtrack
UK45	Uptown Top Ranking	Althia & Donna
UKLP	Abba: The Album	Abba
	WEEK 3	
US45	Stayin' Alive	Bee Gees
USLP	Saturday Night Fever	Soundtrack
UK45	Take A Chance On Me	Abba
UKLP	Abba: The Album	Abba
	WEEK 4	
US45	Stayin' Alive	Bee Gees
USLP	Saturday Night Fever	Soundtrack
UK45	Take A Chance On Me	Abba
UKLP	Abba: The Album	Abba

BOB MARLEY – EASY SKANKING

Bob Marley is an exile twice over: from his native Jamaica where he faces death threats because of the tense political situation there, and from his spiritual home in Ethiopia which is racked by an even more violent civil war.

So he's been recording the follow-up to his hugely successful 'Exodus' album in England. Several of the songs on 'Kaya' were recorded around the same time as 'Exodus', and some of them date back still further.

So what does 'Kaya' mean? 'Erb. Man sometimes seh Kaya because he sell 'erb in the yard and people seh him can't come in because he sell 'erb so he seh kaya.

'This album is about slowin' down and takin' it e-e-easy. Easy skanking y'know? So this is like a rest . . . for some kaya.'

Exodus for Marley

Just when you thought the new wave was wiping out that male chauvinist mentality, along come Blondie. Lead singer Debbie Harry, the blonde bombshell who fronts the band, has become an instant sex object for punks in Britain, where this New York band have made their initial impact. But then what do you expect with a single called 'Rip Her To Shreds'?

'The attitude to women in rock is totally sexist,' affirms Debbie. 'I might not like it when a crowd shouts at me, but I certainly thrive on it.'

Debbie has a past: she escaped from her silver-spoon New Jersey college education to hang out with the avant-garde jazz crowd in Greenwich Village, dropped acid and joined a band called Wind In The Willows at the end of the Sixties, became a heroin addict and a groupie, recovered from both and got together with Chris Stein, the guitarist in Blondie.

So she's inured to anything the sexists have to throw at her and, as the first track on the second Blondie album, 'Plastic Letters', puts it: 'I sold my vision for a piece of the cake/I haven't ate in days.'

'I'd sooner have hecklers than no reaction at all,' she smiles.

MARCH 1978

THIS YEAR'S COSTELLO

Elvis Costello bounded on to the scene last year with a well-defined cynicism that hasn't mellowed with the success of his 'My Aim Is True' album and acclaim for his live shows. He still bears the same grudges on his second album, 'This Year's Model'.

'This job isn't designed to make you nicer or even more mature. People can say, "Oh, he's just immature, he'll soften up" but I f-in' won't. People don't realize that I may not be mature because I don't want to be. I don't know what being grown-up is, see.

'The first album was politics and revenge. This one is politics and fashion. And the songs were written before I became a "fashion". I never wanted that, mind you. I could never imagine a lot of people wanting this ugly geek in glasses ramming his songs down their throats. And that's exactly what I'm in it for. I'm in it to disrupt people's lives.'

THE GRAPEVINE

■ Paul Simonon and Topper Headon of The Clash have been arrested in London for shooting pigeons from the roof of their rehearsal studio.

■ UK punk movie *Jubilee* premieres in London

■ America responds with *American Hot Wax*.

■ 250,000 show up for California Jam II featuring Santana, Dave Mason, Ted Nugent and Aerosmith.

WUTHERING KATE BUSH

Kate Bush is staring doe-eyed and sensuous out of the back of hundreds of London buses at the moment, advertising her first album, 'The Kick Inside' and the single that's taken Kate's extraordinary voice to the top of the charts – 'Wuthering Heights'.

Those high swooping vocals are just one facet of a voice that sounds different on virtually every track of the album. And Kate sings with a self-assurance remarkable for a teenager.

More remarkable still is that Kate signed to EMI three years ago when she was 16, and they've been prepared to wait and let her record in her own time. It helps that she arrived with a personal recommendation from Pink Floyd guitarist Dave Gilmour, who'd sponsored her demo tapes.

After she'd signed, she enrolled at Lindsey Kemp's Mime School. 'He taught me that you can express with your body – and when your body is awake so is your mind.'

She applies the same principle to her voice. 'I always enjoy reaching notes that I can't quite reach. A week later you'll be on top of that one and trying to reach the one above it.

'The reason I sang "Wuthering Heights" so high is that I felt it called for it. The book has a mood of mystery and I wanted to reflect that.'

DE-EVOLUTION

Evolving backwards at speed out of Akron, Ohio, Devo have brought an automaton touch to the new wave. Their robotic cover of the Stones' 'Satisfaction' has been one of the most original singles of the past year – the essentials were stripped bare, becoming naggingly insistent in the process.

On stage, they strut mechanically, clad in industrial cleaning outfits, and they maintain the pose offstage as well.

'We were all basically aliens – alienated aliens – who happened to be in Akron through accidents of birth,' explains architect of the Devo ideology Jerry Casale, who also plays bass.

Akron All Stars Devo

STAR QUOTE
NICK LOWE

'When you're younger you get influenced by people. Nowadays I just steal the stuff. If I hear a good lick I'll just pinch it.'

CHARTS

US45	(Love Is) Thicker Than Water *Andy Gibb*
USLP	Saturday Night Fever *Soundtrack*
UK45	Take A Chance On Me *Abba*
UKLP	Abba: The Album *Abba*

—— WEEK 2 ——

US45	(Love Is) Thicker Than Water *Andy Gibb*
USLP	Saturday Night Fever *Soundtrack*
UK45	Wuthering Heights *Kate Bush*
UKLP	Abba: The Album *Abba*

—— WEEK 3 ——

US45	Night Fever *Bee Gees*
USLP	Saturday Night Fever *Soundtrack*
UK45	Wuthering Heights *Kate Bush*
UKLP	Abba: The Album *Abba*

—— WEEK 4 ——

US45	Night Fever *Bee Gees*
USLP	Saturday Night Fever *Soundtrack*
UK45	Wuthering Heights *Kate Bush*
UKLP	Abba: The Album *Abba*

PATTI PUTS HER NECK BACK ON THE BLOCK

Patti struggles back

'Rock'n'roll is the hardest work any of us in the band has ever done. The physical toil, the mental toil, the 24 hours a day that it has to be lived. Going out on stage is almost the only time that you relax.'

Lenny Kaye is a respected rock journalist and expert of the new wave. He is also guitarist in The Patti Smith Group.

A year ago, Patti Smith fell off stage and broke her neck. She has struggled to regain her fitness, and the band are back on the road, merging rock'n'roll and improvisation into one crucial but speculative performance, night after night.

'Every night something greater happens, we take another risk,' says Patti. 'We go through another membrane, we've been through that one so we're gonna push and push and penetrate another one.'

This is no rock'n'roll band looking for money or fame. They are into exploring instead. 'And when the time comes that we're just going through the motions, there won't be a Patti Smith Group any more,' says Kaye. 'Patti will be the first to cast it into the ocean and move on to something else.'

THE GRAPEVINE

■ Over forty rock performers have petitioned US President Carter to end U.S. commitment to nuclear power, including Bruce Springsteen, Jackson Browne and Tom Petty.

■ The Clash have headlined a massive Rock Against Racism rally in London.

■ The Damned have played their farewell gig.

■ Sandy Denny, singer with Fairport Convention, has died of a cerebral haemorrhage after falling down stairs at her home.

ONE LOVE IN JAMAICA

The gang warfare, murder and violence that characterizes Jamaican politics came to an uneasy truce long enough for Bob Marley & The Wailers and the cream of reggae music to play the One Love Peace concert at the Kingston National Arena.

Youth leaders of the two feuding political parties organized the concert which climaxed with Bob Marley – making a return to his country after an assassination attempt – clasping hands with rival politicians Michael Manley and Edward Seaga in a gesture of solidarity.

Former Wailer Peter Tosh took the opportunity to lecture government officials about marijuana laws while smoking a spliff.

GENERATION X – HONEST PUNKS

The difference between Generation X and every other punk band is that they want to be stars. And maybe they're too honest about it for their own good.

Each of their singles so far – 'Your Generation', 'Wild Youth' and 'Ready Steady Go' – has made the Top 50.

'And they'd have done more if Chrysalis had made us an instant big act by buying us into the Top 30. We asked them to, of course, but they refused,' says guitarist Tony James.

They've taken flak for the lack of punk credibility – bleached blond singer Billy Idol studying English Literature at Sussex University for example – but James reckons: 'There isn't a name punk musician who doesn't have a skeleton in his cupboard.'

Billy Idol is now addicted to the rock'n'roll lifestyle. 'No wonder people in straight jobs can't take rock'n'roll. It must be so-o-o painful to see people enjoying themselves and making a loud noise, and then they've gotta get up and got to work in the morning.'

Hoping to live up to his name, Idol (left) and Generation X

APRIL 1978

CHARTS

US45	Night Fever	*Bee Gees*
USLP	Saturday Night Fever	*Soundtrack*
UK45	Denis	*Blondie*
UKLP	The Kick Inside	*Kate Bush*
	WEEK 2	
US45	Night Fever	*Bee Gees*
USLP	Saturday Night Fever	*Soundtrack*
UK45	Denis	*Blondie*
UKLP	The Kick Inside	*Kate Bush*
	WEEK 3	
US45	Night Fever	*Bee Gees*
USLP	Saturday Night Fever	*Soundtrack*
UK45	I Wonder Why	*Showaddywaddy*
UKLP	20 Golden Greats	*Nat 'King' Cole*
	WEEK 4	
US45	Night Fever	*Bee Gees*
USLP	Saturday Night Fever	*Soundtrack*
UK45	Night Fever	*Bee Gees*
UKLP	20 Golden Greats	*Nat 'King' Cole*
	WEEK 5	
US45	Night Fever	*Bee Gees*
USLP	Saturday Night Fever	*Soundtrack*
UK45	Night Fever	*Bee Gees*
UKLP	Saturday Night Fever	*Soundtrack*

MEAT LOAF LIES DOWN ALL OVER BROADWAY

Meat Loaf is a man who's always known how to go over the top. He's been known as Meat Loaf since he was a kid because of his eating habits. He aims big too.

He played Eddie in *The Rocky Horror Show* movie and soon after ran into songwriter Jim Sheinman, who shared his vision of the outrageous with heavy metal knobs on.

The final piece of the equation is Todd Rundgren, the multi-faceted rock star who never seems to know which of his facets to use next. He produced the 'Bat Out

Of Hell' album, a glorious monument to heavy metal theatrics that nobody believed in but them.

'Record company people kept telling me I wasn't rock'n'roll,' says Meat. 'They said: "We don't wanna hear it, it's Broadway music." That's bullshit, I've done ten shows on Broadway so I know what I'm talking about.'

Epic eventually took the bait, but the record snoozed until they made a video for the title track. Suddenly they have a monster on their hands.

LOWIE BOWIE

Another tour, another personality change; nobody can accuse David Bowie of playing safe these days.

The first hour of his latest tour is taken up with a low-key homage to his 'Low' and 'Heroes' albums, his avowedly conscious rejection of the commercial avenues he opened up with 'Young Americans' and 'Station To Station'. But the crowd at New York's Madison Square Gardens have come for former glories, and they remain restless for all but the title track of 'Heroes'.

'Five Years', 'Soul Love', 'Ziggy Stardust' and 'Suffragette City' are performed slickly, but without any exaggeration. Bowie then takes a left-field turn for the Brecht-Weill Anthem, 'Moon Of Alabama' ('Show me the way to the next whiskey bar').

The tension of his last tour is gone, and so is some of the vital edge.

RICH ROCK FROM CHEAP TRICK

The guy with the home-made T-shirt at the Newcastle Empire Ballroom says it all – 'Cheap Trick. Rocks like nuts.'

Newcastle is four thousand miles from Cheap Trick's hometown of Chicago, but the message travels easy. It's based on good rock'n'roll and good songs,

and it works on new wave, heavy metal and rock audiences alike.

Cheap Trick may look wacky and behave wacky, but they work hard – 300 gigs a year for the past three years and three albums inside the last 14 months.

The band, led by Rick Neilsen (who owns 60 guitars and is re-

puted never to have taken off his baseball cap) play short songs. 'Playing long songs is a waste,' says bassist Petersson. 'Who wants to hear tedious instrumental passages? Most people who aren't musicians don't care, and we know we could do it so we don't care either.'

GABRIEL – DOING IT HIMSELF

Peter Gabriel's second solo album is causing problems. Atlantic can't see a "commercial, immediate single". And in Britain, 'DIY', the likeliest single, has foundered three weeks after release.

The problem is compounded because although 'Solsbury Hill' from the first album was a big British hit, it failed to take off in the US.

So there's no tour being lined up, although Gabriel claims he's got a band ready. Instead, he's being sent out on a tour of American radio stations in the hope that they'll give the album some airplay.

Gabriel admits he refused to listen to nudging whispers from record company executives who wanted 'another album full of "Solsbury Hills".' And he reckons his bank balance is mostly made up of royalties from his former band, Genesis, who have turned into a successful stadium band since he left.

'If I consider my current position realistically, I would say I'd be able to survive in this cottage with my wife and children for another five years. Therefore I am concerned about selling records and being a success. Right now I'm just not compromising, that's all.'

JUNE 1978

BRUCE IS BACK

Finally, the record industry is ready for Bruce Springsteen again. Two and a half years after 'Born To Run', he's back with the follow-up, 'Darkness On The Edge Of Town'.

Most of the time in between has been taken up with legal wrangles to free himself from his former managers. Prevented by court injunctions from recording, Springsteen took to the road, giving bootleggers a field day. He's also written songs for Patti Smith, Southside Johnny and Robert Gordon while waiting to start work on his own album.

On 'Darkness On The Edge Of Town', the blockbuster production techniques and incurably romantic visions of 'Born To Run' have been avoided, although 'Badlands' and 'The Promised Land' are as epic as anything he's written.

Most important of all, however, there's remarkably little hype surrounding 'Darkness On The Edge Of Town'. That is the way Bruce wants it.

GRACE BOTTLES OUT OF STARSHIP

Jefferson Starship do not travel well. Their first trip out of America to Europe for a series of festival appearances has ended in chaos and near disaster with singer Grace Slick literally bottling out of the band.

The trouble started at the Lorelei Festival in Germany when Grace, a reformed alcoholic, hit the bottle again. In the ensuing fracas she stormed out and back to the States. The rest of the band cancelled the show but the 60,000 crowd were already waiting for them and trashed the group's equipment.

Starship fulfilled the final date of their tour – at Britain's Knebworth Festival with Genesis – without Grace, before slinking home to nurse their wounds.

THE GRAPEVINE

■ Bob Dylan's world tour has reached the UK for his first British gigs in nine years.

■ The Rolling Stones have released their 'Some Girls' album and started another US tour.

■ The Sex Pistols have released 'The Biggest Blow' EP, featuring train robber Ronnie Biggs and Sid Vicious' inimitable version of 'My Way'.

■ Peter Frampton has been injured in a car crash in the Bahamas.

Ray Davies

STAR QUOTE

RAY DAVIES
of The Kinks

'I write songs because I get angry, and now I'm at the stage where it's not good enough to brush it off with humour.'

FOREVER DYLAN

They traipsed across the fields in their tens of thousands, just like they had nine years earlier on the Isle Of Wight. That time it was to see Bob Dylan resurrected from his motorbike smash - or whatever it was that had turned him into a recluse for four years.

This time it's to see Dylan coming to terms with his heritage at Blackbushe Aerodrome, 40 miles west of London. His audience are nine years older now, and many of them have brought their children along.

Word of his triumphant London concerts last month has got around, and there are 50,000 people in front of the stage by 11 am when the first band appears. Nine hours later, after Graham Parker, Joan Armatrading and Eric Clapton, Dylan strolls on to a gigantic howl of applause and spends the next two and a half hours running through the last 15 years.

He reworks old favourites like 'Masters Of War' and 'Ballad Of A Thin Man' into powerful rockers, disco riffing through 'Maggie's Farm', lacing 'One More Cup Of Coffee' with large dollops of gospel and getting everyone to sing 'Forever Young' as a farewell anthem.

CHARTS

US45	Shadow Dancing	*Andy Gibb*
USLP	Saturday Night Fever	*Soundtrack*
UK45	You're The One That I Want	*John Travolta & Olivia Newton-John*
UKLP	Saturday Night Fever	*Soundtrack*

— WEEK 2 —

US45	Shadow Dancing	*Andy Gibb*
USLP	City To City	*Gerry Rafferty*
UK45	You're The One That I Want	*John Travolta & Olivia Newton-John*
UKLP	Saturday Night Fever	*Soundtrack*

— WEEK 3 —

US45	Shadow Dancing	*Andy Gibb*
USLP	Some Girls	*Rolling Stones*
UK45	You're The One That I Want	*John Travolta & Olivia Newton-John*
UKLP	Saturday Night Fever	*Soundtrack*

— WEEK 4 —

US45	Shadow Dancing	*Andy Gibb*
USLP	Some Girls	*Rolling Stones*
UK45	You're The One That I Want	*John Travolta & Olivia Newton-John*
UKLP	Saturday Night Fever	*Soundtrack*

— WEEK 5 —

US45	Shadow Dancing	*Andy Gibb*
USLP	Grease	*Soundtrack*
UK45	You're The One That I Want	*John Travolta & Olivia Newton-John*
UKLP	Saturday Night Fever	*Soundtrack*

Lucille Ball: objection

SOUNDTRACK FEVER

Bee Gees in 'Sergeant Pepper' movie

With one bound, The Bee Gees have leapt off the Saturday Night dance floor and into Sergeant Pepper uniforms to become surrogate Beatles for the soundtrack of the *Sergeant Pepper's Lonely Hearts Club Band* movie.

What's that? Yes, that's right, there are only three Bee Gees but there were four Beatles. That's why Peter Frampton has been roped in as the fourth Beatle.

True, they don't look like The Beatles or sound like The Beatles, but neither does Aerosmith's version of 'Come Together'. Which means that the whole soundtrack is a turkey. As is the movie.

Trouble is, the movie industry is obsessed with The Bee Gees. That's why the *Grease* people have drafted in Barry Gibb to write one song for their new film and given him a blockbusting credit for it.

SULTANS OF NEW-WAVE SWING

This is scarcely the time to start parading your J.J. Cale, Bob Dylan and Ry Cooder influences around the London pub circuit. But somehow Dire Straits have made the anachronisms work for them, and prospered amid the new wave.

A demo tape played on BBC Radio London alerted A&R men who finally heard something they could understand. And so did a growing number of punters who started showing up at their gigs.

Singer/songwriter/guitarist Mark Knopfler doesn't subscribe to image or self-analysis. 'We're not on a music-by-mind-and-body trip – getting a synthesizer and playing a few notes just because you've read a book by Herman Hesse.

'Things tend to go wrong when the perspective's directed more towards the artist than what he's doing. What counts is your two per cent: what you're doing!'

VAN HALEN SAY IT LOUDER

'This is the maximum escape trip, because it's so loud you cannot think of anything else but what's in front of you. You can't think about work, you can't think about the wife, the bills, the kids, nothing. Just that music being pounded into your skull.'

Dave Lee Roth is the singer with Van Halen, the 'maximum' heavy-metal band whose self-titled debut album has been firmly lodged in the US Top 30 for weeks.

Roth, guitarist Eddie Van Halen, drummer Alex Van Halen and bassist Mike Anthony, got bored with doing Zeppelin and Sabbath covers in Hollywood bars and took the plunge with their own gigs – renting halls and PAs, printing posters. When they started attracting 3,000 people, Warner Brothers signed them up.

Roth sees it all quite simply. 'We all work for a living, we all fall in love, we all make love, we all feel happy, we all feel sad, pretty much the same ways. Those are the needs that Van Halen caters to.'

Their trick is catering for them extravagantly. 'I like to make spectacles, y'know. We're gonna hire some elephants for our Long Beach Arena show when we get back from Japan. I want Van Halen beach balls!'

CHARTS

US45	Miss You *Rolling Stones*
USLP	Grease *Soundtrack*
UK45	You're The One That I Want *John Travolta & Olivia Newton-John*
UKLP	Saturday Night Fever *Soundtrack*

— WEEK 2 —

US45	Three Times A Lady *Commodores*
USLP	Grease *Soundtrack*
UK45	You're The One That I Want *John Travolta & Olivia Newton-John*
UKLP	Saturday Night Fever *Soundtrack*

— WEEK 3 —

US45	Three Times A Lady *Commodores*
USLP	Grease *Soundtrack*
UK45	You're The One That I Want *John Travolta & Olivia Newton-John*
UKLP	Saturday Night Fever *Soundtrack*

— WEEK 4 —

US45	Grease *Soundtrack*
USLP	Grease *Soundtrack*
UK45	Three Times A Laldy *Commodores*
UKLP	Saturday Night Fever *Soundtrack*

AUGUST 1978

STAR QUOTE

PETE TOWNSHEND

'When the new wave came along it was a great affirmation for me. I thought "Aye aye, we're not dead yet!" It was part of what had been nagging me. It didn't seem that the music business was ever going to get back to rock again.'

THE GRAPEVINE

- Muddy Waters played at Jimmy Carter's White House Picnic.
- Roxy Music are reported to be together again.
- Temptation Melvin Franklin has been shot and mugged in Los Angeles.
- Bebop Deluxe have split.
- New York's chic-est disco, Studio 54, has been busted by members of the narc squad posing as cocaine dealers.

KEEF CLEANS UP

'What can I tell you about it? I can't tell you how it works because they don't even know for sure. All they know is that it works. It's a little metal box with leads that clip on to your ears, and in two or three days – which is the worst period for kickin' junk – it leaves your system.'

Keith Richard has taken the cure. His Toronto bust and the consequences left no alternative. He's used the method that's already worked for Eric Clapton and Pete Townshend, perfected by London doctor Meg Patterson.

And after three days? 'It's up to you.'

Keith hasn't found it a problem, and he confesses that he doesn't even feel that different. But then as he says: 'I've never had a problem with drugs. Only with policemen.'

Keith also has an unresolved problem with the Toronto Justice Department, where he faces heroin charges. But the fact that he's finally cleaned himself up should help his case.

TELEVISION'S MEDIA BURN

Television have switched off, just weeks after playing six sell-out shows at New York's Bottom Line. The band's four-year career has been punctuated by ego clashes, management problems and general temperamental instability.

Leader Tom Verlaine forced Richard Hell out of the band before they even landed a record contract, and guitarist Richard Lloyd left twice, only to return each time within a week.

Their debut album, 'Marquee Moon', was hailed as a new-wave masterpiece, but the recent follow-up, 'Adventure', got the full force of a critical backlash.

Lloyd says that after the Bottom Line gigs, 'It was clear none of the band wanted to continue together.' Verlaine says: 'There was a full moon that night. Moby Grape broke up on a full moon. So we decided to do the same.'

Townshend: not dead yet

1978

CHARTS

US45	Grease	Soundtrack
USLP	Grease	Soundtrack
UK45	Three Times A Lady	Commodores
UKLP	Saturday Night Fever	Soundtrack
	WEEK 2	
US45	Boogie Oogie Oogie	Taste Of Honey
USLP	Grease	Soundtrack
UK45	Three Times A Lady	Commodores
UKLP	Night Flight To Venus	Boney M
	WEEK 3	
US45	Boogie Oogie Oogie	Taste Of Honey
USLP	Grease	Soundtrack
UK45	Three Times A Lady	Commodores
UKLP	Night Flight To Venus	Boney M
	WEEK 4	
US45	Boogie Oogie Oogie	Taste Of Honey
USLP	Grease	Soundtrack
UK45	Dreadlock Holiday	10cc
UKLP	Night Flight To Venus	Boney M
	WEEK 5	
US45	Kiss You All Over	Exile
USLP	Grease	Soundtrack
UK45	Dreadlock Holiday	10cc
UKLP	Grease	Soundtrack

KEITH MOON TAKEN AWAY

On the cover of The Who's new album, Keith Moon is sitting on a chair inscribed 'Not to be taken away'. But the seemingly indestructible drummer has died – from the drug he was taking to get him off the drug that was most likely to kill him: booze.

After an evening with his girlfriend Annette Walter-Lax at the premiere, of *The Buddy Holly Story* movie, and a party with Paul McCartney, Keith went home to his Mayfair flat. Annette found him dead the next morning. A post-mortem revealed an overdose of Heminevrin.

Pete Townshend's reaction was immediate: 'No-one could ever take Keith's place and we're not even going to try to replace him. But we're more determined than ever to carry on.'

The Who have just finished making a film documentary of their career called *The Kids Are Alright*, and Moon's last gig for the band earlier in the summer was filmed for the movie.

According to Keith: 'People often say to me, "Keith, you're crazy." Well, maybe I am, but I live my life and I live out my fantasies, thereby getting them all out of my system.'

THE DEAD'S PYRAMID PRANK

Grateful Dead and the pyramid – American rock and bedouin wailing

When The Grateful Dead discovered last March that it was possible to stage a gig at the Egyptian pyramids, their vibes were tickled. When they discovered that there would be an eclipse of the moon there on the evening of September 16, they nearly blew their cosmic minds.

They've landed up playing three nights to 3,000 people on the stone Apron theatre of the Giza Son Et Lumière Theatre in front of the Pyramid. And on the third night, three hundred San Franciscans flew in to see the show. As the moon began to darken, the wind rose, blowing sand from the desert and the noise of bedouin tribesmen wailing in their caravans across the theatre, mingling with the Dead's supremely self-indulgent American rock music.

'This is The Grateful Dead's annual Pyramid prank. It's great, I love it,' says Jerry Garcia.

FEELS LIKE FOREIGNER

Latest band to clean upon the American melodic heavy rock circuit are Foreigner, whose two albums have sold over 7½ million 'units' (that's industry-speak for copies sold).

The relentlessly old-wave band have had minimal press coverage during their sudden rise. In the mid-Sixties British-born guitarist Mick Jones wrote and recorded hits for French heart-throb Johnny Halliday. After spending ten years on the fringes of the US scene with Gary Wright, a reformed Spooky Tooth and Leslie West, he wrote the first Foreigner album before recruiting the band.

He picked an unknown singer, American-born Lou Gramm, ex-Ian Hunter drummer Dennis Elliott and original King Crimson keyboard player Ian McDonald.

'What we've got is not just a blend of Britain and America,' says Mick Jones. 'But a blend of relative experience and relative inexperience. I think that's important.'

Not to mention successful.

SID VICIOUS ON MURDER CHARGE

The Sex Pistols saga is turning from hype to horror. On October 13 Sid Vicious's girlfriend Nancy Spungen was found dead from abdominal stab wounds in their room at the New York Chelsea Hotel.

Sid, suffering from the effects of heroin, barbiturates and alcohol, was charged with second degree murder and taken to the hospital wing of Riker's Island Prison.

Nobody knows what really happened in their hotel room, including Sid. The pair, who had been together since the spring of 1977, were a volatile but inseparable couple, fuelled by a shared and growing heroin habit.

When The Sex Pistols broke up, they returned to London and became registered addicts, adding a severe methadone habit to their problems. Just before they left for New York, where Sid was planning to get a band together with former New York Doll and fellow dope fiend Johnny Thunders, 19-year-old John Shipcott OD'd at their flat and died.

While Sid was waiting to be released from Rikers Island on bail, he tried to commit suicide.

STAR QUOTE

JOHN LYDON

'It's power that runs any country; you can't change things overnight with a hit record. Rock singers getting into politics is rather stupid . . .'

THE GRAPEVINE

■ Peter Tosh acquired a broken arm and head wounds needing 20 stitches while being detained overnight by Jamaican police on marijuana charges.

■ Aerosmith's Steve Tyler and Joe Perry were injured by a cherry bomb thrown on stage at Philadelphia.

■ The Clash have fired their manager Bernie Rhodes.

Peter Tosh

KEITH OFF THE HOOK

Keith Richards has been given one year's probation by a Toronto court for heroin possession. An earlier charge of trafficking was dropped after he entered a guilty plea to possessing 22 grams of heroin. Richards has also agreed to play a benefit concert for the blind in Toronto.

Meanwhile, The Stones have run into charges of racism from the Rev. Jesse Jackson over their 'Some Girls' single. The Stones reply: 'It never occurred to us that our parody of certain stereo-typical attitudes would be taken seriously by anyone who has heard the entire lyrics of the song. We sincerely apologize.'

SPRINGSTEEN'S ON FIRE

Bruce Springsteen is slumped in the dressing room of the New York Palladium after a four-hour show. He seldom does less these days, and often spends a couple of hours soundchecking beforehand.

It's the last of three nights in front of a partisan crowd. During the summer he did three Madison Square Gardens and in between he's been pummelling the road promoting his 'Darkness On The Edge Of Town' album.

Night after night he drives himself beyond the brink of exhaustion. His shows have become almost a religious celebration of the spirit of rock'n'roll.

'Yeah, there's a lotta morality in the show,' he says. 'And it's a very strict morality. Anybody that works for me has gotta understand that. I know how I'd feel if I'd paid money to see a show and what I wanted wasn't delivered.'

The managerial trials and tribulations that have blighted his career for the past two years have left him stronger than ever. And it's reflected in his songs.

'I couldn't do an innocent album like "Born To Run", because things ain't like that for me anymore. The characters on the new album ain't kids, they're older – you been beat, you been hurt – but there's still hope. There's always hope.'

DRIVE, SHE SAID

The Cars are a tight piece of machinery, a pop-driven new-wave model that's found favour with radio programmers. In the past six months the Boston quartet have scored a Top 20 hit with 'Just What I Needed', a platinum debut album and a second hit single with 'My Best Friend's Girl'.

Fortunately, singer/song-writer/guitarist Ric Ocasek has no illusions. 'All written words are fiction,' he declares.

The Cars deliberately aimed for the charts by getting Roy Thomas Baker, the doyen of 'clean' producers, to produce them. 'We figured he knew how to mix for radio – more than us,' says Ric.

Drummer Dave Robinson, formerly of The Modern Lovers, gave the band their name. Ric approves: 'Cars are great; they go through all the changes that musicians do, too. They all wear out, they get broken parts, some are better than others and some go in the junkyard . . .'

THE JAM'S MOD CONS

'I feel that the mod scene was very close to the punk thing; wholly youth – like going out with green hair. It changed you, made you something. It's something every kid goes through. You just want to be noticed, to be recognized.'

Paul Weller sits on the edge of the bed in his hotel room, chain-smoking, anxious to be understood. On stage with The Jam it's the same nervous need to communicate to legions of fans.

Like the mods, the Jam are a very British phenomenon. 'I wrote a load of songs when we were in America, but they were all crap. We went through Harlem, which is really inspiring,

but that has nothing to do with me. I've got no right to write about it. We've got Harlems of our own – go up to Glasgow.'

But doesn't he worry about becoming too complex and introverted for his audiences to relate to?

'Sometimes yes, but I don't think that should necessarily stop you. I mean, I'd be too embarrassed to write something like "We're all going down the pub" (from 'Hurry Up Harry', current UK hit for punk rabble rousers Sham 69) 'even though that is probably very real to thousands of kids. I just feel that I should reach for something higher.'

POLICE GIVE EVIDENCE

'This band have had a really hard time from the press. We've been accused of "bandwagon punk" and now we're accused of "bandwagon reggae"'.

Police guitarist Andy Summers may complain but as an ex-guitarist with Zoot Money's Big Roll Band, Eric Burdon, Kevin Ayers and Kevin Coyne, he's nobody's idea of a punk, despite his bleached hair.

Neither is singer/bassist

Sting, previously with Newcastle jazz-rock big band Last Exit. Or drummer Stewart Copeland, ex-Curved Air.

But their attitude is new-wave and Sting who wrote their hit singles 'Roxanne' and 'Can't Stand Losing You', admits the reggae influence. 'They're not reggae all the way though. Both of them go into straight rock'n'roll. You can't expect us to play old Led Zeppelin riffs now . . .'

THE GRAPEVINE

■ Chic have their second gold record of the year with 'Le Freak'.

■ The disco boom has reached out to pull in hits from 'legendary' soul/R&B names like Jerry Butler (from The Impressions), Gene Chandler, Gladys Knight, Joe Simon and The Temptations.

■ The Jam's Paul Weller has been arrested for assault while staying at the same hotel as the Australian rugby league team.

The Jam: (l to r) Rick Buckler, Paul Weller, Bruce Foxton

CHARTS

US45	You Needed Me	*Anne Murray*
USLP	Living In The USA	*Linda Ronstadt*
UK45	Summer Nights	*John Travolta/Olivia Newton-John*
UKLP	Grease	*Soundtrack*

— WEEK 2 —

US45	MacArthur Park	*Donna Summer*
USLP	Live & More	*Donna Summer*
UK45	Summer Nights	*John Travolta/Olivia Newton-John*
UKLP	Grease	*Soundtrack*

— WEEK 3 —

US45	MacArthur Park	*Donna Summer*
USLP	52nd Street	*Billy Joel*
UK45	Rat Trap	*Boomtown Rats*
UKLP	Grease	*Soundtrack*

— WEEK 4 —

US45	MacArthur Park	*Donna Summer*
USLP	52nd Street	*Billy Joel*
UK45	Rat Trap	*Boomtown Rats*
UKLP	Grease	*Soundtrack*

THE CLASH SORT IT OUT

Most of '78 has been a battleground for The Clash. Their UK tours became prey to all kinds of random violence from the audience and band alike; they've been in constant conflict with CBS over the recording of the second album, 'Give 'Em Enough Rope'; and they were constantly made to feel 'second best' to The Sex Pistols as their respective managers bitched over the title of 'Svengali Of Punk'.

But the T-shirts for the band's year-end tour display a new attitude. The message reads 'The Clash – The Sort It Out Tour', and the band appear to be doing just that.

On stage, the band are channelling their energies into their music, although the behaviour of their fans still manages to keep many gigs on a knife-edge. The UK chart success of 'Give 'Em Enough Rope' has resulted in a truce with their record company. And they've parted company with manager Bernie Rhodes.

Guitarist Mick Jones, who recalls 'breaking down in tears all the time' during the band's bleakest hours, admits that the band fell into a time-honoured rock'n'roll trap.

'Two years ago I did the band's first major TV interview and I was all young and naive. I blamed bands taking too many drugs for the great mid-Seventies drought in rock. I remember saying it really well. And a year or so later I found myself taking as many drugs as them.'

THE (DE) HUMAN FACE OF DISCO

'The disco sound is not art, or anything so serious. Disco is music for dancing and I know that people will always want to dance.'

Giorgio Moroder is the man responsible for the synthetic wizardry behind Donna Summer's 'Love To Love You Baby', 'I Feel Love' and 'MacArthur Park', and is fast becoming the hottest name in disco.

Italian-born Moroder fashions his records at Munich's Music machine in Germany, adding the gloss in Los Angeles or London. He acknowledges the influence of The Philly Sound and, like Gamble & Huff, maintains a house band.

He's not worried about accusations of dehumanizing disco. 'Disco is the soul and R&B sound of today,' he declares.

Donna Summer

CHARTS

US45	You Don't Bring Me Flowers	*Barbra Streisand & Neil Diamond*
USLP	52nd Street	*Billy Joel*
UK45	Rat Trap	*Boomtown Rats*
UKLP	Grease	*Soundtrack*

— WEEK 2 —

US45	Le Freak	*Chic*
USLP	52nd Street	*Billy Joel*
UK45	Do Ya Think I'm Sexy	*Rod Stewart*
UKLP	20 Golden Greats	*Neil Diamond*

— WEEK 3 —

US45	Le Freak	*Chic*
USLP	52nd Street	*Billy Joel*
UK45	Mary's Boy Child	*Boney M*
UKLP	20 Golden Greats	*Neil Diamond*

— WEEK 4 —

US45	Le Freak	*Chic*
USLP	52nd Street	*Billy Joel*
UK45	Mary's Boy Child	*Boney M*
UKLP	Grease	*Soundtrack*

— WEEK 5 —

US45	Le Freak	*Chic*
USLP	52nd Street	*Billy Joel*
UK45	Mary's Boy Child	*Boney M*
UKLP	Grease	*Soundtrack*

Kenny Jones: replacing Moon

STILL LOOKING FOR NUMBER ONE

A year ago, Bob Geldof was bragging that The Boomtown Rats would be a No. 1 band in a year's time. They'd already had UK chart success by then, but the difference between a Top Ten hit and a chart topper is bigger than they knew – and 'Rat Trap' stalled at No. 6.

But that hasn't stopped Geldof being a star. He was a rock journalist before he formed the Rats, and knows not to bullshit the media. Or his audiences. Which is why The Boomtown Rats are drawing huge crowds as they tour the UK on their wittily titled 'Seasonal Turkey Tour'.

'The Rats are the band I sing with,' he says. 'It's a job. I don't consider myself to be a big deal. But rock'n'roll, along with TV and the movies, is a great twentieth-century art form.'

By 1975, a new generation of British teenagers began to reject the current chart fodder, preferring the uninhibited attitudes of people like Patti Smith, The New York Dolls and Iggy Pop to the seamless success of groups like The Eagles.

Malcolm McLaren, who ran a shop in London's trendy Kings Road, recognized this trend and decided to try to manage a group which involved a kid who worked in the shop on Saturdays and some regular customers who were always hanging around the place. McLaren had got the music biz bug from managing the New York Dolls in that group's death throes, and after noting that the most interesting band from New York at the time was Television, led by two kids who had renamed themselves Tom Verlaine and Richard Hell, and played with little regard for the state-of-the-art perfection of Boston, Pink Floyd or the other "dinosaurs".

Into this self-satisfied status quo charged The Sex Pistols, (a name guaranteed to annoy), a quartet fronted by a surly youth who clearly was neither able to sing nor interested in learning; Johnny Rotten was well-named – a sinister figure screaming abuse at an audience of his own contemporaries, who were lapping it up!

It wasn't long before British record labels sensed potential profits, and eventually McLaren signed them to Britain's oldest company EMI. Their first single, 'Anarchy In The UK', crashed into the Top 50 of the UK chart at the end of 1976.

It all started to go wrong (or maybe right?) when the group appeared on an early evening TV show and were interviewed by a reporter who made little secret of how repugnant he found the Pistols and encouraged them to swear at him. British newspapers continued to report on every move the group made, and EMI, under pressure from its establishment shareholders, paid them off and withdrew the hit from the nation's stores.

By mid-March, 1977, the Pistols – now featuring a new bass player known as Sid Vicious – had signed a new recording contract with A&M Records on tables set up outside Buckingham Palace to draw attention to the fact that their first A&M single would be 'God Save The Queen'.

Before the single was properly released, A&M had paid off McLaren, who was again free to milk the record industry and the media for all he could. Finally, Richard Branson's Virgin label released the single in the same week as Britain celebrated its monarch's Silver Jubilee. The NME listed it as being number one, but other charts – including the one used by BBC Radio One, the national pop network – did not grant it the chart-topping accolade.

In November, 1977, came the album, 'Never Mind The Bollocks', which topped all the UK LP charts.

The Pistols' next moves were a shambolic US tour, during which Rotten left the group, and production of a feature movie which was threatened by his departure. In an act of apparent desperation, McLaren contrived to involve an escaped English convict named Ronnie Biggs, who was exiled in Brazil, and 'The Great Rock & Roll Swindle' finally limped out.

A decade later, Rotten has reverted to his real name, John Lydon, and leads an idiosyncratic combo known as Public Image Limited (PIL), while Sid Vicious died of a heroin overdose while out on parole, accused of murdering his girl friend, Nancy Spungen.

Not all the punks faded away, however. Some, like The Clash, belatedly convinced the US that there was something in their music, while The Damned split up and reformed regularly. The most successful punk acts were the Americans Blondie, fronted by the eye-catching Deborah Harry, The Ramones and Talking Heads. In exactly the same way as The Stones had reminded America of its own music by refining it and sending it back, so the USA eventually profited more from punk than the UK.

The DAMNED

the PiSTols' JohNny Rotten

BOLLOCKS

UK Punks 1977

the Clash

the Sex Pistols

BLOndie's Debbie Harry

Sid 'n' Nancy

1979

SEX AND DRUGS AND ROCK'N'ROLL

'Sex and drugs and rock and roll/Is all my brain and body needs/Sex and drugs and rock and roll/Is very good indeed.'

Last year's rock'n'roll anthem across Britain and Europe never made the charts. But 'Sex And Drugs And Rock And Roll' by Ian Dury & The Blockheads sums up the perennial fantasy of the rock generation – and the gruesome reality for a select few.

Ian Dury, the ex-art-school lecturer who rasps the song in a half-spoken hoarse Cockney accent, is a Great British Eccentric. Known to The Blockheads as Raspberry – Cockney rhyming slang: raspberry ripple = cripple – he wears his affliction, caused by polio, like a badge. He limps round the stage and clutches the mike stand with his withered hand while throwing knotted handkerchiefs around with his other.

And all the while The Blockheads are pumping out sandpaper-textured funky riffs written by keyboard player Chas Jankel, whose ear for a catchy hook has hit paydirt.

Their latest single, 'Hit Me With Your Rhythm Stick', barrelled its way through the UK Top 40 during December and up the Top 10 this month to hit No. 1 after two weeks at No. 2.

Ian Dury and the Blockheads

BEDROOM FEVER

America's latest fad for the nouveau riche is the disco bedroom. Affluent Travolta types are forking out up to $20,000 to instal a full disco and light show to bolster their egos in the boudoir.

Jack Ransom, head of MGM Stage Equipment, a leading disco supply company, reckons it's a new twist on the age-old art of seduction, and says the playboy types 'are willing to pay top dollar to indulge their whims'.

Even the oil-rich Arabs are succumbing to Saturday Night Fever, converting sections of their palaces into discos.

STAR QUOTE

ELVIS COSTELLO

'If two days go by without an idea for a song, I become obsessive about writing. That's what taking it up as a career does, as opposed to it merely being a hobby.'

Elvis giving up his hobby

CHARTS

US45	Too Much Heaven	Bee Gees
USLP	Greatest Hits Volume 2	Barbra Streisand
UK45	Y.M.C.A.	Village People
UKLP	Greatest Hits 1976-1978	Showaddywaddy

— WEEK 2 —

US45	Too Much Heaven	Bee Gees
USLP	Greatest Hits Volume 2	Barbra Streisand
UK45	Y.M.C.A.	Village People
UKLP	Greatest Hits 1976-1978	Showaddywaddy

— WEEK 3 —

US45	Le Freak	Chic
USLP	Greatest Hits Volume 2	Barbra Streisand
UK45	Y.M.C.A.	Village People
UKLP	Greatest Hits 1976-1978	Showaddywaddy

— WEEK 4 —

US45	Le Freak	Chic
USLP	52nd Street	Billy Joel
UK45	Hit Me With Your Rhythm Stick	Ian Dury
UKLP	Don't Walk, Boogie	Various

THE GRAPEVINE

■ Sid Vicious has been sent for trial for murdering his girlfriend Nancy Spungen.

■ The Clash have released their first US single, 'I Fought The Law'.

■ Jazz giant Charlie Mingus has died of a heart attack, aged 56.

■ Singer Donny Hathaway died after falling from the 15th floor of his New York hotel.

MARVIN GAYE'S ALIMONY ALBUM

All proceeds from Marvin Gaye's new album will go to his ex-wife Anna Gordy, daughter of Tamla Motown founder Berry Gordy. The album is on Tamla Motown. It's called, not without irony, 'Here, My Dear'.

The divorce has left Marvin bankrupt. And the songs on the album are a loser's guide to love and marriage. Even Marvin's staunchest fans aren't arguing that it's his best to date, but it's remarkably candid about his own reality – admittedly different from most people's reality.

'I think this is man's last-ditch effort to maintain whatever supremacy we have,' Gaye declares, although he maintains that he bears his ex-wife no personal ill-will.

'Although there is some bitterness on the album, there are also respectful cuts that tell of a wonderful love,' he says. 'It was just lack of compatibility . . . in a marriage compatibility is everything.'

Marvin Gaye: loser in love

SID DID IT HIS WAY

The predictable death of Sid Vicious came early on February 2 – from a heroin overdose.

He was at a party given by his current girlfriend Michelle Robinson and his mother Ann Beverley, to celebrate his release from jail pending a hearing of his murder trial.

While in prison, Sid was put on a detoxification course and, as a result, his tolerance to heroin was lowered. Sid collapsed after being given the drug, but recovered before the party broke up and went to bed around 3 am. Ann Beverley found him dead in his bed the following morning. A syringe and spoon were found near the body.

Sid would have been 22 in May.

Just to prove that The Sex Pistols are also dead, John Lydon has forced Malcolm McLaren's Glitterbest management company into liquidation. A receiver is being appointed to sort out the group's financial affairs, with authority to release *The Great Rock and Roll Swindle* film and album, into which most of Glitterbest's money has been invested. The judge said the film represented 'the only realistic hope of any substantial funds being rescued for anyone'.

Anyone except Sid, that is.

CHARTS

US45	Le Freak *Chic*
USLP	Briefcase Full Of Blues *Blues Brothers*
UK45	Hit Me With Your Rhythm Stick *Ian Dury*
UKLP	Don't Walk, Boogie *Various*
— WEEK 2 —	
US45	Da Ya Think I'm Sexy? *Rod Stewart*
USLP	Blondes Have More Fun *Rod Stewart*
UK45	Heart Of Glass *Blondie*
UKLP	Parallel Lines *Blondie*
— WEEK 3 —	
US45	Da Ya Think I'm Sexy? *Rod Stewart*
USLP	Blondes Have More Fun *Rod Stewart*
UK45	Chiquitita *Abba*
UKLP	Parallel Lines *Blondie*
— WEEK 4 —	
US45	Da Ya Think I'm Sexy? *Rod Stewart*
USLP	Blondes Have More Fun *Rod Stewart*
UK45	Heart Of Glass *Blondie*
UKLP	Parallel Lines *Blondie*

Village People: cottage industry

VILLAGE PEOPLE'S COTTAGE INDUSTRY

The Indian, the cowboy, the labourer, the cop, the army bloke, the leather man – all of them treading the line between what is deft and what is daft with a visual onslaught that cannot fail to leave you uncommitted one way or the other.

Village People are the brainchild of French-born New York producer Jaques Morali, and their 'YMCA' disco blast has been tucked in at No. 2 in the US charts for three weeks. In the UK it's No. 1.

The boys in Village People may complain that people are only interested in whether or not they're gay, but they should have thought about that before they started putting on such butch costumes and started singing songs like 'Macho Man', 'YMCA', and 'I Am What I Am', with lyrics that are so camp they have to be held down with tent pegs.

THE GRAPEVINE

■ A US Grand Jury has been investigating alleged links between Chicago (the band) and the mafia.

■ One hit wonder Sgt Barry ('Ballad Of The Green Berets') Sadler also facing a Grand Jury investigation after shooting songwriter Lee Bellamy dead; Sadler claims he aimed to miss.

■ 10cc's Eric Stewart has suffered serious head injuries in a car crash.

■ The Clash start their first US tour.

Chicago – under investigation

JOE JACKSON LOOKS SHARP

'Look Sharp' is the title of Joe Jackson's debut album and the tall, thin man with a truculent baby face looks just that.

His songs have energy, wit and melody. His first single, 'Is She Really Going Out With Him', proves the point perfectly and has alerted enough people to mark him down as one to watch this year.

His lyrics are defiant, idealistic and ironic. 'I want to get away from all that macho shit, but at the same time I don't want to do the Elvis Costello god-I've-been-hurt-in-love thing either,' he explains.

He's pitched his album quite deliberately. 'I didn't want your typical '77/'78 new wave band sound. I wanted more of a reggae mix, where you have a very upfront bass and drums and a thin sounding guitar that goes in and out. The idea is to leave a lot of gaps to let the song really come through.'

1979

US45	Da Ya Think I'm Sexy? *Rod Stewart*
USLP	Spirits Having Flown *Bee Gees*
UK45	Heart Of Glass *Blondie*
UKLP	Parallel Lines *Blondie*

— WEEK 2 —

US45	I Will Survive *Gloria Gaynor*
USLP	Spirits Having Flown *Bee Gees*
UK45	Tragedy *Bee Gees*
UKLP	Parallel Lines *Blondie*

— WEEK 3 —

US45	I Will Survive *Gloria Gaynor*
USLP	Spirits Having Flown *Bee Gees*
UK45	Oliver's Army *Elvis Costello*
UKLP	Parallel Lines *Blondie*

— WEEK 4 —

US45	Tragedy *Bee Gees*
USLP	Spirits Having Flown *Bee Gees*
UK45	I Will Survive *Gloria Gaynor*
UKLP	Spirits Having Flown *Bee Gees*

— WEEK 5 —

US45	Tragedy *Bee Gees*
USLP	Spirits Having Flown *Bee Gees*
UK45	I Will Survive *Gloria Gaynor*
UKLP	C'Est Chic *Chic*

Twisted Sister: selling out

THE JACKSONS – ON THE WALL

Jackson 5 heading for destiny

Ten years after bounding into the charts with 'ABC' and 'I Want You Back', Michael Jackson still refuses to grow up. He's no longer the youngest of the Jackson 5 – Randy is three years younger – but he remains the Peter Pan of the group.

He's totally dedicated to his profession because he knows no other way of life. From the age of five, when he started singing and dancing with the group, he has grown in an environment so com-pletely cloistered that he can only regard the imaginary as reality.

On stage, the band create real magic, from the infectious 'Let Me Show You The Way' to the up-market soul of 'Destiny'. They even get away with a hurried medley of their old hits.

Off-stage, Michael is closely guarded to prevent unnecessary contact with the real world. Far from turning him precocious and arrogant, he gets off on the simple things of life, like swimming in the hotel pool after dark. And his biggest thrill right now is holding the record attendance at the Houston Astrodome. There's even a commemorative plaque to prove it.

'It makes me feel really good when other bands who've played there meet us and tell us they've seen our plaque,' he says.

THE GRAPEVINE

■ David Bowie has finished filming *Just A Gigolo* and has set out on a US tour.

■ Twisted Sister sold out the 3,000-capacity New York Palladium without a record deal or radio play.

■ Punk riots have come to the US when Los Angeles police broke up a Zeros gig at Elks Hall.

■ Elvis Costello was punched by Bonnie Bramlett in a Columbus, Ohio, hotel bar after allegedly making racist remarks.

TOTO AIM FOR THE MEGA BUCKS

Toto are the latest American radio rock stars. Their debut single, 'Hold The Line', was a monster hit and their debut album has cleaned up a million copies in four months.

The six-piece band are all seasoned West Coast session musicians, and their approach is practical to say the least. 'The way the rock field is set up right now, you either don't make a nickel or you make over two million dollars,' says drummer Jeff Porcaro.

'There's no making half a million dollars. It's just not worth it. It's too much trouble. You either make a lot of money or get out of the business.'

He's scathing about punk too: 'All new wave music and punk music is bullshit. The music's ugly and the people are ugly.'

JOAN ARMATRADING'S ENIGMATIC EMOTIONS

Joan Armatrading has become Britain's most successful singer/songwriter over the last couple of years, yet she remains an enigma.

After a critically acclaimed but poor-selling debut album in the early Seventies, she signed to A&M where she continued to gather plaudits for her 'Back To The Night' and 'Joan Armatrading' albums and finally landed a UK Top 10 single with the powerful and emotive 'Love And Affection' at the end of 1976.

Since then her 'Show Some Emotion' and 'To The Limit' albums have consolidated her reputation as a perceptive writer experimenting with reggae, gospel and blues styles.

But she reveals little of herself in her songs, preferring to write from personal observation rather than personal experience.

'Although they're not personal, I do get very involved in the songs,' this self-confessed loner contends. 'It's not just a bunch of words. They have to mean something to me.'

THE POLICE – BORN IN THE FIFTIES

Still ignored in the UK where they've been accused of bandwagon jumping, The Police are making inroads in America where their 'Roxanne' single and 'Outlandos D'Amour' album have just cracked the Top 30.

Significantly, they are doing better than The Clash, The Sex Pistols, The Stranglers, The Boomtown Rats and all the other British new-wave bands. They've achieved the breakthrough by playing a shoestring tour of the East Coast, where college radio took 'Roxanne' to its airplay bosom.

They've just completed a second tour climaxing with a series of gigs at New York's Bottom Line, where their reggaefied new-wave sound has lured the

likes of Robert Fripp, Return To Forever drummer Lenny White, and Mick Jagger.

The word is out: the Police can actually play.

'We're too young to have been into Woodstock and all that, and we're too old to be punks,' explains Sting. 'We're stuck with

being wise in one way and naive in another.

'We didn't elect the dinosaurs of rock. They've been put up there by people older than us. Our generation has to establish itself and we're not going to vanish just because we're over 23. What do people expect us to do?'

The Police: too young for Woodstock and too old for punk

LOU REED CAN'T DANCE

Lou Reed should be an idol for the punk generation, but instead he's rubbing them up the wrong way. His new LP, 'The Bells', has been panned as 'a delusion disguised as an album', and the London show on his European tour was dismissed as 'a crushing, oppressive, indulgent thrash'.

His behaviour became increasingly unpredictable during the German leg of the tour. In Berlin he enthralled the audience with a three-hour show. But in Frankfurt he stormed off after less than an hour, demanding that a GI be removed from the hall. When he returned 40 minutes later, he knocked down and kicked a girl who'd climbed on stage before beating a hasty retreat.

Lou spent the night in police custody on an assault charge.

STAR QUOTE

MIKE OLDFIELD

'People are very complicated machines – to get them to do what you want, you have to be very careful. You have to behave towards them in a very definite sequence.'

Mike Oldfield works out another definite sequence of behaviour

SQUEEZING OUT HITS

Squeeze freely admit they rode the new wave to get a record deal although they were never really a part of it. Their latest and biggest UK hit to date, 'Cool For Cats' is a jokey, lightweight song with some rude lyrics which have somehow escaped the censorious minds that control UK radio.

'A lot of people find it hard to categorize us,' says Chris Difford, one of the band's singers, 'and that puts them off.'

Squeeze are a six-piece quirky pop band from Catford, south London who now have two singles and a confessedly 'patchy' debut album to their credit. They are more pleased with their second album, also called 'Cool For Cats'.

'It's one of the best I've heard,' says Glenn Tilbrook, who co-writes most of the songs with Difford. 'It's intelligent, both musically and lyrically, and the playing is great. It's just that the general public don't happen to realize it at the moment.'

Lou Reed not fearing for whom the bell tolls, it's for him

1970

WHO'S NEXT?

The Who are back – as defiant as ever – with a film documentary of their illustrious career so far, a movie version of their 'Quadrophenia' rock opera, and gigs with their new drummer.

Kenny Jones faces the unenviable task of replacing Keith Moon for the first time at London's Rainbow Theatre – a gig announced with two days' notice. He succeeded by avoiding comparison and playing in his own style.

A few days later at the Roman amphitheatre in Frejus, in the South of France, Kenny was even more confident, stamping his own identity on the band who in turn responded with rejuvenated energy.

After all, they've nothing to lose now. Their past is behind them, neatly encapsulated on celluloid. *The Kids Are Alright* is the story of The Who from TV and film clips dating back to 1964. It never tries to put a gloss on the band, so the result is a perceptive documentary that's as much about the era of The Who as The Who themselves.

The Who hang on

J GEILS BAND SEEK SANCTUARY

For nearly a decade The J Geils Band have been touted as America's answer to The Rolling Stones. In fact, they came closest on their debut album back in 1970, but nobody's ever forgotten the connection, which ultimately hasn't done the band many favours.

They've had more than a few of the right connections too: managed by Dee Anthony before he came alive with Peter Frampton, road managed by Fred Lewis until he drove off with The Cars, and produced by Bill Szymczyk until he flew off with The Eagles.

Everybody around them made it big except The J Geils Band. But they've kept their integrity, and nobody was ever able to tell them what to do.

'We made it a rule to care about ticket prices, the sound, the comfort, the security,' says singer Peter Wolf. 'If a guy brings his girl to a show, we want to know there won't be some goons around to spoil their fun.

'And that goes for recording, the pressing, the cover. And each other. See, we've only got one career, we have to be protective of it.'

Maybe they've been over-protective. There have been albums when they've pandered to their fans. But their latest album, 'Sanctuary', puts a tougher resolve into their adventurous music and sets them back on the right road.

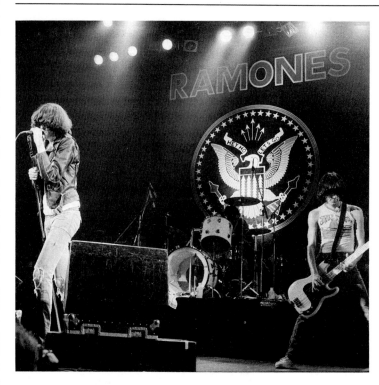

THE RAMONES GRADUATE

Rock 'n' Roll High School, featuring The Ramones, is bidding to become the cult film of American punkhood and bring da brudders the fame which has so far eluded them in the U.S.

The movie was shot in three weeks by Roger Corman, undisputed master of the B-movie – including *Attack Of The Crab Monsters*, *The Day The World Ended*, *The Wild Angels* and nearly 200 others.

A tale of teen romance and adolescent anarchy, *Rock 'n' Roll High School* is a perfect celebration of The Ramones and all they stand for.

Da brudders: preppy punks

STAR QUOTE

DEBBIE HARRY
Blondie

'I wouldn't mind being a mom. I already am a housewife. I guess I vacuum once in a while.'

THE GRAPEVINE

■ Led Zeppelin have announced their first gig for nearly two years – at the Knebworth Festival in August.

■ Falling LP sales have forced record companies to cut back on the quantity of releases.

■ Jefferson Starship begin to pick up the pieces with a free gig in San Francisco and new vocalist, Mickey Thomas.

■ Elton John has played gigs in Israel and Russia.

CHARTS

US45	Reunited	Peaches & Herb
USLP	Minute By Minute	Doobie Brothers
UK45	Bright Eyes	Art Garfunkel
UKLP	The Very Best Of Leo Sayer	Leo Sayer

— WEEK 2 —

US45	Reunited	Peaches & Herb
USLP	Minute By Minute	Doobie Brothers
UK45	Bright Eyes	Art Garfunkel
UKLP	The Very Best Of Leo Sayer	Leo Sayer

— WEEK 3 —

US45	Reunited	Peaches & Herb
USLP	Breakfast In America	Supertramp
UK45	Pop Muzik	M
UKLP	The Very Best of Leo Sayer	Leo Sayer

— WEEK 4 —

US45	Reunited	Peaches & Herb
USLP	Breakfast In America	Supertramp
UK45	Bright Eyes	Art Garfunkel
UKLP	Voulez Vous	Abba

DIRE STRAITS – THAT'S THE WAY YOU DO IT!

In a business that can cheerfully blow £50,000 'repackaging' a disco artist you never heard first time round, Dire Straits have achieved the biggest-selling debut album in the US by any British band for a £15,000 production bill and a miniscule promotional budget.

The promotional budget would have been bigger, but by the time Warner Brothers had analysed the radio station feedback, the album was already the most-played on radio, coast-to-coast.

Rhythm guitarist David Knopfler says he once jumped stations to hear three different tracks being played simultaneously. The album literally sold itself into the charts, peaking at No. 2, just behind the Bee Gees.

At least America released the album. Some countries, like Canada and Germany, didn't want to know. But every country that did reported the same reaction.

Unconcerned, Dire Straits set about their follow-up: a more expensive affair at Nassau, with Jerry Wexler and Barry Beckett supervising. By the time their debut was turning several shades of platinum in America, they'd finished the follow-up.

But Warners wanted to delay the second album to give them more time to milk the first. 'No deal,' said Dire Straits, aware of

Dire Straits left their record company standing with the fastest selling debut album in America

the danger of over-exposure. They set a June release date in Europe, leaving Warners to catch up or face massive imports.

Warners caught up. Undeterred, they are already making promotional plans for the third single from the album.

NO STOPPIN' McFADDEN & WHITEHEAD

'Look, soul music is only some guy singing his songs. I know you folks believe it's some cat with all gravel in his voice and stuff singing about hard times, but that ain't soul music. Most of those guys are singing someone else's songs so how in hell can they be feeling soul? No – soul music is any cat who feels enough to sing what he wrote himself.'

John Whitehead is busy putting the media right about soul. Together with Gene McFadden he's just scored a massive hit with the monumental 'Ain't No Stoppin' Us Now'.

It's a real break for them. They've been an integral part of the Philly sound, writing for the O'Jays and Harold Melvin & The Blue Notes. Now it's their turn, and the success is all the sweeter after they tried and failed to go it alone before. They've fulfilled their own definition of soul.

STAR QUOTE
IAN DURY

'If somebody's looking at me with rapture all over their face I want to throw a bucket of water over them.'

HEADBANGING BABES

Headbanging can start earlier than you think.

Respected UK medical journal *The Practitioner* reveals that headbanging can afflict children from six months to four years, and is started by the child trying to rock itself to sleep.

Doctors call it rhythmic motor habits, but they were surprised to find that Ted Nugent fans at a recent London concert were exhibiting the same symptoms: 'Most headbangers, as with head rollers, adopt an "on all fours" position when banging. A few, however, sit bolt upright.'

Ain't that a real mutha for ya?

Ted Nugent reverts to childhood

CHARTS

US45	Hot Stuff	*Donna Summer*
USLP	Breakfast In America	*Supertramp*
UK45	Sunday Girl	*Blondie*
UKLP	Voulez Vous	*Abba*
	WEEK 2	
US45	Love You Inside Out	*Bee Gees*
USLP	Breakfast In America	*Supertramp*
UK45	Dance Away	*Roxy Music*
UKLP	Voulez Vous	*Abba*
	WEEK 3	
US45	Hot Stuff	*Donna Summer*
USLP	Bad Girls	*Donna Summer*
UK45	Ring My Bell	*Anita Ward*
UKLP	Voulez Vous	*Abba*
	WEEK 4	
US45	Hot Stuff	*Donna Summer*
USLP	Breakfast In America	*Supertramp*
UK45	Ring My Bell	*Anita Ward*
UKLP	Discovery	*Electric Light Orchestra*
	WEEK 5	
US45	Ring My Bell	*Anita Ward*
USLP	Breakfast In America	*Supertramp*
UK45	Ring My Bell	*Anita Ward*
UKLP	Discovery	*Electric Light Orchestra*

THE GRAPEVINE

■ Chuck Berry is facing prison after pleading guilty to evading $200,000 in taxes, one week after performing at The White House.

■ Jefferson Starship have lured Grace Slick back into their ranks.

■ Little Feat have broken up after ten years ... two weeks later, mainman Lowell George is dead of a heart attack caused by obesity and drug problems.

THE PRETENDERS TURN THE DIAL

They've played less than 50 gigs and only had a couple of singles so far, but already The Pretenders are being swamped with media praise.

They are an odd matching of Chrissie Hynde, a precious, Iggy Pop-fixated tomboy from Akron, Ohio, who came over to Britain just before punk struck, and three boys from Hereford, a market town near the Welsh border.

'There was nothing to do there but get wasted,' says guitarist James Honeyman-Scott, who admits the band has saved him from becoming a rabid speed freak.

Their first single was a jangly cover of The Kinks' 'Stop Your Sobbing', which failed to break into the UK Top 30, while the second, 'Kid', has scarcely done better. It's a major leap forward

Chrissie Hynde tunes in

for the band however, as Chrissie wrote it.

She's been accused of leaning on the Sixties but says her only influence was the radio. 'I was in a very advantageous position living where I did. I could lay down at night and just . . . with my hand on the radio . . . with the slightest flick of the wrist . . . get another station; Nashville, Chicago, New York, Cleveland.'

GOING DIGITAL

Fleetwood Mac, Giorgio Moroder, Stephen Stills, Ry Cooder, Randy Newman and Bonnie Pointer are the first artists to discover the benefits of a new breakthrough that's being hailed as the biggest advance since stereo-digital recording.

Instead of simply storing sound on tape, the digital recorder samples the noise – 40-50,000 times per second – and stores the information in an electronic shorthand of binary numbers. So what you get back is exactly what you played.

It ain't cheap though, as Fleetwood Mac have discovered. You have to go through an expensive production system which costs around $100,000.

VAN HALEN'S ENERGY DRIVE

Dave Lee Roth is a fireball of energy, onstage and off. Onstage, his frenzied antics have propelled Van Halen into the heavy-metal mega-league with 'Van Halen II' a top ten album and 'Dance the Night Away' a top 20 single. Off-stage, his mouth works just as hard promoting the band to anyone in earshot.

The fact that Van Halen play the kind of hard rock that makes Led Zeppelin sound sluggish helps give his extravagant claims some substance.

'We're out to establish Van Halen as the most energized band on the planet. And I'm talking about a constant output of natural high energy, not coked-out high energy,' he proclaims.

'Sure, I've been up two or three nights at a time, but when the time comes to move on I just throw back a load of vitamins and like, OK, show me to the next gig. I tell ya, there's none that can keep up with us. Groupies, dealers – you name it, they hang around for a couple of days and then it hits 'em. They're flaked out and we're awake, heading for the next gig!'

Vitamin time for Van Halen

STAR QUOTE

DAVID BYRNE
of Talking Heads

'Anyone who tries to be naive these days is a fool. I know that most of this business is just merchandise.'

THE GRAPEVINE

■ Chicago DJ Steve Dahl burned a pile of disco records during a White Sox double header, and the ensuing riot caused the second game to be cancelled.

■ Van McCoy has died of a heart attack, aged 38; Minnie Riperton is also dead of cancer, aged 31.

■ Scott Cantrell, a 17 year old staying with Keith Richards' girlfriend Anita Pallenberg, shot himself dead in her bedroom.

Minnie Ripperton: still lovin' you

RY COODER – BOPPING TIL HE DROPS

There are four great reasons for getting into Ry Cooder's music: unbeatable artistry, funky humour, warmth and a genuine introduction to America's most vital genre of popular music. And you'll find them all on his new album, 'Bop Til You Drop'.

Cooder's music draws on the American blues experience – country, gospel, uptown R&B and the folk styles of Texas, Mexico, Hawaii and the Bahamas.

He neither plagiarizes nor bastardizes other people's work. He keeps the music alive and undiminished, and he's lucky enough to have a major label – Warner Brothers – that's prepared to support him in his efforts.

'If I did it on a little label, no one would pay a bit of attention,' he admits. 'But I've been lucky to grease by with some stuff that normally wouldn't be a part of anyone's roster.

'I don't want to be thought of as unmarketable – y'know, weird and eccentric. Because then you're in a bad position, you're unable to work.'

So far, his seven albums haven't produced the return that Warners might have liked. But 'Bop Til You Drop' is his most accessible and commercial offering yet. And so far neither Cooder nor Warner's patience has run out.

WHALES FOR MINGUS

Joni Mitchell was the last person to record with Charlie Mingus. He wrote six songs which feature on her new album, 'Mingus'. The album has given Joni jazz kudos which she finds remarkable, but not as remarkable as Mingus himself.

'He died aged 56 in Mexico,' she says. 'And on the day he was cremated, 56 whales beached themselves on the Mexican coast. The locals didn't know what to do, so they burned them too. There was a lot of mojo in his life.'

Mitchell meets Mingus: the last album of the jazz bass pioneer

THE GRAPEVINE

- Led Zeppelin packed the Knebworth Festival two weeks running for their first UK gigs in four years.
- The Cars played to half a million people in New York's Central Park.
- British rocker Nick Lowe has married Johnny Cash's daughter Carlene.
- The surviving members of Little Feat and friends staged a benefit for Lowell George in Los Angeles.
- Stan Kenton, modern jazz band leader, has died, aged 67.

Zeppelin still pack 'em in

JOY DIVISION's DREAM WORLD

The themes of Joy Division's music are sorrowful, painful and sad, with sometimes harrowing glimpses of confusion and alienation.

Not that this Manchester band are giving any clues. They refuse to put a lyric sheet with their debut album, 'Unknown Pleasures', even though it's obvious that they've got something to say.

'Haven't you ever been listening to a record where you've been singing a certain line, and when you find out what it really is you feel let down?' asks bassist Peter Hook.

Joy Division are insular and possessive about their music. Signed to the Manchester independent label Factory, they recorded their album for £8,500, mistrusted the rave reviews and now wait dispassionately for the backlash.

'I used to work in a factory, and I was really happy because I could daydream all day,' says shy singer Ian Curtis. 'All I had to do was push this wagon with cotton things in it up and down. I didn't have to think. I could dream about the weekend, imagine what I was going to spend my money on, which LP I was going to buy . . . You can live in your own little world.'

Taj – for the old cats

CHARTS

US45	Bad Girls	*Donna Summer*
USLP	Bad Girls	*Donna Summer*
UK45	I Don't Like Mondays	*Boomtown Rats*
UKLP	The Best Disco Album In The World	*Various*

WEEK 2

US45	Bad Girls	*Donna Summer*
USLP	Get The Knack	*The Knack*
UK45	I Don't Like Mondays	*Boomtown Rats*
UKLP	The Best Disco Album In The World	*Various*

WEEK 3

US45	Good Times	*Chic*
USLP	Get The Knack	*The Knack*
UK45	I Don't Like Mondays	*Boomtown Rats*
UKLP	The Best Disco Album In The World	*Various*

WEEK 4

US45	My Sharona	*The Knack*
USLP	Get The Knack	*The Knack*
UK45	I Don't Like Mondays	*Boomtown Rats*
UKLP	Discovery	*Electric Light Orchestra*

STAR QUOTE

TAJ MAHAL

'You get off-days when you think: "I've been banging this out for 20 years and what does it amount to?" But the quality of life is where it's at. That's why I enjoy covering old blues tunes – hoping to send those old cats six or eight thousand dollars.'

THE SPECIALS – 2-TONE RUDE BOYS

Rude boys out of Coventry, England, The Specials are a curious mixture of old and new. Their musical inspiration comes originally from the Jamaican ska and rock-steady styles of the Sixties and they include covers of Prince Buster, The Skatalites, The Maytals and The Pioneers in their set.

But there's also a bunch of songs written by keyboard player Jerry Dammers with a contemporary intelligence all of their own. Like 'Gangsters', the biggest-selling independent single of the year on their own 2-Tone label, 'It's Up To You', 'Stupid Marriage', and the new single,

The Specials look smart

'Too Much Too Young'.

'Ska is just somewhere to start,' says Dammers. 'It's dead simple, but there's so many variations you can make out of it.'

But it's not just the music. 'The clothes are almost as important,' states singer Terry Hall. 'We're not a mod band or a skinhead band. The rude boy thing is a real mixture.'

Rude boy? 'He's a rebel that don't go around causing unnecessary trouble,' says co-singer Neville 'Judge Roughneck' Staples. 'He enjoys himself and dresses nice. And he's cool. If he goes around kicking people, then he's no rudie.'

STAR QUOTE

VAN MORRISON

'I reckon that anything that anybody wants to know about Van Morrison they'll find out in my records.'

THE GRAPEVINE

■ Bruce Springsteen, Jackson Browne, The Doobie Brothers, Bonnie Raitt, James Taylor and Carly Simon have played a five-night series of 'No Nukes' shows at Madison Square Gardens.

■ The Clash, Country Joe, Peter Tosh, Robert Fripp and Canned Heat play the Second Annual Tribal Stomp at Monterey.

■ Jimmy McCulloch, guitarist with Thunderclap Newman and Wings, has died in London from 'undetermined causes' aged 26.

REGATTA DE BLANC

Brought to you by the same team that made 'Outlandos D'Amour', The Police have realized the potential of their second album in contrast to the first which nobody really understood.

As a result, the trio's distinctive style – Sting's reggae voice, Stewart Copeland's dub rhythms and Andy Summers' stripped down guitar – are reinforced as an investment for the future.

Their brilliance is too erratic to survive over an album's worth of songs but it confirms The Police as a great pop singles band as 'Message In A Bottle' and 'Walking On The Moon' clearly demonstrate. For this The Police are dependent on Sting's singer/ songwriter/hitmaker image, his charismatic dry, strained voice and his skill in concocting 'original' melodies and hooklines – 'original' because the origins are buried too deeply in people's subconscious to identify.

DISCO CRUSADERS

Currently topping the US disco and jazz charts with their 'Street Life' single and album, The Crusaders are veterans of thirty albums and eight solo efforts. They were The Jazz Crusaders until the beginning of the Seventies, when they grew out of their Texan jazz roots and into the growing funk movement.

They've had an awesome studio reputation for years and have worked with The Rolling Stones, Steely Dan, Joni Mitchell, Marvin Gaye, Diana Ross, The Jackson Five, Barry White, Sarah Vaughan and Buddy Miles.

But their own progress has been hampered by the lack of a permanent singer. Which is by choice, not by accident.

Instead, they pick and choose, and the girl who's been lucky enough to be at the microphone as they suddenly tap into the disco market is Randy Crawford. The combination is the classiest thing you can dance to.

Randy Crawford stirs up disco fever, courtesy of the Crusaders

THE CLASH TAKE THE FIFTH

After a short dip in the spring, The Clash are back for their first major tour of America. Called the Take The Fifth Tour, it's as much of a crusade as a tour.

'I want to reach the kid in high school,' says Joe Strummer. 'The one with the Kansas and Kiss albums in his bedroom. I feel he should have a dose of us.'

Paradoxically, it's a quest that The Clash can never fulfil without destroying the purpose of the crusade. 'If all we achieve is someone wanting my autograph, then we've gone wrong,' admits Strummer.

Commercial success would be another problem. 'If we were just going to be another Stones or a Who, it would be a bit of a bore. That's why we're going to try and turn left where we should have turned right.'

The confusion that surrounds The Clash is certainly helping them make a few left turns. There is confusion over management, which means that conflicting advice is being given to each member of the band. And their record company is being cautious. Tour subsidies are hard to come by.

The uncertainties and distractions are causing frustrations, but the positive aspect is that the essence of The Clash is not set and sealed. There is nothing certain about The Clash. Nothing comfortable.

And that includes the reaction of the American public they've come to find.

THE GRAPEVINE

■ **The Rose**, starring Bette Midler as a James Joplin-like rock singer, has opened, in Los Angeles.

■ Madison Square Gardens has had an eventful month: Jethro Tull's Ian Anderson was hit in the eye by a rose thrown by a fan, 15 people were arrested for mugging at an Earth Wind & Fire concert, but Elton John played eight nights without incident.

BLONDIE EAT THE BEAT

Blondie rode in on the crest of the new wave, and now they're riding the crest of the discowave, courtesy of their 'Parallel Lines' album and the monstrously successful 'Heart Of Glass' single – a perfect merger of pop and the disco beat.

And to judge from Debbie Harry's comments, it seems the new wave has learnt nothing from the old when it comes to avoiding the perils of the rock'n 'roll business. The band are still counting the cost of extricating themselves from less than satisfactory label and management deals.

'People playing stupid little games . . . Yuck! It really disturbs me. It's horrible when you actually see it happen. For me, the only good thing about all of this is going into the studio, because you're isolated and surrounded by all this electricity and all you have to think about is what you're doing.

'The next best thing is the hour or so you're on stage in front of an audience. Take it from me, the rest of it sucks,' says Debbie

vehemently.

She's not over-enamoured at her sex-symbol image either: 'In America they put girls in two categories. Either you're a sweet clean-cut girl or a real nasty bitch. And I know which one they've figured me out to be.'

Blondie's new album is 'Eat To The Beat', and although guitarist Chris Stein admits that there isn't another 'Heart Of Glass' to send the disco crowd crazy, he's convinced that it's their best album to date.

CHARTS

US45	Sad Eyes *Robert John*
USLP	In Through The Out Door *Led Zeppelin*
UK45	Message In A Bottle *Police*
UKLP	The Pleasure Principle *Gary Numan*

— WEEK 2 —

US45	Don't Stop 'til You Get Enough *Michael Jackson*
USLP	In Through The Out Door *Led Zeppelin*
UK45	Message In A Bottle *Police*
UKLP	The Pleasure Principle *Gary Numan*

— WEEK 3 —

US45	Rise *Herb Alpert*
USLP	In Through The Out Door *Led Zeppelin*
UK45	Video Killed The Radio Star *Buggles*
UKLP	Regatta De Blanc *Police*

— WEEK 4 —

US45	Rise *Herb Alpert*
USLP	In Through The Out Door *Led Zeppelin*
UK45	Video Killed The Radio Star *Buggles*
UKLP	Regatta De Blanc *Police*

STAR QUOTE

SAMMY HAGAR

'I don't want to be a fake star y'know. I wanna legitimately be the baddest mother up there.'

Big bad Sammy Hagar

137

1979

FROM BABYLON TO HARLEM

'Tell me Bob, why are you playing the Apollo Theater in Harlem? Is there any significance in that?' asks the elegant black lady from the TV station.

'Well, Marcus Garvey was there,' begins Bob Marley before launching into an unintelligible diatribe that ends with an abrupt 'Rastafari!' at the camera crew. The lady looks baffled.

Later, one of The Wailers' entourage explains it more simply: 'The Apollo is an important part of our black heritage. There isn't a single major black star who hasn't played there at one point – from Bessie Smith and Billy Holiday to all the soul stars. Bob had to play there, to put him in that tradition for people to understand.'

Bob Marley is carrying the message of reggae to the soul of black America. The slower, more considered pace of his latest album, 'Survival', allows him to concentrate on the lyrics and connect with his audience.

He uses three stage backdrops to reinforce the message: the Ethiopian flag, a portrait of Emperor Selassie, and a collage of Marcus Garvey and other black freedom fighters.

Harlem gets the message.

Bob Marley carrying his heritage

CHARTS

US45	Pop Muzik	M
USLP	In Through The Out Door	Led Zeppelin
UK45	One Day At A Time	Lena Martell
UKLP	Regatta De Blanc	Police

— WEEK 2 —

US45	Heartache Tonight	Eagles
USLP	The Long Run	Eagles
UK45	You're In Love With A Beautiful Woman	Dr Hook
UKLP	Regatta De Blanc	Police

— WEEK 3 —

US45	Still	Commodores
USLP	The Long Run	Eagles
UK45	You're In Love With A Beautiful Woman	Dr Hook
UKLP	Regatta De Blanc	Police

— WEEK 4 —

US45	No More Tears (Enough Is Enough)	Barbra Streisand & Donna Summer
USLP	The Long Run	Eagles
UK45	You're In Love With A Beautiful Woman	Dr Hook
UKLP	Greatest Hits	Rod Stewart

STAR QUOTE

HUGH CORNWELL
of The Stranglers

'We're never going to use a producer again. They are just shitty little parasites. All they're good for is telling jokes. And we know better jokes than any of 'em.'

Shalamar crack the Solar system

DISCO BUSINESS

Solar stands for Sound Of Los Angeles Records, an independent disco label set up by writers/producers Dick Griffey and Leon Sylvers, who sell their product with hefty dollops of Californian 'sincerity' and business acumen.

'You gotta understand that disco is a positive music, it's not gloomy. You won't hear a sad disco song. People want positive music,' they say.

They may be selling it like soap powder, but Solar has some of the best disco music of the moment coming from acts like Shalamar, Carrie Lucas, Dynasty and The Whispers.

Most of the young acts have an almost religious attitude to the music business. 'I want to become one of those all-round entertainers known for giving his all to show business,' gushes Jeffrey Daniel of Shalamar.

But Scotty of The Whispers believes that marketing is sometimes winning out over the music. 'Blacks in this business are running scared. I hear the young blacks saying that you've gotta bend to the companies, and it's deplorable.

'But it's gonna come, ain't no getting away from that.'

THE LAST BRICK?

Is 'The Wall' the last brick in Pink Floyd's own towering edifice? Having constructed their own wall around themselves, this double album finds them rather shocked by the realization of this fact – that rock and roll is not the autonomous wonderland they had assumed it to be.

It's a seemingly fatalistic piece of work, a monument of self-centred pessimism. Its 'point' is everywhere and nowhere. Roger Waters' lyrics, set in stark relief against their targets, sink into dogged depths of self-expression and social concern – 'Hey teacher, leave those kids alone'.

'The Wall' is the rock musician's equivalent of the tired executive's toy, a gleaming, frivolous gadget that serves to occupy midspace. It's misplaced boredom with graphics by Gerald Scarfe.

THE GRAPEVINE

■ Bob Dylan was booed by San Francisco fans at the start of his 'Slow Train Coming' Tour.

■ Chuck Berry released from prison after two months of his four-month sentence.

■ Marianne Faithful has been arrested for possession of marijuana in Norway.

■ Anita Pallenberg has been cleared of murder charges over the death of Scott Cantrell at her house.

WALKING ON THE CHARTS

Suddenly The Police are the latest teenybop sensation in the UK. After a lengthy struggle for any kind of recognition, the band have hit paydirt with two singles from their 'Regatta De Blanc' album.

'Message In A Bottle' made No. 2 in August, and its successor, 'Walking On The Moon', has stormed to No. 1 to coincide with the band's 10th tour of the year – a dozen-date shindig that's produced mass hysteria at every stop.

'I never thought we'd get that kind of teenage audience,' grins guitarist Andy Summers. 'But we haven't compromised at all. Some of our music is definitely not teenage-oriented, but I don't mind. You get a tremendous amount of enthusiasm with kids of that age.'

Sting: original moonwalker

Sting is the object of most of this pubescent adulation. 'To a lot of people, teenyboppers are a sub-species not even to be entertained. I don't agree. If you can transcend the screaming, you can take a generation with you into something else. It's a real challenge.'

The tour climaxed with two shows in London on the same night – the seated Hammersmith Odeon and the standing-only Hammersmith Palais – with the band travelling between the two in an armoured personnel carrier.

And they still had enough energy to slot in a charity show afterwards.

THE GRAPEVINE

■ The Who, Paul McCartney, Elvis Costello, The Clash, The Pretenders and The Specials have played benefit gigs for the people of Kampuchea.

■ The Eagles, Linda Ronstadt and Chicago have staged a benefit for the presidential campaign of Linda's boyfriend, Governor Jerry Brown.

■ The Clash have won their battle with CBS to sell their album, 'London Calling,' at a reduced price, by taking lower royalties.

HEADS DOWN NO NONSENSE FEAR OF MUSIC

Talking Heads' 'Fear Of Music' is not an easy listening album. It has a disquieting tonal quality, some bizarre conceits and unappealing song titles like 'Life During Wartime', 'Animals', 'Air', 'Paper' and 'Mind'.

But the album has been nestling in the lower reaches of the US Top 30 and provided the

ELEVEN FANS KILLED AT WHO GIG

The Who's comeback tour of America has been struck by tragedy in Cincinatti.

Thousands of fans arrived early for their Riverfront Coliseum gig to grab the best seats. But only two doors were opened to let them in, and in the ensuing crush 11 fans were trampled to death and 20 more taken to hospital.

The Who played unaware of the disaster, because police feared a riot if the show was cancelled. But afterwards they were in a state of emotional turmoil.

Roger Daltrey: 'If it had happened on stage – if just one person had been killed because of us – I would have been on the first plane back home and never played another gig in my life.

band with the bridgehead they need to reach a mass audience.

'The first two albums used up all the songs I had, so I had to compose a whole new set,' says David Byrne.

Musically, Talking Heads are reaping the fruits of their collaboration with Eno on their second album. Not surprisingly, he's co-produced the new one, too.

Lyrically, Byrne is honing his stark, conversational style. 'It's not so much what is said as how it's put across. I can't stand all those unnecessary embellishments, the idea of lyrics as poetry that demands reams of verses, all of them superfluous or just pointless.'

STAR QUOTE

JOE JACKSON

'You know, I looked at myself in the mirror this morning and I just laughed.'

Talking Heads: if the cap fits

CHARTS

US45	No More Tears (Enough Is Enough) *Barbra Streisand & Donna Summer*
USLP	The Long Run *Eagles*
UK45	You're In Love With A Beautiful Woman *Dr Hook*
UKLP	Greatest Hits, Vol. 2 *Abba*

— WEEK 2 —

US45	Babe *Styx*
USLP	The Long Run *Eagles*
UK45	Walking On The Moon *Police*
UKLP	Greatest Hits, Vol. 2 *Abba*

— WEEK 3 —

US45	Babe *Styx*
USLP	The Long Run *Eagles*
UK45	Another Brick In The Wall *Pink Floyd*
UKLP	Greatest Hits, Vol. 2 *Abba*

— WEEK 4 —

US45	Escape *Rupert Holmes*
USLP	The Long Run *Eagles*
UK45	Another Brick In The Wall *Pink Floyd*
UKLP	Greatest Hits, Vol. 2 *Abba*

— WEEK 5 —

US45	Escape *Rupert Holmes*
USLP	The Long Run *Eagles*
UK45	Another Brick In The Wall *Pink Floyd*
UKLP	Greatest Hits, Vol. 2 *Abba*

Joe 'Pretty Boy' Jackson

SEVENTIES CHARTBUSTERS

These top records and artist listings have been calculated from the peak chart positions they reached and the number of weeks they spent on the chart. In cases where a record is by two artists, i.e. 'Stumblin' In' by Suzi Quatro and Chris Norman, then both artists receive full credit. In calculating the Top Album acts no various artist albums (including original casts or soundtracks) are included. Since these lists are chart-based rather than sales-based they tend to favour records that spent a long time on the charts over those that may have sold more but did so in a shorter period of time. The 'One-Hit Wonders' lists include all artists whose only Top 50 UK or Top 40 US single hit made the Top 5.

US ONE-HIT WONDERS OF THE '70s

	Artist	Title
1970	BLUES IMAGE	Ride Captain Ride
	EDISON LIGHTHOUSE	Love Grows (Where My Rosemary Goes)
	FREE	All Right Now
	NORMAN GREENBAUM	Spirit In The Sky
	EDDIE HOLMAN	Hey There Lonely Girl
	IDES OF MARCH	Vehicle
	JAGGERZ	The Rapper
	MUNGO JERRY	In The Summertime
	SHOCKING BLUE	Venus
	R. DEAN TAYLOR	Indiana Wants Me
	TEE SET	Ma Belle Amie
1971	LYNN ANDERSON	Rose Garden
	FREE MOVEMENT	I've Found Someone Of My Own
	JANIS JOPLIN	Me And Bobby McGee
	JEAN KNIGHT	Mr. Big Stuff
	OCEAN	Put Your Hand In The Hand
	UNDISPUTED TRUTH	Smiling Faces Sometime
1972	ARGENT	Hold Your Head Up
	CLIMAX	Precious And Few
	JONATHAN EDWARDS	Sunshine
1973	DEODATA	Also Sprach Zarathustra (2001)
	CLINT HOLMES	Playground In My Mind
	VICKI LAWRENCE	The Night The Lights Went Out In Georgia
	HURRICANE SMITH	Oh Babe What Would You Say
	STORIES	Brother Louie
	SYLVIA	Pillow Talk
	TIMMY THOMAS	Why Can't We Live Together
	ERIC WEISSBERG & STEVE MANDELL	Dueling Banjos
1974	WILLIAM DeVAUGHN	Be Thankful For What You Got
	CARL DOUGLAS	Kung Fu Fighting
	DAVID ESSEX	Rock On
	FIRST CLASS	Beach Baby
	MARVIN HAMLISCH	The Entertainer
	TERRY JACKS	Season In The Sun
	DAVE LOGGINS	Please Come To Boston
	BYRON MACGREGOR	Americans
	SISTER JANET MEAD	The Lord's Prayer
	MFSB	TSOP (The Sound Of Philadelphia)
	PAPER LACE	The Night Chicago Died
	BILLY SWAN	I Can Help
1975	ACE	How Long
	JESSIE COLTER	I'm Not Lisa
	MAJOR HARRIS	Love Won't Let Me Wait
	SAMMY JOHNS	Chevy Van
	VAN McCOY	The Hustle
	PILOT	Magic
	MINNIE RIPERTON	Lovin' You
	PHOEBE SNOW	Poetry Man
1976	WALTER MURPHY & THE BIG APPLE	A Fifth Of Beethoven
	ELVIN BISHOP	Fooled Around And Fell In Love
	RICK DEES & HIS CAST OF IDIOTS	Disco Duck
	PRATT & McCLAIN	Happy Days
	JOHN SEBASTIAN	Welcome Back
	STARLAND VOCAL BAND	Afternoon Delight
	WILD CHERRY	Play That Funky Music
1977	DEBBY BOONE	You Light Up My Life
	BILL CONTI	Gonna Fly Now (Theme From 'Rocky')
	FLOATERS	Float On
	PETER McCANN	Do You Wanna Make Love
	ALAN O'DAY	Undercover Angel
	DAVID SOUL	Don't Give Up On Us
1978	ALICIA BRIDGES	I Love The Night Life (Disco 'Round)
	NICK GILDER	Hot Child In The City
	RANDY NEWMAN	Short People
	SAMANTHA SANG	Emotion
1979	M	Pop Muzik
	FRANK MILLS	Music Box Dancer
	DAVID NAUGHTON	Makin' It
	SUZI QUATRO & CHRIS NORMAN	Stumblin' In
	AMII STEWART	Knock On Wood
	RANDY VANWARMER	Just When I Needed You Most
	ANITA WARD	Ring My Bell

UK ONE-HIT WONDERS OF THE '70s

	Artist	Title
1970	CLARENCE CARTER	Patches
	FRIJID PINK	House Of The Rising Sun
	NORMAN GREENBAUM	Spirit In The Sky
	HOTLEGS	Neanderthal Man
	LEE MARVIN	Wand'rin' Star
	MATTHEWS SOUTHERN COMFORT	Woodstock
	MR. BLOE	Groovin' With Mr. Bloe
1971	LYNN ANDERSON	Rose Garden
	ASHTON GARDNER & DYKE	Resurrection Shuffle
	CURVED AIR	Back Street Luv
	CLIVE DUNN	Grandad
	TAMI LYNN	I'm Gonna Run Away From You
	MIXTURES	The Pushbike Song
	PIGLETS	Johnny Reggae
	REDBONE	Witch Queen Of New Orleans
	WALDO DE LOS RIOS	Mozart Symphony No. 40 In G Minor
	SPRINGWATER	I Will Return
	TITANIC	Sultana
1972	CHELSEA F.C.	Blue Is The Colour
	CONGREGATION	Softly Whispering I Love You
	HOT BUTTER	Popcorn
	PYTHON LEE JACKSON	In A Broken Dream
	SHAG	Loop Di Love
	FARON YOUNG	It's Four In The Morning
1973	HOTSHOTS	Snoopy vs. The Red Baron
	SIMON PARK ORCHESTRA	Eye Level
	BOBBY 'BORIS' PICKETT & THE CRYPT KICKERS	Monster Mash
1974	JOHNNY BRISTOL	Hang On In There Baby
	EDDIE HOLMAN	(Hey There) Lonely Girl
	ANDY KIM	Rock Me Gently
1975	MORRIS ALBERT	Feelings
	MIKE BATT	Summertime City
	JASPER CARROTT	Funky Moped/Magic Roundabout
	JIM GILSTRAP	Swing Your Daddy
	TAMMY JONES	Let Me Try Again
	GREG LAKE	I Believe In Father Christmas
	LAUREL & HARDY	The Trail Of The Lonesome Pine
	MINNIE RIPERTON	Loving You
	TYPICALLY TROPICAL	Barbados
1976	J.J. BARRIE	No Charge
	YVONNE FAIR	It Should Have Been Me
	LAURIE LINGO & THE DIPSTICKS	Convoy GB
	C.W. McCALL	Convoy
	HANK MIZELL	Jungle Rock
	OUR KID	You Just Might See Me Cry
	ROBIN SARSTEDT	My Resistance Is Low
	SHERBET	Howzat
	R & J STONE	We Do It
	GEORGHE ZAMFIR	(Light Of Experience) Doina De Jale
1977	LA BELLE EPOQUE	Black Is Black
	BRIGHOUSE & RASTRICK BRASS BAND	The Floral Dance
	EMERSON LAKE & PALMER	Fanfare For The Common Man
	FLOATERS	Float On
	MARY MACGREGOR	Torn Between Two Lovers
	DANNY MIRROR	I Remember Elvis Presley
	DAVID PARTON	Isn't She Lovely
	SPACE	Magic Fly
	JOE TEX	Ain't Gonna Bump No More
1978	ALTHIA AND DONNA	Up Town Top Ranking
	BRIAN & MICHAEL	Matchstalk Men And Matchstalk Cats And Dogs
	CLOUT	Substitute
	JAMES GALWAY	Annie's Song
	JILTED JOHN	Jilted John
	TASTE OF HONEY	Boogie Oogie Oogie
	JOHN PAUL YOUNG	Love Is In The Air
1979	JANET KAY	Silly Games
	LENA MARTELL	One Day At A Time
	McFADDEN & WHITEHEAD	Ain't No Stoppin' Us Now
	MILK & HONEY	Hallelujah
	QUANTUM JUMP	The Lone Ranger
	ANITA WARD	Ring My Bell

US TOP SINGLES OF THE '70s

	Title	Artist	Label	Year
1	YOU LIGHT UP MY LIFE	Debby Boone	WARNER	1977
2	NIGHT FEVER	Bee Gees	RSO	1978
3	TONIGHT'S THE NIGHT (GONNA BE ALRIGHT)	Rod Stewart	WARNER	1976
4	SHADOW DANCING	Andy Gibb	RSO	1978
5	LE FREAK	Chic	ATLANTIC	1978
6	MY SHARONA	Knack	CAPITOL	1979
7	THE FIRST TIME EVER I SAW YOUR FACE	Roberta Flack	ATLANTIC	1972
8	JOY TO THE WORLD	Three Dog Night	DUNHILL	1971
9	BRIDGE OVER TROUBLED WATER	Simon & Garfunkel	COLUMBIA	1970
10	ALONE AGAIN (NATURALLY)	Gilbert O'Sullivan	MAM	1972
11	BEST OF MY LOVE	Emotions	COLUMBIA	1977
12	I'LL BE THERE	Jackson Five	MOTOWN	1970
13	MAGGIE MAY/REASON TO BELIEVE	Rod Stewart	MERCURY	1971
14	SILLY LOVE SONGS	Paul McCartney	CAPITOL	1976
15	BAD GIRLS	Donna Summer	CASABLANCA	1979
16	IT'S TOO LATE/ I FEEL THE EARTH MOVE	Carole King	ODE	1971
17	KILLING ME SOFTLY WITH HIS SONG	Roberta Flack	ATLANTIC	1973
18	ONE BAD APPLE	Osmonds	MGM	1971
19	I JUST WANT TO BE YOUR EVERYTHING	Andy Gibb	RSO	1977
20	STAYIN' ALIVE	Bee Gees	RSO	1978

UK TOP SINGLES OF THE '70s

	Title	Artist	Label	Year
1	SAILING	Rod Stewart	WARNER	1975/6*
2	YOU'RE THE ONE THAT I WANT	J. Travolta & O. Newton-John	RSO	1978
3	BOHEMIAN RHAPSODY	Queen	EMI	1975
4	MULL OF KINTYRE	Paul McCartney	CAPITOL	1977
5	LEADER OF THE PACK	Shangri-Las	VARIOUS	1972/6*
6	IN THE SUMMERTIME	Mungo Jerry	DAWN	1970
7	SUMMER NIGHTS	J. Travolta & O. Newton-John	RSO	1978
8	THE WONDER OF YOU	Elvis Presley	RCA	1970
9	SAVE YOUR KISSES FOR ME	Brotherhood Of Man	PYE	1976
10	HOT LOVE	T. Rex	FLY	1971
11	I HEAR YOU KNOCKING	Dave Edmunds	MAM	1970
12	DANCING QUEEN	Abba	EPIC	1976
13	BROWN GIRL IN THE RING	Boney M	ATLANTIC	1978
14	DON'T GO BREAKING MY HEART	Elton John & Kiki Dee	ROCKET	1976
15	BAND OF GOLD	Freda Payne	INVICTUS	1970
16	BYE BYE BABY	Bay City Rollers	BELL	1975
17	BRIGHT EYES	Art Garfunkel	CBS	1979
18	LONG HAIRED LOVER FROM LIVERPOOL	Little Jimmy Osmond	MGM	1972
19	MAGGIE MAY	Rod Stewart	MERCURY	1971
20	KNOCK THREE TIMES	Dawn	BELL	1971

Appeared in Top 20 in both years

US TOP ALBUMS OF THE '70s

	Title	Artist	Label	Year
1	RUMOURS	Fleetwood Mac	WARNER	1977
2	SATURDAY NIGHT FEVER	Soundtrack	RSO	1978
3	TAPESTRY	Carole King	ODE	1971
4	THE WALL	Pink Floyd	COLUMBIA	1980
5	SONGS IN THE KEY OF LIFE	Stevie Wonder	TAMLA	1976
6	GREASE	Soundtrack	RSO	1978
7	FRAMPTON COMES ALIVE!	Peter Frampton	A&M	1976
8	BRIDGE OVER TROUBLED WATER	Simon & Garfunkel	COLUMBIA	1970
9	ELTON JOHN – GREATEST HITS	Elton John	MCA	1974
10	THE LONG RUN	Eagles	ASYLUM	1979
11	COSMO'S FACTORY	Creedence Clearwater Revival	FANTASY	1970
12	PEARL	Janis Joplin	COLUMBIA	1971
13	CHICAGO V	Chicago	COLUMBIA	1972
14	GOODBYE YELLOW BRICK ROAD	Elton John	MCA	1973
15	52ND STREET	Billy Joel	COLUMBIA	1978
16	HOTEL CALIFORNIA	Eagles	ASYLUM	1977
17	IN THROUGH THE OUT DOOR	Led Zeppelin	SWAN SONG	1979
18	WINGS AT THE SPEED OF SOUND	Wings	CAPITOL	1976
19	AMERICAN PIE	Don McClean	U.A.	1972
20	CAP'N FANTASTIC & BROWN DIRT COWBOY	Elton John	MCA	1975

UK TOP ALBUMS OF THE '70s

	Title	Artist	Label	Year
1	BRIDGE OVER TROUBLED WATER	Simon & Garfunkel	CBS	1970
2	SATURDAY NIGHT FEVER	Soundtrack	RSO	1978
3	THE SINGLES 1969-73	Carpenters	A&M	1974
4	GREASE	Soundtrack	RSO	1978
5	GREATEST HITS	Abba	EPIC	1976
6	ELTON JOHN'S GREATEST HITS	Elton John	DJM	1974
7	20 ALL TIME HITS OF THE FIFTIES	Various	K-TEL	1972
8	ARRIVAL	Abba	EPIC	1977
9	20 GOLDEN GREATS	Beach Boys	CAPITOL	1976
10	THE BEST OF THE STYLISTICS	Stylistics	AVCO	1975
11	20 DYNAMIC HITS	Various	K-TEL	1972
12	BAND ON THE RUN	Wings	APPLE	1974
13	ATLANTIC CROSSING	Rod Stewart	WARNER	1975
14	THE ALBUM	Abba	EPIC	1978
15	20 GOLDEN GREATS	Diana Ross & The Supremes	MOTOWN	1977
16	THAT'LL BE THE DAY	Various	RONCO	1973
17	ELECTRIC WARRIOR	T. Rex	FLY	1971
18	DON'T SHOOT ME I'M ONLY THE PIANO PLAYER	Elton John	DJM	1973
19	20 GOLDEN GREATS	Shadows	EMI	1977
20	40 GREATEST HITS	Perry Como	K-TEL	1975

TOP ALBUM ACTS OF THE '70s

	UK Charts		US Charts
1	DAVID BOWIE	1	ELTON JOHN
2	ELTON JOHN	2	ROLLING STONES
3	ROD STEWART	3	CHICAGO
4	ROLLING STONES	4	PAUL McCARTNEY/WINGS
5	PAUL McCARTNEY	5	LED ZEPPELIN
6	BOB DYLAN	6	BOB DYLAN
7	STATUS QUO	7	CAROLE KING
8	ELVIS PRESLEY	8	BEE GEES
9	LED ZEPPELIN	9	BARBRA STREISAND
10	ABBA	10	NEIL DIAMOND
11	QUEEN	11	JOHN DENVER
12	CARPENTERS	12	EAGLES
13	PINK FLOYD	13	BEATLES
14	YES	14	ROD STEWART
15	ANDY WILLIAMS	15	LINDA RONSTADT
16	WHO	16	JETHRO TULL
17	DIANA ROSS	17	STEVIE WONDER
18	EMERSON, LAKE & PALMER	18	EARTH, WIND & FIRE
19	T. REX	19	CAT STEVENS
20	SIMON & GARFUNKEL	20	FLEETWOOD MAC

TOP SINGLES ACTS OF THE '70s

	UK Charts		US Charts
1	ABBA	1	ELTON JOHN
2	ROD STEWART	2	BEE GEES
3	SLADE	3	PAUL McCARTNEY
4	ELVIS PRESLEY	4	CARPENTERS
5	T. REX	5	STEVIE WONDER
6	PAUL McCARTNEY	6	JACKSON FIVE
7	ELTON JOHN	7	THREE DOG NIGHT
8	SHOWADDYWADDY	8	EAGLES
9	MUD	9	BARRY MANILOW
10	DAVID BOWIE	10	OLIVIA NEWTON-JOHN
11	GARY GLITTER	11	DONNA SUMMER
12	SWEET	12	JOHN DENVER
13	ELECTRIC LIGHT ORCHESTRA	13	NEIL DIAMOND
14	BAY CITY ROLLERS	14	BARBRA STREISAND
15	10CC	15	HELEN REDDY
16	BONEY M	16	DIANA ROSS
17	STYLISTICS	17	AL GREEN
18	STATUS QUO	18	COMMODORES
19	HOT CHOCOLATE	19	MARVIN GAYE
20	QUEEN	20	SPINNERS

INDEX

PICTURE ACKNOWLEDGMENTS

The Publishers gratefully acknowledge the tremendous assistance of London Features International in providing the majority of photographs for this book:
London Features International: Half title, Title, 6 TL,CL&BL, 7 TR,CR&BR, 9 T, 10 BL, 11 T&BR, 12 T,C&B, 13 CL,CR&B, 14 T&B, 15 B, 16 T, 17 T,C&B, 18 T&B, 19 T, 20 L,TR&BR, 21 TL,TR&BL, 24 C, 25 TL&B, 26 T,BL&BR, 27 T&BL, 28 C&CR, 29 BL&BR, 30 T,BL&BR, 31 T&B, 32 T&BR, 33 B, 34 T, 35 T&B, 36 T&B, 37 T,BL&BR, 38 T&B, 39 T&C, 40 TL,TR&BL, 41 TL&B, 42 BL, 44 T&BR, 45 B, 46 T,C,&B, 47 BL&BR, 48 T, 49 BL, 50 T,C,BL&BR, 51 T, 52 TL&B, 53 T, 54 BL&BR, 55 T&B, 56 TL, 57 T&B, 58 B, 59 T, 60 T,C&B, 61 T&B, 62 L,R&C, 63 T,CR&B, 64 C&B, 65 T&BR, 66 TL,TR&BR, 67 TC,TR&BR, 68 T&B, 69 BL, 70 T,C&B, 71 T&BL, 72 L, 72-3 B, 74 T, 75 B, 76 T&B, 79 T&B, 80 T&BL, 81 T&B, 82 T&B, 84 T&C, 85 T,C&B, 86 TR,CR&BR, 87 TL,CL&BL, 88 T&C, 89 CL&CR, 90 T,BL&BR, 92 T&BL, 93 B, 96 T,C&B, 97 T&C, 98 T, 99 BL&BR, 100 T,C&B, 101 BL, 102 T&C, 103 B, 104 L&R, 106 B, 107 T, 110 B, 111 T&B, 112 T&C, 113 T,C&B, 116 C&B, 118 T&B, 119 BL&BR, 120 T, 121 B, 122 T&LB, 123 R, 127 L&TR, 128 BR, 129 R, 130 T&B, 131 T, 132 B, 133 T, 134 T&R, 135 TR&B, 137 T&B, 139 C.
Michael Ochs Archive/LFI 8 T, 10 T, 22 B, 25 TR, 27 BR, 28 B, 34 B, 35 C, 37 BR, 38 C, 39 BL&BR, 40 BR, 41 TR, 42 T&BR, 49 C&BR, 53 B, 54 TL&TR, 55 C, 57 C, 58 T, 66 BL, 69 T, 71 C, 84 B, 117 T.

The publishers would like to thank the following organisations for their kind permission to reproduce additional photographs in this book: *Barratt's:* 16 B; *Camera Press:* PR Francis; 15 T; Terry O'Neill: 10 BR; *Chrysalis Records Plc:* 9 B; *The Hulton Picture Company:* 127 TC&AC; *The Kobal Collection:* 8 B, 21 CR, 45 T, 76 C, 101 TL&R.